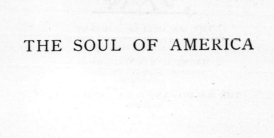

THE SOUL OF AMERICA

THE MACMILLAN COMPANY
NEW YORK · BOSTON · CHICAGO · DALLAS
ATLANTA · SAN FRANCISCO

MACMILLAN & CO., LIMITED
LONDON · BOMBAY · CALCUTTA
MELBOURNE

THE MACMILLAN CO. OF CANADA, LTD.
TORONTO

THE SOUL OF AMERICA

A CONSTRUCTIVE ESSAY IN THE SOCIOLOGY OF RELIGION

BY

STANTON COIT

New York
THE MACMILLAN COMPANY
1914

Norwood Press
J. S. Cushing Co. — Berwick & Smith Co.
Norwood, Mass., U.S.A.

To

MY WIFE ADELA

TABLE OF CONTENTS

PART I

RELIGION AND NATIONALITY

vii

PART II

CHRISTIANITY TO BE REINTERPRETED IN THE LIGHT OF SCIENCE AND AMERICAN IDEALISM

PART III

THE author acknowledges his indebtedness to Messrs. Williams and Norgate, of London, for permission to incorporate in Parts II and III of this volume the substance of several chapters of his book entitled "National Idealism and a State Church," published by them in 1907.

PART I

RELIGION AND NATIONALITY

THE SOUL OF AMERICA

CHAPTER I

A PROSPECTUS, NOT A FORECAST

1. *Moulding the Future*

OUR age has produced many religious Forecasts and Outlooks; but, so far as I am aware, no Prospectuses have been issued. Outlooks and forecasts are the work of spectators who stand aloof and watch the trend of forces, without pretending or wishing to guide them or to increase or diminish their momentum. They are written from the point of view that the future of religion is nothing which the observer can be responsible for. The writers are simply reporters of what would take place even if they were not to note and record. But this book is of a different nature; its attitude towards the future of America — especially of its religion — is somewhat like that of the preliminary advertisement of a business proposition. Except that it is on a spiritual and not a material plane, it is analogous to the prospectus of a manufacturing or mining or railway enterprise. In this respect, it is not unlike General Booth's book entitled "In Darkest England, and the Way Out," which was published because its author wished to raise a million dollars for his great plan of Social Reform. Mine, similarly, is an attempt to induce men and women to invest their time, money, and mental and physical energy in the scheme which it outlines. I therefore

3

stand to the future which I depict, as the first dreamer, let us say, of a canal across the Isthmus of Panama stood to the fact which is now on the eve of complete actualization. A prospectus attempts to bring into existence the idea it presents.

2. *The Word Spiritual*

This book submits to the public a scheme for conserving and developing the Spiritual Resources of America. The specific nature of the scheme will be disclosed later; but at the outset a word may be in place as to what I mean by Spiritual Resources. The very context in which the word spiritual appears shows that it does not point, as it sometimes does in general literature, to some spirit-world outside of time and space or beyond death. Nor does it point to any occult or transcendent faculties of the human mind or to the influx of the infinite spirit of the Creator into the sphere of mortal mind. The word spiritual here refers, as it does in the language of religious piety, to a kind of life. We divide our world into that of the senses and of the soul; and we say that a man is spiritually minded when to him principles of justice, honour, purity, and the like, and visions of a perfect society are as real and present as are the ground he walks on, the bread he eats, or the water he drinks. We say of a woman that she is spiritually minded if, when the practical alternative is presented to her of loyalty to her own ideal of womanhood on the one hand, and on the other the sacrifice of this to luxury, display, and physical comfort, she without an instant's hesitation finds herself siding with her own inward standards of honour. The suggestion that she should disregard these is to her as if it were proposed that she should walk straight through a granite wall. It is the sense of the reality of the unseen universe of principles and ideals that constitutes spirituality.

The proposition, then, how to conserve and develop the spiritual resources of America is the proposition how to conserve and develop the sense of the reality, the potency, the pressure and power of those principles and ideals which have emerged in the history of the American people as manifestations of its essential and unique moral genius. It is a question as to what is the American type of manhood and womanhood. It is further the question as to what is the high calling or inherently preëstablished destiny to which the unprecedented origin, geographical location, and opportunity, and the unforeseen and unforeseeable events in the nation's career have been calling her citizens.

The spiritual resources of America thus understood are clearly seen to be not unrelated to her commercial, political, and domestic life. On the contrary, the motive of this book springs from the conviction, which I believe many readers will share with me, that the ultimate dynamic of all thorough reform in domestic life, in economics and politics is to be found in the sense of the reality and urgency with which moral principles and social ideals are invested. Even the conservation of the material resources of America requires the development of its spiritual energy and insight.

This prospectus for the development of the Soul of America arises out of the belief that her moral potencies are at present running enormously to waste or lying idle, and are therefore practically as if they were in great part non-existent. My propositions assume that it would be possible to develop almost infinitely the spiritual potencies of the nation by organizing them and lifting them into self-consciousness, and that when so developed they would be able to sweep away rapidly and forever national defects and wrongs and causes of suffering and disease which now alarm every true statesman and patriot.

I began by referring to religion, because the spiritual

resources of the world have always been the concern of organized religion. It has always been religion which has given spiritual sanctions — the sense of the reality of an unseen order — to the practical conduct of a people and its customs and laws concerning property, life, the family, politics, truth, and religion itself.

3. *Statesmanship in Religion*

When we look at the place which intelligent foresight and statesmanship have taken in the history of religion, it becomes the more astonishing that in our day writers should occupy themselves with outlooks and forecasts instead of prospectuses. This peculiarity of present-day writers on religion would seem to argue some sort of degeneracy or blindness or some aberration as to the real character and significance and purpose of religion; for in its periods of creative and beneficent activity religion has been full of the plans of patriots and statesmen. Possibly the greatness of the past has overpowered us so that we can no longer originate, but only imitate and repeat. We must imitate and not repeat; that is, we must imitate the originality and constructive statesmanship of the great religious geniuses of the past. Primarily we must remember that religions start with ideas which gradually become facts. It was an idea in the mind of Jesus — an idea of the nature of a prospectus or scheme of salvation — from which emanated the Christian churches. But the scheme of Jesus was supplemented by another of St. Paul and his contemporaries. There was constructive enterprise of statesmanship at work to conserve and develop the spiritual resources of society. The great religious geniuses never assumed the rôle of spectators, nor did they practise an aloofness, as if the religious drama of the world would unroll of itself before them. They were not spectators, but the actors in the drama. They felt that, with themselves left out, the issue of the plot would fail to manifest its inherent meaning.

If we look beyond Christianity to ancient Judaism, we note the same conspicuous office performed by the enterprises of statesmanship and the entire absence of any rôle assigned to mere onlookers; nor was there any thought of an evolution of religion as a thing uncaused by human effort and design. For instance, religious patriots and politicians first threw out the idea that the Jewish nation was weakened and decentralized in character by the scattered "high places" of worship over the land; and then they agitated for the abolition of remote altars and the concentration upon Mount Zion in Jerusalem as the one point of national worship. Coming forward again in history, we are startled by the fact that the Roman Catholic Church, which declares itself not only to be heaven-born, but continuously inspired from on high, is the world's chief instance of men's intelligent foresight in mapping out the kind of future they wish to see created and constraining the forces of human nature to actualize their scheme. Even the present policy of the Roman Church in centralizing itself in the Vatican and in this way unifying the Roman Catholic world is but a repetition on a larger scale of the prospectus of Jewish politicians in the eighth, seventh, and sixth centuries before Christ.

Not to prolong to too great length my historical argument, I would cite only two more instances of the place of prospective enterprise in religion. Richard Hooker, at the close of the sixteenth century, in his "Ecclesiastical Polity," marked out a scheme which has had structural effect upon the religious organization of England, and which seems destined to have still more decisive influence. My last instance is American. It was the practical organizing statesmanship of John Wesley that caused him, as soon as the United States were established, to assume the rôle of bishop and, by sending out preachers, transplant to American soil his whole system of religious discipline. Thus he brought into being, and did not simply foresee or forecast, the present-day fact that the Methodist denominations of America possess a greater membership than any other one group of Protestant churches.

If I mistake not, there have again appeared in America during the last five years evidences of a recognition of the significance of practical statesmanship in conserving and developing the spiritual resources of the nation as distinct from faith in supernatural providence. I am therefore the bolder in laying stress upon the enterprise-launching nature of this book; but I have another reason for doing so. The clue to its literary style and structure can only be found in the fact that it is a prospectus, and that I am, as it were, trying to float a practical undertaking. Only this object and the peculiar character of the enterprise can explain the composition of the book. They alone will justify both what I have included and what I have excluded. Another person writing on the Soul of America, or I myself writing from a different point of view, would have presented many facts here omitted and shown even those here presented in quite different relations and with different values. For instance, my giving a great part of the space of this volume to a humanistic reinterpretation of Christianity and to the psychology of public worship is wholly justified, if I am right in thinking that the churches in the future are to be the chief instrumentalities for the conserving and developing of America's spiritual resources, and if religious rites and ceremonies must be the chief means for bringing home to the citizens of America the reality of the ideal order of her life.

CHAPTER II

1. *An Argument from Personal Experiences*

THERE was a time when the champion of any fundamental idea anxiously attempted to demonstrate to his readers that his philosophy was in no wise coloured by his own private experience. He tried to show that it was purely objective, and might have originated in the mind of any one; but, happily, in our day we have come to see that even profound and universal truths are never discovered and brought to self-conscious definition, except by some rare opportunity, and even because of some peculiar emotional experience and bent of the individual's will. No philosophy is now counted worthy of attention that was not, in the first instance, an outgrowth of some one person's peculiar individuality and experience; and no thinker is fully trusted who is not perfectly aware of the subjective and incidental occasion that disclosed to him the universal truth which he is advocating.

Accordingly, before proceeding to impersonal grounds to justify the main thesis of these pages, I wish to offer as an argument in favour of it those experiences of my own which first thrust it into the foreground of my attention and so diffused it over my mind that it has now become the formative principle of all my thought on social problems.

Until my twenty-third year, it had never occurred to me that such a person as myself, with such a point of view concerning life and its meaning, with such presupposi-

9

tions, spontaneous reactions and recoils, and with such a
scale of values and standards of judgment, might not have
been born and reared at any time, in any place on the face
of the globe, or even on the planet Mars. So self-evident
had I been to myself that it seemed to me as if an infinite
Creator might have projected me, full-grown, into space
and time at any point, and that I should have felt myself
at home anywhere, irrespective of antecedent courses of
local and temporal events. My notions of self-respect
and duty, of liberty and temperance, manliness and woman-
liness seemed to me to be such as must appear immediately
right and rational to any intelligent will, human or angelic,
finite or infinite.

At the age of twenty-two, however, leaving for the first
time my own national *milieu*, I went as a student to Germany. Only then did I gradually become aware that the
most impersonal and universal characteristics of my inner
selfhood could never have been brought into existence except
in the United States of America — in the Middle West —
and at the exact point in her history when I was born and
had lived there. Then for the first time I saw that almost
everything in morals, religion, and even manners, that had
seemed to me to go without saying, needed argument and
justification beyond itself before it could appeal to any
German. I thus became aware that every native student
in the University of Berlin differed from me in all the
spontaneous reactions of his nature against the occasions
that call for judgment and decision, by as much as the whole
history of Germany for three hundred years has differed
from the entire tradition and experience of America from
the time of the landing of the Pilgrim Fathers until the
year in which I was born — the year before that in which
Abraham Lincoln had awakened America by saying of it
that a house divided against itself could not stand, and that
the United States must become either all free or all slave.

It was revealed to me that America, despite her original descent from England and her continued intercourse with Europe, was a world in herself — a psychic sphere of creative energy, enveloping her citizens, but that she herself was not in the same way comprehended under any larger moral sphere that overarched her as she spans her own geographical sections, her States, counties, cities, families, and individual men and women. And I became aware that Germany constituted for her subjects an equally self-contained sphere of active psychic influence, and in the same way furnished an outer circumference or surface up to which the duties and responsibilities of her subjects extended, but beyond which they suddenly decreased almost to the vanishing point. I realized that beyond that point where one nation stops and another begins on the surface of the earth, the nation and not the individual mind becomes the moral agent which is to deal with neighbouring nations. I saw the profound wisdom of the aphorism of Mazzini, that nations are to humanity as individual men and women are to nations. I saw that reverence for all nations was as essential to the idea of universal brotherhood as reverence for all individual human beings irrespective of race, nationality, colour, sex, or religion. I saw that the brotherhood of *nations* was the true meaning of the brotherhood of man, and that those were the enemies of men as well as of nations who interpreted universal brotherhood in the sense of the obliteration instead of the sanctification of national differences.

After two years and a half of study in Berlin, my debt to Germany had become so great that I have never since been able to think of the "Fatherland" without awe, reverence, and deep personal gratitude. But I am quite certain that what I gathered from the Imperial University was totally different from what any German student would have drawn. It was the contrast with everything I had been accustomed to that gave for me a peculiar significance to German philosophy, political economy, art, and social customs, and brought out a new meaning in all things American. I tingled with awareness of characteristics which did not challenge the attention either of stay-at-home Germans or Americans. I am convinced, and have been ever since my student days in Berlin, that the ratio of a man's points of quickening contact with his own nation to those of his possible contact with any foreign country is at least ten thousand to one. I do not deny the one point. I am fully aware that everybody receives into his mental and moral composition elements and energy derived from other nations, nor do I undervalue these factors; but I do say that even when the specific influences have originated in foreign countries or have had historic roots abroad, they become so transmuted and reorganized by entering the new national atmosphere, as to constitute in their psychic effect a totally different environment. A person, also, who has never left his native country, or at best has travelled abroad only for holiday diversion and not for work and coöperation, inevitably remains blind to the fact that almost all the influences that have moulded him have emanated from within the confines of his own nation.

2. *America Super-political*

The purpose of this book seems to justify me in giving space here for only one instance of the many characteristics of America as a nation that were brought home to my mind by Germany. I became aware after a half year's sojourn in Berlin of the pervading presence, and what seemed to me then omnipotence and omniscience, of a spiritual reality the like of which I had never felt and never could have felt in America. I became aware of the presence of what is called the State. In America, if no individual person is watching you for some private reason of his own, you are unobserved and have a corresponding sense of being alone. In Germany everybody is not only being observed, but is being tracked by the State. I realized that with a million eyes and with instruments and with agencies adequate in power to its purposes, the State was above me, below me, in front and behind, and on both sides, protecting me from others and others from me. I began to perceive the immensity of the difference between a Nation and a State, which my professors in Political Science had pointed out, but which hitherto I had counted as nothing more than an academic distinction. Some of the Political Economists of Germany describe the same thing as the difference between Society and the State. I saw that what I had known and felt in the land of my birth was a Society, a Nation, but scarcely a political organization.

I gradually began also to realize the beneficence and moral necessity of the strong State as a guardian of each person and of the community as a whole, and to deplore its absence in America. The Will of the People, I saw, could never become truly coherent and sovereign, could never fully express itself and execute its plans; the working people would instead become victims of dominant individuals and classes, unless the State stepped in as the agent of the Nation and preserved the human claims of all as against the aggressions of the few. It was Germany that turned my individualistic Democracy into Social Democracy. The German State added to my belief in the good of *all*, a belief in the good of the *whole* as being equally the end of the State.

Foreign observers of America still note a prevalent lack of the sense of the State throughout America. In a democracy preyed upon by plutocratic enemies from within, this is an alarming defect, which as such must be brought to acute self-consciousness; for the State cannot become powerful and wise in the interests of the people — that is, it cannot really exist — except as the conscious need of it encourages it into existence. Only an enormous increase of the power of the State in the interests of the whole community can ever beat back the unblushing and unashamed exploitation of the national wealth by the few, to the detriment of the millions. For instance, there has been no greater menace to America than the pretence of promoters of industry that when benefiting themselves in bringing immigrants to these shores they are also acting for the benefit of the Nation. The public does not seem yet to see the difference between the immediate private benefit of the controlling classes, or of all, and the permanent good of America as a whole; and it accordingly has been ready to sacrifice the total and abiding nation to the rapid development of private enterprises in commerce. Otherwise there could not have been so undisguised an appeal to individual self-interest in summoning immigrants to America. To all the oppressed of Europe America herself still says: "Come over here, here is your country. This country is *your* opportunity to get rich, to rise in the world, to make much of yourself, to be somebody. Come, bleed me." Does America, then, exist for individuals who are not equally to exist for America? Is she merely a means and they wholly the ends? My impression in the course of recent journeys across the United States is that there are more human beings in America preying upon the resources of their nation from a motive of undisguised self-interest than is the case with any country in Europe. Not only do these American citizens batten upon her wealth, but also upon her naïve faith in human nature and individual liberty; nor do the poor in America differ in motive and intent from the rich. More of America's nurslings, of all classes and of whatever origin, feed upon her vitals than is the case with any other national brood in the

world.   It cannot be accounted for in any other way than
negatively, that is, by the absence of the State and the sense
of the State as an instrument in the service of the People
as a whole; there must spring up a political government
to express and administer the Will of the whole people
in the interests, not of all individually, but of the whole as
an abiding totality, of the nation as an organic unit of life.

But my student years in Germany did far more for me
than reveal merely the characteristics, positive and negative and good and bad, of America; the contrast of Germany with the United States, as I have already said, gave
me the formative principle of all my thinking since then
upon social problems.

3. *When Religion builds States*

It required only a few months of sojourn in Germany
to reveal to me the fact that in our dependence upon con-
tinuity of environment our minds belong spiritually to the
plant order of creation.   Our characters, our hearts and
wills grow by means of roots which we put down into the
soil, or rather the soul, of the nation in which we are born
and where we pass our years of infancy and adolescence.
To transplant a man from one country to another is to
tear him up by the roots and to remove the most sensitive
fibres and tendrils of his being from the sources whence
he has drawn his vitality and the peculiar substance and
form of his nature.   In proportion as a man possesses
individuality and virility, he suffers exquisite torture by
expatriation.   In the strongest natures, homesickness in
a foreign land is liable to become not only normally painful, but pathologically dangerous.   It is exile from home
that first reveals to oneself not only one's love of home, but
one's psychic dependence upon it.   One's sense of personal identity may almost be overborne and obliterated

by a change of environment from one's native country to a land where the speech, the customs, the wit and humour, and the ethical valuations are different. A love of one's own country thus awakened will never sink into unconsciousness again. Of all the spiritual energies of the human mind, the sentiment of patriotism aroused by exile is the deepest and most powerful. In depth and potency it is the one spiritual momentum which can be classed with the primal instincts and appetites, such as those of hunger, thirst, the reproductive instinct, curiosity, anger, imitation, and the love of self-display. Women are equally responsive with men to the sentiment of patriotism; but the careers open to men have made it chiefly a masculine characteristic.

The craving to return to one's native environment and the conscious sense of dependence upon it, when once awakened, constitute not only the most powerful of spiritual motives, but also the most cohesive of social forces. It would therefore seem that if somehow the religion of the churches could in each country identify itself with the conscious sense of dependence upon one's nation as the source of one's spiritual life, Christianity and the churches would enter upon a new period of beneficent activity, unprecedented in the world since the first two centuries after Christ — a period of masculinity and virility as well as of a new tenderness and respect for the poor, for women, and for all the unfortunate. It would seem that if the churches could link up their aim with that of patriotism, religion would become again the greatest State-building power in the world. It would reorganize and reconstruct cities and institutions of commerce and education and the laws of marriage and of the ownership of land and capital. Such is the belief in the religious significance and power of awakened patriotism which was engendered in me by the contrast of Germany with America. My experience of the difference in these two nationalities prepared my mind to accept as

the most significant lesson of universal history the identity
of religion in all its great epochs with the higher patriotism.

I saw for the first time why religion among the ancient
Jews was such a dominant national asset; I saw how it was
that Judaism — his religion — made the Jew and gave him
such vitality that 2000 years of foreign oppression and
inhumanity has not been able to extinguish him or his
national idealism.   It was all because with the ancient
Jews religion was patriotism and patriotism was religion.
The God the Jews worshipped was the socializing spirit
of the tribe and nation; Jahweh was the indwelling moral
genius of the Jewish people.   He was the creative soul of
Israel.   The moral genius of this people had brought the
Jews out of the house of bondage and out of the land of
Egypt, had preserved them in the desert, and had kept the
remnant of the righteous together during the seventy years
of the exile in Babylon.   It was the consciously awakened
loyalty of the Jews to the indwelling spirit of their nation
that constituted their religion while in Babylon and brought
them back to their own country and induced them to establish a theocracy when they were denied an independent
political state.   The *throne* of their God, as one of their
psalmists says, was in the praises of his people.

Nobody denies that national idealism was the religion of
Judaism; but many who concede this historic fact are accustomed to assert that with the advent of Christianity
religion became distinct from patriotism, and that this
separation was a moral and spiritual advance.   But the
new psychology and sociology of religion are throwing a flood
of light upon historic Christianity and showing an unexpected identity of it with patriotism.   This identity
for the first thousand years explains the organizing and
virile power of Christianity.   Had it not become the indwelling, socializing, moralizing spirit of a great nation,
Christianity would not have survived and would not have

c

deserved to survive. What happened was this: the Roman Empire was in need of a soul, it was the body without the spirit of a nation. It had only military unity. All the conquered peoples paid tribute unto Cæsar; but there was no cultural unity, and the Roman Empire would soon have become a disintegrating corpse. Even the emperors and courtiers saw this. Constantine and his advisers appreciated the strategic significance of the little groups of Christians worshipping underground throughout the Empire. They must be made the Soul of the nation. And this was what happened: They conserved and developed the spiritual resources of the Roman Empire. They gave it a common ideal of manhood and of life — the ideal found in the New Testament together with the standard of national loyalty presented in the Old. Thus Europe became spiritually unified. In Christianity, then, religion did not cease to be identical with national idealism; on the contrary, it assumed the task of creating a nation — of breathing into it the breath of life. That is the reason Christianity lived and deserved to live. Paul ceased to be a Jew, but he became a Roman citizen; the moral genius which he now worshipped as God was indeed no longer that of Israel, but it was that of Rome.

In like manner, Protestant interpreters have for the most part been quite blind to the true significance of the Reformation. The Reformation was not an assertion of private conscience and of the individual's right to think for himself, but the assertion of Germany's will to become an organic unit of spiritual life and free itself from the dictation of a foreign bishop. Luther is at the same time the genius of the Reformation and the genius of the spiritual resources of Germany; yet not because he was a genius in two directions, but because the Reformation was the awakening of Germany to spiritual self-consciousness.

Analogous was what happened in Scotland and in England; but I cannot here prolong the story. It is clear that religion whenever it has been creative and beneficent has been identical with patriotism. God has always been the indwelling moral genius of a people, the Holy Ghost has always been the socializing power that quickens individual men and women into glad self-sacrifice and service for the good of the whole group to which they belong.

4. *Sir John Seeley's Teaching*

But the interpretation of history which I have just given was by no means a discovery of my own. The awakening to self-consciousness of my own patriotism through the contrasts which I saw between Germany and America only prepared my mind and made it receptive and enthusiastically sensitive to this doctrine of the identity of true religion with the higher patriotism which I found expressed in masterly fashion by Sir John Seeley in his book on "Natural Religion," which was first published in 1883. Sir John Seeley is, in the judgment of many, the most original genius both in the sphere of religious insight and of historic imagination which England produced in the nineteenth century. He more than anyone else was able (in his book entitled "Ecce Homo") to present the human aspect and the human and natural significance of the personality of Jesus Christ. He also, so far as I am aware, was the first to point out the nationalizing genius of Christianity through the Roman Catholic Church and the identity of Protestantism in its several branches with the awakening self-consciousness of the nations of the North.

It was such passages as the following that illuminated and justified to me my personal sense of the exalted significance of patriotism : —

Look almost where you will in the wide field of history, you will find Religion, whenever it works freely and mightily, either

giving birth to and sustaining States, or else raising them up to
a second life after destruction.   It is a great State-builder in the
hands of Moses and Ulfilas and Gregory and Nicholas; in the
ruder hands of Mohammed and many another tamer and guide
of gross populations, down to the prophet of Utah, it has the
same character; the same, too, in the hands of the almost forgotten Numas and propagators of the Apollo-worship who laid
the foundation of Roman and Greek civilization, and of the
Pilgrim Fathers who founded New England.   In the East to
this day nationality and religion are almost convertible terms;
the Scotch national character first awoke in the adoption of a
new Religion, and afterwards expressed itself more than once
in national covenants; the Reformation itself may be represented as coming out of the German national consciousness,
and it has been proposed to call the various forms of Protestantism by the collective name of Teutonic Christianity.   Lastly,
in Christianity itself, in Romanism, and partly also in Mohammedanism we find religion in the form of an aggressive or
missionary nationality, bringing foreign nations into a new
citizenship.

All this being overlooked, the very outlines of European
developments almost disappear from our view.   In losing sight
of the connection between Religion and Nationality, we lose the
clue to the struggle between Church and State, which is the
capital fact in the development of Europe.   As in the first part
of the struggle we overlook that the Church is but another
aspect of the Empire, and Catholicism but the embodiment of
the Roman nationality, so in the later stages of it, in the modern
struggle between Catholicism and that which calls itself the
State, we are blind to the fact that under the so-called State
there lurks a new, yet undeveloped, Church.

On account of my own individual experience, the passages in Sir John Seeley's book which have most endeared
his moral insight to me are those in which he points out the
awakening and deepening effect upon patriotism of exile from
one's native land.   He made me realize that whatever
special sensitiveness it was on my part which had converted

my patriotism into a religion was no eccentricity nor abnormality of mine; for a similar experience in thousands of hearts in all ages has proved of untold significance and beneficence to the world.

A civilization [says Sir John Seeley] which to those who live in the midst of it is imperceptible as an atmosphere, becomes distinctly visible in contrast with the outer world.

Greeks felt their Hellenism in contrast with barbarism and Jews their election in contrast with Gentiles. When the contrast becomes intense a condition of unstable equilibrium is created . . . and one of those great spiritual movements takes place which mark at long intervals the progress of humanity, such as the conversion of all nations to Judaism, to Romanism, to Hellenism.

It would even seem that Seeley had not failed to observe cases of American patriotism like mine; for he says:—

Not otherwise at this day the American who finds himself in Europe translates of sheer necessity his American ways of thinking into a creed. He can think and talk of nothing else. To every European he preaches, like St. Paul, in season and out of season, America, America!

I hope I may not seem to be falling into too personal a vein instead of keeping to my argument when I cite the present volume as perhaps the latest instance of an American in Europe preaching America. Nor can I deny that my case is still more aggravated than those referred to by Seeley, for I am here presuming to preach America, America, not to Europeans, but to Americans themselves. I would, however, plead excuse and justification on the ground of the exile which my specialized work has imposed upon me; and if I need further justification, I would hide behind that fine aphorism of Mr. Rudyard Kipling with which he shielded himself against the adverse judgment of those who thought that he, having sojourned in remote India, should

not presume to criticise or instruct England. In retort
he exclaims : —

What should they know of England, who' only' England
know?

5. *America Super-historical*

But I have not finished the argument from personal
experience with which I said I wished to introduce the
thesis of this book. After student days in Germany and a
brief return to America, my special task called me to England, and there I settled ; and I have lived and worked there
since the year 1888. From the first I delighted in those
qualities of English life — mellow as her summer sunshine
— which always enchant and often permanently enchain
visitors from the New World. But here I wish only to give
my testimony as to the increasing consciousness which my
knowledge of England brought about as to the deeper
meaning of America in particular and of National Idealism
the world over as the redemptive trend in history. In
England, I again found myself in a new world, a world as
different from both Germany and America as I had found
these two unlike each other. England, in my judgment, is
spiritually a different sphere from America, as much as
Mars is physically different from the Earth. All the
planets, no doubt, have the same chemical nature and manifest the same laws of physics, and all of them are in the same
solar system ; but life in Mars, if there be any, and the
forms engendered there by natural selection, must be as
different from those of Earth as is her place in the solar
system. Both Englishmen and Americans, let us grant,
participate in the same primal instincts and psychic constitutions ; but the men and women in England who are
surrounded by a social atmosphere more than a thousand
years deep, through which the whole of the Past presses
upon them, inevitably find the American, with his short

national tradition and memory, almost a human curiosity; and *vice versa*. As with my impression of Germany, so of England; my arguments here permit me to specify only one characteristic of America as distinct from England, and it is again a negative quality. The absence of the sense of the Past, and the absence of the pressure of it upon the American imagination and will, are unique in the life of the great modern nations, just as is the absence from the American mind of the sense of the State and of the pressure of the State as a living reality. This sense in a nation of escape from the Past is a negative quality of the highest significance for the whole future of America. It is a form of liberty, I believe, which to the end of all time will mark her; having once got into her blood, it will propagate itself like an antitoxin. The consciousness of being free from the Past and therefore of relative contempt for the Past is one of the chief elements in the American sense of liberty. The absence of the Past and of a sense of it, will make America forever predisposed to undertake enterprises which have no precedent in the world's history. America, from a motive of utilitarian idealism, will always be ready in the spirit of Nietzsche's philosophy to become superhistorical. I could cite many instances of communities in America which have quite readily, and without any misgiving or apprehension, passed laws of a wholly untried and unprecedented nature, laws which the British would have felt that their very sanity — meaning their historic sense — forbade them to pass. Here, then, we find, although of a negative nature, a characteristic common to all Americans: the lack of the historic sense and the absence of the pressure of history. This negative characteristic of American life begins immediately to have effect upon the heart of every immigrant or casual visitor, making it light, and upon the will, making it brave. Thus is every American differentiated from the stay-at-home subjects of every other government in the world.

I count typical of all America, and therefore an allegory or parable, an answer to a question of mine which was made many years ago by a youth in one of my boys' clubs in New York City. He had made some remark which seemed to reveal so superficial a sense of history that I asked him: "But how old do you suppose the world is?" With surprise and some bewilderment he answered with the return question: "Wasn't the world created in 1776?" No youth ever spoke more wisely! The world in which *he* lived, the world of the United States, the Soul which brooded over him, the Soul of America, was, as an ordered cosmos, as a spiritual providence, created in 1776.

If we contrast the great historic fact of the identity of patriotism and religion with the present state of things in America, we cannot help being startled by what seems to be an absolute divorce between religion in America and American patriotism. In America religion is one thing; and patriotism, where it exists, is altogether another and a different thing. They are not even two things that interpenetrate or move in the same direction or advance to the same end. There probably never was a country in the world that lived so long and that prospered so well where there was so little identification, conscious or unconscious, of religion with patriotism. But its history thus far has been wholly unique; and now the unique conditions are at an end. Its divorce, therefore, of religion from patriotism is no proof that either Christianity or American patriotism or even the material conditions of the United States will go on prospering if the divorce continues. It is possible that, from now on, the one national asset that will save America from internal disruption and from moral decay will be the making of religion henceforth identical with the nation's sense of high destiny and sublime responsibility.

CHAPTER III

1. *Pioneers, O Pioneers!*

SOME recent students of life in the United States have
declared that America is lacking in any central vitalizing
power that gives unity of culture, community of vision and
aim, and harmony of values to all her citizens. For instance, Mr. A. E. Zimmern, until recently a Don of Oxford,
in a brilliant paper entitled, "Seven Months in America,"
which appeared in the *Sociological Review* for July, 1912,
says: "Another common political fallacy needs to be
mentioned. Current ideas . . . assume that America is
a nation. . . . America consists at present of a congeries
of nations who happened to be united under a common
federal government." He adds, "No, America is not a
melting pot. . . . To meet image with image, I would
reply, 'America is not a melting pot; it is a varnishing pot,'
or, in the words of Freiherr von Wolzogen, 'America is a
sausage machine, for grinding out Equality sausages.' . . .
'There is all the difference in the world,' said a young Jewish
philosopher to me, 'between an American Jew and a Jewish
American. A Jewish American is a mere amateur Gentile,
doomed to be a parasite forever.'"

Where is the truth in this matter? Has it been an illusion of self-conceit and vanity on the part of America to
believe that the very spirit embodied in the Constitution
and history of the United States penetrates through a
thousand different avenues into the centre of the soul of
every child born here and of every immigrant that is landed

here, and that it then, from the throne of each person's
selfhood, begins to construct his character in accordance
with the organic law of the nation's being?

Mr. Zimmern's denial that America gives cultural unity
to her people can in the first place be refuted out of his own
mouth. In the very same essay, of which the object is to
deny that America is a nation, occurs the following lavish
delineation of that disposition of will, that quality of heart,
that type of intellect which, according to Mr. Zimmern's
own confession, marks not only the successive generations,
but all the geographical groups of the United States: —

Every one knows what the American pioneer qualities are;
most Europeans admire or even envy them, as the middle-aged
envy the young, while laughing a little up their sleeve. Yet it
is worth while trying to define them, indefinable though they
are. An inexhaustible fountain of kindness and good nature,
which makes a journey in America seem like a passage from
friend to friend; a wonderful alertness and adaptability,
through which the hostess grasps the situation, the financier
closes with a bargain, the citizen takes the law into his own
hands, in as brief a moment as it took their ancestors to sight
and shoot the Red Indian who was climbing the stockade; an
undaunted self-confidence, which will plant a city in a treeless
wilderness, as the Mormons did in Utah, or descry a business
prospect when the Easterner can see only a castle in Spain; a
ferocious optimism which seems to welcome difficulty and disaster, bankruptcy and earthquake, for the fierce joy of overcoming them; an ingenuous delight in novelty for the mere
sake of experiment, which replaces the philosophic " Why? " of
Europe by the unanswerable "Why not!" a nonchalant venture-
someness which gambles with life and fortune as gaily as the
reprobates among ourselves would risk a handful of money on a
racecourse; a strength of purpose and a vigorous tenacity in
action unexampled in any one people, even the Scotch, but
explicable as the result of three generations of social selection
from among the stronger wills of Europe; a complete absence of
self-consciousness or reflectiveness or any kind of deeper in-

sight, and an inclination, developed by their education into a
habit, towards using the mind as a quick-firing gun; all the
qualities of childhood except reverence, with a continent for a
nursery, its easy emotions and rapid tempers, its lively curiosity,
its sunny expansiveness, its irresistible buoyancy, its short and
fickle memory, its disobedience, its ruthlessness, its almost
tragic capacity for laughter in the face of grave issues, its in-
satiable appetite for sweetness and light, in the shape of con-
fectionery and electric sky signs; above all, and a redemption
of all, its intense and abounding and infectious vitality, its instinctive loyalty and comradeship in action, its idealism in the
darkest hours, shedding immortal lustre on some disaster which
its own unwisdom has failed to avert, when in a moment, as
under Lee and Lincoln, at the bidding of destiny the scattered
band of 'boys' becomes an army of men — this, this is the American spirit; and Walt Whitman is its prophet. *Pioneers, O
Pioneers*, is the song of successive generations of young Americans, novitiates into the Dionysiac spirit of transatlantic life.

The only possible explanation which I can find for Mr.
Zimmern's self-contradiction in describing the character
of America, and yet denying to her a dominant unifying influence, is that if a nation's genius is of the pioneer
sort, he thinks it must be only a passing phase of mental
life and not enduring enough to be a nation-building power.
He seems to imply that the moment pioneer opportunities
of material exploration have ceased, it is preposterous to
suppose that the qualities of the pioneer may continue to
dominate. But here, in my judgment, the sociology of this
student of America is defective in three vital points. Some
unique circumstance in a nation's career, although itself
not lasting for more than two or three lifetimes, may
generate a temper, a vision, a standard of values, that will
live on and mould the people for centuries to come. Even
Mr. Zimmern opens his essay with the affirmation that,
although she is not a nation, America is "a state of mind."
Now, my contention is that the state of mind which is

America is a permanent creative spirit, giving unity of vision, a sympathetic understanding, and comradeship of will to all the dwellers on American soil. It was generated under conditions unique in the history of mankind; those conditions are rapidly becoming a thing of the past. But that spirit which they engendered is mightier throughout the United States to-day than ever before. Not only this; it is spreading throughout the world. Japanese scholars caught it in American colleges and took it back to Japan. Sun Yat Sen and his fellow-students carried it to China. And we know what it has already achieved in both these countries. This Dionysiac spirit, begotten into immortality by the pioneer life in America, sets quickly on fire the proletariats of all the nations of the world. For three generations it has drawn something like a million persons a year to the American shores. Now it is taking root in foreign soils and is engendering revolutions there — like the recent one in China. Let us, then, concede that primitive pioneer conditions have ended. But let us not be blind to the gigantic fact that before they ended, they let loose a Spirit which bids fair to become everlasting and universal. It is probable that from now on throughout the world for all time the dominant disposition of Humanity will not cease to be that of the Pioneer Spirit.

The second error which I think must lurk at the root of Mr. Zimmern's self-contradiction is that pioneering work is over when once the primeval forests have been owned and cut down. The facts of American history justify as against such a view the belief that the moment the pioneering spirit has nothing more to achieve on the purely physical plane of material wealth, it immediately rises to the mental, moral, and spiritual plane. There it discovers one new vision after another that needs actualizing and one old world after another that requires to be annihilated in order that there may be room for the new ideal. The real and the highest pioneer work has only begun in America. Note the recent transformations of the Constitutions of the United States and of the several States, whereby these have been made more plastic and supple instruments of the sovereign will of the people. Who is so literal and materialistic, as to deny that the adoption of the Initiative, the Referendum, the Recall, and of Woman's Suffrage has been in each case an enterprise that has given full scope to all the live qualities of the pioneer spirit? It was as late as 1903 that Mr. H. G. Wells unfortunately committed himself to saying of America: "No national Income Tax is legal; and there is practically no power, short of revolution, to alter that." And yet the pioneer spirit has altered "that," already, and far short of revolution in the sense of violence and disorder.

It was Mr. Walter Bagehot in his book on " The English Constitution," who, criticising the American Constitution a generation ago, said that the defect of it was that just when you most wanted to find the sovereign will of the people there was no way of discovering it. He therefore maintained that England, with its government by Cabinet and its Electoral Appeal to the people whenever the Cabinet lost the support on any vital issue of the majority of the House of Commons, was far more democratic in method than America. But the pioneer spirit of America in the last five years has been able to find means for the expression of the sovereign will of the people, and there is ample evidence to justify the belief that in another generation America will be in reality, as well as in boast, the most democratic nation in the world.

2. *A Falsehood that will be made True*

My allusion to the boast of Americans that their country is a democracy suggests to me what I count a third vital fallacy implied in Mr. Zimmern's sociological reasoning. In one place he says: "The schoolboy is taught in his text-book, and repeats to every passing stranger, that America, being a republic, is a free country and that she is a pure democracy, and that she offers perfect liberty to her citizens, that she knows no distinctions of rank and class, that, giving votes to all, she is governed by all. All this is false to-day, if it ever was true."

My knowledge of the dynamics of national life has helped me to see that the fallacies about itself which a nation sincerely believes to be true are of greater worth as a national asset and are therefore in a sense more true than those exactly literal facts which an unsympathetic stranger is quite capable of detecting even in less than a seven months' visit. Let it be conceded that America is not by any means governed by all, although she gives votes to all; that she knows inhuman, bitter, and wholly unjustifiable distinctions of rank and class; that there is nothing she offers which even remotely resembles perfect equality among her citizens; and that she is not either a free country or a pure democracy. Still, there is more hope for a land that is not free in fact, but is so in ideal, than for a land that is in fact free, but is not so in ideal. A nation that teaches in its text-books to every schoolboy, so that he can repeat it to every passing stranger, that his country is free, is storing up a dynamic of liberty that will prove irresistible when once it strikes consciously against economic inequalities of opportunity. The future of a country does not come out of what it is at present or what it was in a past generation, — such a notion is a mere pedantry of academic sociology. The future of a country comes out of what its teachers tell its schoolboys that it is. For, when in later life they find that the country is not what the teachers prepared them to expect, the teachers' statement will be transformed by the younger generation into fiery prophecy.

When Americans awake to the illusory nature of what had been taught them in childhood as very fact, it will be the newly detected facts and not the illusion which they will repudiate as impossible. They will transform the Great Illusion into a Greater Fact.

The most wonderful characteristic of that state of mind which is America is the teaching of this fallacy that America is a free country. There is no other land in the world where the boys and girls have been so taught from the beginning of the nation's existence that their nation offers perfect equality to its citizens. Russia has not taught that, Prussia has not taught that; and I can testify from twenty-five years of close observation of what is given by teachers to the children of England that no child born in Great Britain has ever been told by parent, teacher, or preacher that in England there are no distinctions of rank and class, that the country is free and offers equality to all, and that she is governed by all. One reason why economic equality as regards the ownership of land comes so slowly in England and why women's suffrage has seemed to many of the best women in England as if it were an instalment of justice that never could be brought about except by violence and terror, is because in England no educators have been indiscreet enough to perpetuate the explosive fallacy that all men are created free and equal.

Could there be any greater proof that it is a mistake to deny a homogeneous culture to America than the fact that the United States has for a hundred and forty years taught, in season and out of season, in every section of the land, to all children and adults, and teaches now more than ever, the doctrine of equality? Americans have been setting up that false notion, — false to the facts, — and making it the standard by which they will condemn all conflicting facts. That false doctrine will never be yielded up simply because it is false; it will make itself true. Sociologically, there could be no greater error than to laugh at the Declaration of Independence and the Preamble of the Constitution of the United States as if they were mere words or mere paper or mere ideas, simply because the economic conditions of America do not tally with them. That Declaration and that Preamble are as yet not facts, and in this sense are only ideas. But some ideas act as stimuli to the primal instincts and cravings in human nature, they awaken an active thirst for self-realization. They cannot therefore be called merely ideas, as if they were not actual potencies, for they are incentives which build and unbuild States. The conviction, "I am free," striking unexpectedly against the flinty fact, "I am not free," generates a spark from whence a revolution may be kindled.

But, happily, in this America, which is said not to be a nation but only a congeries of nations, the idea that she is free is not an absolute falsehood. There are some actual institutions in the United States that not only are free, but are open doors to a larger freedom. Those clauses in the Constitution of the country which made it possible to introduce the Income Tax without the violence of revolution are footholds on which the Spirit of Liberty can stand and lift the whole people into economic equality.

3. *America true to the Law of her own Being*

It is to be regretted that many present-day students of American life, instead of noting that the United States is evolving from within according to the organic law of its own being, are simply struck by the fact that great changes are taking place. They see the new phases of life, but do not seem to detect the inner law from which they issue. The new phases accordingly seem to them incidental, accidental, or arbitrary. But I should like to record, for what it is worth, my judgment that, as compared with England and

Germany, America is not being transformed more rapidly than either of these other two countries, nor in the changes which she is effecting is she less true to the genius of her historic past.   There is no more occasion to write a book on "Changing America," as one American has done, than for a German to write a book on changing Germany; likewise, it is a great mistake to imagine that America in 1914 is a new world, any more than is the England of the same year, as compared with that of 1814.   Berlin, Düsseldorf, and Munich, London, Manchester, and Liverpool are no more like what they were even fifty years ago than is New York like its former self, or San Francisco and Chicago like themselves.   The sanitary conditions, the municipal laws, the habits and tastes of the people have undergone as great a revolution throughout Germany and England as throughout America.   What is more, the changes have been, on the whole, in the same direction.   One cannot say that Germany and England have become Americanized, although they both have become democratized and socialized in education, politics, economics, and in mental characteristics.   German democratization is of an essentially German kind; that of England bears all the marks of the peculiar dialectical process by which for a thousand years England has zigzagged forward; while America has become more social-democratic in a manner which only her peculiar problems and her particular traditions could have occasioned.   It is therefore altogether superficial and uncritical to interpret the rapidity of the changes in America as due to a lack of cohesiveness or a deficiency of unifying power in the moral genius of the nation.   It would seem as if some sociological visitors from abroad become bewildered by the complexity and extent of American social life, as if their brain power was not equal to detecting the inward unity which embraces all the differences and even dictates the changes, manipulating them in the interests of the nation.   But it is surely

D

a fallacy to infer that there is no coördination in an external complex, because one's own mind lacks the unifying faculty of apperception.

As a proof of increasing anarchy and chaos, and as support to the assertion that America is not a nation, it is stated that during the last decade the restlessness of the working-classes is greater. They shift more often from city to city and from State to State than they did thirty years ago. From this the critic infers that they do not remain long enough in any one locality of the United States to receive a unity of culture or to feel a local attachment. But such an interpretation presupposes that, when they shift from State to State, they come under another type of moral and social influence, and that the locality to which they are becoming attached may not be America as a whole. In journeying to and from New York and San Francisco I have been astonished to find almost an absolute identity in the degree and kind of culture that exists over the whole continent. I have heard very much friendly bantering of the inhabitants of one section towards those of another, as if there were colossal differences; but I am certain that as I passed from Boston to Los Angeles there was no downward slope to a lower or any ramification to a different culture. The only place in which I became aware of a drop in tone and a different type of civilization was in Utah, especially Salt Lake City; but whoever has read the Book of Mormon and knows all the circumstances will understand how Mormonism has acted as a barrier, shutting out from Utah the full influence of modern critical thought and social education.

The very increase in the shifting of populations from locality to locality itself tends to cultural unification and lifts the lowest of the population above the dull unconsciousness of self in which the proletariats of European nations have slept until the last thirty years. One of the striking

contrasts between the middle- and the working-class populations in a country like England is the greater mobility
(because they can afford it) of the middle classes from section to section. The shifting, then, of the wage-earners in
America simply means that they already have the cultural
opportunity of the trading classes of England.

In the preceding paragraphs I have tried to show that
the differences in American life that seem to point to a lack
of unity are really purely superficial, or are actually causes
of unity; and I have also shown that the preaching of
liberty, equality, and fraternity is universal, and always
has been since the winning of independence by the American
Colonies. In a later chapter, likewise, I shall make it
clear that the subsidiary patriotisms of the various national
groups of American immigrants give an interesting and
delightful variety without destroying in the least the
cultural unity of the United States, or her dominance as
a formative power. I have also pointed out two negative
characteristics of America which cause all her citizens,
in common, to escape two of the mightiest pressures that
have shaped the characters of people in all the other great
nations of the world. One is the absence, relatively, of
the State and therefore the lack of the sense of the State;
the other is the absence of any concrete monuments of the
civilization of the world prior to 1606 and of all such
customs, habits, and traditions as were left behind in the
Old World and all such as pilgrim and immigrant have
preferred to forget. There is reason to believe, as I have
already said, that a nation which during its first century
and a half of existence is comparatively free from these two
pressures, will never desire to submit to the State or to
revere it, or to be brought under that mighty Past from
which it in great part escaped. It seems quite reasonable
to conjecture that however rapidly the State develops in
power and enters into the details of the lives of individuals,

the individuals will never forget that they themselves devised the laws and enforced them; and that they themselves, as a nation, that is, as a Society, were the original protoplasm, as it were, which differentiated itself into a State, and that they can at any time, being still alive and creative, slough off all laws and traditions that have become dead, and can afresh shape other laws to meet the present and the future need. And as America sees an ever deepening past of her own stretching behind her, that past, being her own, will be increasingly a power on the side of those ideas which first dictated and then adapted her political structure.

With no pretence of a systematic or exhaustive presentation of the positive influences that play upon the minds of all American citizens alike, let me mention three more which have a direct relation to the fundamental purpose of this book.

4. *Where the Poor do not look up to the Rich*

The first is the universal attitude of the American poor to the rich. While in all other great historic nations, and in America as well, the rich look down upon the poor, America is the only great nation where the poor do not inwardly, that is, with real respect and reverence, look up to the rich or to the ruling classes in general. An English gentleman visiting in the United States misses a certain deference to which he has always been accustomed. He sometimes receives the very opposite; but in the end, if he pierces to the motive forces of social democracy and if he respects democracy and believes in it, he will interpret what at first seems to him contempt for persons of a higher social station as being in reality the American workingman's enormously greater respect for himself. It is not that he respects the rich and powerful less than the British workman, but that he respects himself infinitely more. The social atmosphere of America engenders in him a fearlessness towards anybody and everybody. He becomes superbly oblivious to any conventional barriers with which the rich of America attempt to secure themselves against easy approach. He may notice difference of dress and bearing and of speech; but these by no means impress or overpower him. Nothing can be more astonishing to a European of high social position as he moves among the rank and file of the American public than to find the perfect readiness with which persons will speak to him on a basis of social equality while belonging to a class who in Europe would not dream of making any social approach. I may be allowed to cite as typical of hundreds of experiences that are likely to befall any visitor to the United States one of my own. I have selected it as illustrative of a general temper among the wage-earners of America, and as an exhilarating expression of the general absence of social deference. This experience was provided me by the conductor of an electric street-car in a city of the Middle West. It was a summer evening and the open car was crowded. As the car was brilliantly lighted, I was for an instant too dazzled to detect whether there still remained one vacant seat or not; accordingly, as the conductor stood near on the outer rail where I mounted the car, I asked him in a tone no louder than necessary, "Is there an empty seat?" "An empty seat?" exclaimed he in a voice that attracted the attention of every one in the car, "Can't you see for yourself? Haven't you got any eyes?" Whereupon all my fellow-passengers riveted theirs upon me. As I took my seat, I fixed my gaze upon the conductor, when he again broke out with, "That's right, stare at me! My name's McCarthy and my number is 243." Again my fellow-passengers focussed their vision upon me. Some twenty minutes later every one else had got out, but I

remained, as I was going to my brother's house beyond the
terminus of the electric line. I was looking off into the
dark and wishing myself back in effete England, when
suddenly I felt two hands, like those of a suppliant, placed
upon my knees; and there stood the conductor, who in
subdued and gentle voice began: "See here! I understand
you are Colonel Coit's brother. I hope you won't peach
on me; for if you do, I shall get the sack." "I shall not
say anything," I replied, "but it is a pity if a foreigner —"
"There now!" he interrupted, "do you know, I *thought*
you must be a foreigner! No American would ever have
asked such a damn-fool question as you did!" In America
wage-earners not only count themselves as good as anybody else, but will allow no one, I have learned, to intrench
upon their time a moment beyond what is nominated
in the bond. American working-men regard themselves
simply as men, as fellow-citizens, and not as members of
the economic class to which for the moment they belong.
Not a day can be passed by a visitor from Europe without
being reminded of the universal fact throughout America
that there is no horizontal stratification of society and that
no one seemingly at the bottom feels any superincumbent
weight of the classes above him pressing out of him not
only the ability, but even the desire to rise. If the traveller
from Europe chances to put up at the best hotels, for
instance, in the Yellowstone Park, he may observe, as I
did, among the guests at the evening dance given for them in
the dining room, the women who during the day have
been serving at the tables. Bewildered by this circumstance,
he may apply to the hotel clerk to inquire whether this
be a servants' or a guests' dance; and he will be informed
that it is both! He will be assured that if the waitresses
were not admitted to the dance, they would immediately
strike. Upon his return to the East, if he cites such experiences as typical of American life, his friends will explain

that the waitresses in the Yellowstone Park were not ordinary "hired help," but were probably school-teachers taking their summer holidays. Yet to him, this explanation only reveals the more palpably the astonishing absence of any horizontal classification of social grades in America. I have said that the American working-man never looks up to the rich and to the ruling classes and he feels no barrier in approaching nor any shyness in seeking access. This is the more remarkable, considering the enormous respect paid to riches; and it is only explicable on the ground that the respect for the riches is impersonal. It is the money the American reveres, and not the man who owns it. It would seem that even the richest men in America are not so vain as to imagine that it is they and not their riches which are sought after. In his "Inspired Millionaires," Mr. Gerald Stanley Lee with exquisite humour depicted the American plutocrat who is only rich and nothing more. He represents such a millionaire as forced in mere self-pity to become something else besides rich; for he cannot induce any one, least of all the poor, even though he come with open cheque-book in hand, to have him for a friend and companion. The public hold aloof because they look down upon him, not because they look up.

Now there is no other nation on the earth where the poor do not with genuine reverence and sincere respect look up to the rich. In Germany the Social Democratic Party has been trying for forty years to prevent the poor from doing this, but has not succeeded except through terrorization. In England, in spite of the organization of the aristocracy of labour into proud trade-unions, the average working-man still has social contempt for members of his own order. He has a sincere deference for the members of the so-called "gentleman class," and prefers to have gentlemen represent him in the House of Commons. The contempt of the working-man in America for the rich merely as the rich is

the greatest dynamic factor in the evolution towards social
justice that the world possesses to-day; while the reason
that liberty and equality halt so long in their advance over
Europe is because the wage-earners respect their "superiors"
and believe in them more than they respect and believe
in themselves.

5. *Intuition versus Instinct and Intellect*

The second unique element that is diffused throughout
the entire moral atmosphere of America and gives to it
a tonic effect is the universal faith in the power of the
experienced mother-wit of every average individual to
cope with unforeseen difficulties, and in the corresponding
power of the combined mother-wit of the nation to enlist
ultimately all the resources of the universe into the service
of humanity. Perhaps I cannot better bring out the exact
character of this pervasive feature than by calling the attention of my reader to the distinction, as M. Bergson
makes it, between intuition on the one hand, and on the
other instinct and intelligence.

Adopting the Bergsonian distinction, we may say that
England is proverbial the world over for her reliance upon
instinct. This accounts for her fumbling and her faith in
fumbling. She trusts to accident and happy chance and
to improvised hand-to-mouth judgments. Britishers believe in the subconscious trend in themselves; their intelligence is tied down to the immediate present, and they
trust to its spontaneous reaction against the unanticipated
circumstances which confront them. In this way they
have moved for ages through crises and have moved out
of long epochs exactly as the birds in the north of Scotland
pass in the autumn southward over Europe to Egypt; and
the result has thus far justified them in trusting to their
almost automatic reaction in coping with adverse environ-

ments which have no precedent. On the other hand, the British have no historic experience to justify them in trusting either to their logical intelligence or their intuition. Mr. Gladstone has given classic recognition to this instinctive character of the British genius in a passage in which he contrasts the Constitution of England with that of America. "The two Constitutions," he says, "of the two countries express rather the differences than resemblances of the two nations. The one is a thing grown, the other is a thing made; the one, the offspring of tendency and indeterminate time, the other of choice and of an epoch. But, as the British Constitution is the most subtle organism which has proceeded from the womb and the long gestation of progressive history, so the American Constitution is, as far as I can see, the most wonderful work ever struck off at a given time by the brain and purpose of man. It has had a century of trial under the pressure of exigencies caused by an expansion unexampled in point of rapidity and range; and its exemption from formal change, though not entire, has certainly proved the sagacity of the constructors and the stubborn strength of the fabric."

America has not been an outgrowth of instinct; but neither does it illustrate the action of logical or abstract intellect. For a nation typical of the logical understanding, in the Bergsonian sense, we must look to Germany. Here we see a nation which is at the same time the least instinctive and also the least intuitive nation on earth. Germans believe universally in abstract reasoning and even in deductive inference when once they have carefully built up their generalizations. Modern Germany has been made according to a highly elaborated design, just as a building is put up according to the architect's plans. As compared with Englishmen and Americans, Germans never trust either instinct or intuition. They will not even trust a man whom they have seen and with whom they have talked by the impression he makes directly upon them, but require paper credentials and the testimonials of teachers and employers, and these evidences they will accept even against their own immediate impression. The Germans have become so impregnated with the habit of exact and quantitative knowledge such as science demands, that they find it difficult to act in any direction until they have attained a definition and an algebraical formula. They seem, therefore, both to the Englishman and the American, to be victims of a pedantry that bids fair to paralyze whatever mother-wit they may have been endowed with at birth. Even the Social Democratic Party, although consisting chiefly of untutored working-men, illustrates this national characteristic. The Social Democratic Party was derived directly from the university discipline and studies of two middle-class thinkers, and all along it has been led by doctors of philosophy from the universities. It is the most rationalistic, metaphysical, self-conscious, and theoretical organization in the world, and is the least instinctive and the least intuitive. It is absolutely encoffined in the metaphysical dogma of Karl Marx. Such Socialism can see no facts that run counter to Marx's fiction; and, unless new life be brought to it from some genius who, like Edward Bernstein, has been in touch with the instinctive method of England, the Social Democratic Party is doomed to practical ineffectuality. Its Utopia is an abstract construction of logical intellect, which will be shattered the moment its leaders come into power and try to meet the demands of concrete life. Schopenhauer protested against this kind of death-engendering intellectualism of Germany, and so did Nietzsche. Bernstein, even within the Congresses of the Social Democratic Party, has now for more than a decade cried protest in the name of instinct and intuition.

But Bergson counts both the method of instinct and the

method of the logical intellect as inferior to intuition. Intuition, as he defines it, has all the self-consciousness of understanding and yet that closeness of spontaneous reaction to the instant circumstance which characterizes instinct in the lower animals. Now America as a nation is equally distrustful of the *cul de sac* of instinct and the designed canals of the logical understanding; and, instead, she chooses the lightning path of intuition. This has been characteristic of America from the first. Even the Constitution which Gladstone so admired was struck off by tact, by concrete thinking, by supreme self-reliance.

Americans seem to believe in education, but their real trust is in each man's immediate insight and in his ability to anticipate the demands of the concrete situation that confronts him. Americans seem to believe in science; but they never allow her to become the mistress; she is only the handmaid of their mother-wit. Intuition is where instinct and scientific intelligence fuse into a new point of illumination. This new illuminating force would be impossible if both the trained intellect and the blind instinct were not there and did not come together. As illustrative, I would cite the peculiar blend of theory and of practical application in the methods of Edison and Burbank. They are both instances of the intuitive character of the American mind. It was equally manifested in the financial methods of Americans like Harriman and Pierpont Morgan. These men comprehended the markets of the world with an eagle's sweep of vision, but with equal agility darted to the strategic point of central control. Unlike Germans, Americans suspect all custom and tradition and all authority in every walk of life; and yet even in business their utilitarianism is idealistic. They know that yesterday's knowledge is already obsolete this morning. On the other hand, they have no mystic faith, like that of the English, in the somnambulism of instinct.

Another instance of the intuitive character of the American mind is that very American movement in commercial enterprise called "Scientific Management." This method of avoiding all possible waste in manufacture and in business, when closely examined, is found to consist primarily in concentrated observation of the actual practices already in vogue, in an alert challenge and beating back of routine habits and devices that may have outlived their efficiency, and in a casting out of every element in accepted methods that cannot justify itself by its utility in the present circumstance. It is gratifying to observe in America that this same method of scientific management is already beginning to be taken over from the sphere of material wealth to that of the nation's mental and moral resources, with an eye to doubling the output of the nation's spiritual insight and efficiency. America believes in an intuitive mastery of facts in the interests of utilitarian idealism, and will discard in religion as well as in industry both the blindness of instinct and the mechanism of intellect. Facing the immediate facts, she will allow the divining will of the people to advance without chart or compass. M. Bergson points out that the method of the creative artist is never that of logic or of instinct, but is always that of intuition. In the United States business men, the leaders of political parties, and the champions of religion are beginning consciously to realize that their method must be that of constructive and creative imagination — the method of poets. And now that her preachers and teachers, philosophers and statesmen have caught this psychic secret of the makers of her original Constitution, and of the triumphant materialism that has mastered her economic opportunity, it is easy to believe that the human day in her creative evolution has come.

6. *Where the Educated, Leisured, and Revered Class consists of Women*

The transition from the foregoing characteristic of the American nation to the third and last which I wish to point out here, is a natural one.   One-half of mankind are proverbially intuitive.   The social position of women in America and the moral attitude of men towards them are, in my judgment, unprecedented in the world's history, and are fraught with deepest significance for the future of the nation, especially for the future of its Soul and of the part which organized religion will play in the developing of its spiritual resources.

Probably next to the women of the United States those of England are the best educated in the world; yet to anyone well acquainted with the educational aspects of the two countries it must seem that for one woman with a college education in England, there are a thousand in America.   Now, to be subjected for four consecutive years to systematic instruction and study produces an enormous effect upon the power of voluntary control over the intellect and upon the systematization of one's acquired knowledge.   Throughout America one is continually meeting women who immediately pigeonhole and tabulate in their college-learned scheme of things any chance remark that one may make; so that one becomes aware that one is being placed in the classified universe in which one's interlocutor lives.   A person with a four years' college education has an enormous advantage over those who have not enjoyed any such opportunity.   But the more remarkable circumstance about the intellectual position of women in America is that there is no corresponding class of men.   I do not know the exact figures as to the relative number of men and women who receive a college education; but it is no uncommon thing to meet with families who send their sons into business, while they send their daughters to college. The real educational superiority, however, of the women of America is due to the fact that, after they leave their academic halls, they continue through the rest of their lives their acquaintance with philosophy, history, literature, art, and science, while the men from the same families do not. These go into business and work from morning till night so exhaustively that they have neither time nor mental energy left for the continued pursuit of purely intellectual interests. As more than one friend of mine has said to me, "I have read nothing since I left college; ever since I have been married, I have handed over the 'culture' to my wife." For the first time in the history of the world, so far as I know, one is confronted in America with the fact that the men are inferior to the women of their own social set as regards philosophic outlook, historic insight, universal information, and the qualities of mind due to a disinterested pursuit of the ideals of truth, beauty, and character. No visitor from abroad, acquainted with the facts I am presenting, can fail to realize that they disclose something distinctively and universally American. By a typical incident the intellectual life of the well-to-do women of America was brought home to me recently in New York City. Having learned that my friend Professor Zueblin was to deliver a discourse at eleven o'clock, Tuesday morning, on "The Conservation of the Natural Resources of America," I made my way to the theatre where the lecture was to be given. Having paid a fashionable price for a ticket, I found myself in a large auditorium, one of some eight hundred human beings. But, with the exception of Zueblin and myself, there were only women present. After the admirably constructed and informing discourse had been finished, I approached the lecturer with the remark: "But how preposterous that you should be talking on the Conservation of the Natural

Resources of America to nearly a thousand persons, no one of whom has any political office or any directive power in the organized industries of the nation, and not one of whom can vote. Why waste your time? Why not, instead, lecture to men?" "Ah, but you forget," was the reply, "that the well-to-do men of America are too busy; only the women have the leisure or the mental energy to attend lectures. But it is not so futile to speak to them; for they go home and tell their husbands; and their husbands do what they tell them!" This kind of thing exists throughout the length and breadth of America. The women are everywhere organized into clubs, where they hear the great questions of modern thought presented, while the men, so I am informed, have no time for such pursuits. Perhaps the only exception, as regards the men, is that of the ever increasing groups, in all the larger cities, of those who have founded clubs devoted to civic reforms and where the members, lunching together, spend upwards of an hour a week in the consideration of problems of importance. On the whole, however, the men are absorbed in earning a livelihood or acquiring a fortune; while their wives, sisters, and daughters are equally strenuous in pursuing those ends for which one earns a living.

The women of America, so far as I am aware, are the only class of human beings in the world who have equipped themselves intellectually with no scope for action. For, while America has provided and lavished upon them opportunities of intellectual discipline and acquisition, it has furnished no more outlet for the will of women than any other country has provided. To one who is accustomed to the new psychological interpretation of the Intellect as a mere instrument of the human will in the execution of its designs, it seems a moral enormity that the women of America, who have no more scope for voluntary self-realization in politics, law, medicine, religion, business, or handicraft than the women of the Old World, yet constitute the intellectual aristocracy of their nation. The men of the country so will it. This, on their part, is either a national madness, or else they have been, unconsciously, prophetically, and without knowing it, preparing their womankind for some great and significant responsibility which they had not designed and have not even foreseen. It is often true that unique national trends make for several generations towards no foreseen goal, and yet they arrive at a point of destination which, when discerned, is immediately recognized as a full justification for what seemed a meaningless drifting. If, now, the vote should be granted to all women in America, they will be the best-prepared class in the world, as regards their knowledge of the ultimate ends and ideals of human existence. At the same time, the new responsibility will open up avenues of volitional self-realization, which will justify their mental equipment and will save them from the pathological effects of being without scope for the will. But, I repeat, intellectually the equipment of women in America is unique.

The women of America, also, have more freedom from engrossing cares and responsibilities than have the women of any of the older nations of the world. It would seem here, again, that the menfolk of a nation who are ready to slave that the women of their families need not work, must be, in some mystic way, the instruments of a cosmic or collective trend of humanity. It is unprecedented in history that men should not care to share in the freedom which they secure for their wives and daughters. When American women get the vote, the significance of the revolution will consist in the fact that, relatively to the present voters, they are persons of education and leisure.

But there is one other national peculiarity of the attitude of American men towards the mental and moral qualities of the women of their class. In one of my many voyages to America from England I overheard a German, an Englishman, and an American discussing the relative character and ability of women. The German gave true utterance to the tradition of his nation in maintaining that women were by nature inferior and should hold a correspondingly subordinate social position. The Englishman maintained that men and women were equal, however different, and should be comrades on the same level. He pleaded that for a man to place all women on a pedestal was degrading to himself and that for women to be encouraged to think themselves superior would tend to destroy their most beautiful characteristics. But the American insisted that there was something peculiarly holy and divine in the nature of womanhood and that men ought to know it; women were to be worshipped. Whether such an attitude be one of folly or not, it is undeniable that in America the spiritual relation of the sexes is different from what it is anywhere else in the world. And as regards the conservation and development of the spiritual resources of the nation, this difference gives a tremendous significance to the approaching political emancipation of women and the opening of the intellectual professions to them. In a nation where the menfolk for three generations have had no leisure and no surplus brain energy to devote to politics or to religion, a class of human beings better educated than the present voters, more leisured and highly revered by the community at large, is suddenly to receive equal powers of initiative. I prophesy, therefore, that in America the granting of the vote to women will advance the spiritual life of the nation far more than it will in England. In the interests of democracy and of humanistic religion I rejoice that the half of the population which has the better intellectual equipment and the more leisure and is the more respected and trusted is about to enter into full civic opportunity.

E

CHAPTER IV

THE JEWS IN AMERICA

1. *Jewish Enthusiasm for America*

ONE of the most interesting narratives in Mr. Wells' book on "The Future in America" is his account of how one of the women leaders of a college settlement in New York City led him to the building of the Educational Alliance, a Jewish Institution in East Broadway, to show him how the little immigrant children were being transformed into enthusiastic patriots of their new home. There he witnessed the ceremony, performed by recently arrived Jewish children, of the Salutation of the American Flag. Each child, it seems, held two small specimens of this symbol of the soul of the new country to which they had come; and in the midst of the ceremony the children repeated aloud in unison these words: "Flag of our great Republic, inspirer in battle, guardian of our houses, whose stars and stripes stand for bravery, purity, truth, and union, we salute thee! We, the natives of distant lands, who rest under thy folds, do pledge our hearts, our lives, and our sacred honour, to love and protect thee, our country, and the liberty of the American people forever." After quoting these words Mr. Wells gives the following comment: "The Educational Alliance is, of course, not a public institution; it was organized by Hebrews, and conducted for Hebrews, chiefly for the benefit of the Hebrew immigrants. It is practically the only organized attempt to Americanize the immigrant child."

I am here reminded that a Jewish Rabbi in New York City, after listening to my theory that religion in America

50

should be essentially the higher patriotism of the country, remarked: "We Jews in the United States have been charged with going too far in that direction already." In that same direction some Jews in Boston also seem to have moved. I recall that a few years ago a Jewish Rabbi there gave up his synagogue and established an organization which in its printed circular declared in so many words that the essence of its religion was American idealism. Its formula ran thus: —

Religion should answer the insistent questionings of the human mind, should relate itself to the universe and human beings to one another. An American religion must meet the needs of our peculiar civilization, and must grip and govern the facts of life for us here and now. A nation is in danger whose doings and aims are not given meaning through ideal purposes.

We believe that real religion is practical idealism, not apart from, but a part of, the everyday life and the actual interests of the people; we believe that our homes must harbour mutually respecting equals, that education must help to call forth and harmonize all the powers of the individual, that science and art must prove their use to man, that law must serve the ends of absolute justice, that politics must express the will of the people, that the Press must be the honest agent of publicity, that business must be made moral and human; in short, that every social interest and undertaking must further the democratic purpose of America, — to make strong, creative men and women, and to give them larger and fuller life.

Our aim is to dignify the life of America, so that every individual may know and work for its spiritual greatness and splendour, — through the dedication of each to all, the devotion of all to each, and our common consecration to all the nobler ends of life.

Recently Rabbi Hirsch of Chicago has been urging wholehearted devotion to the United States, so that the patriotism of all immigrants should be unqualified, and that they should call themselves simply Americans and never Italian

or Swedish or Jewish Americans. I have heard other Jews
in America express a similar sentiment in saying that to
them "America is Zion"; nor can there be any doubt that
the national ideality of the Jews is deeply stirred when
they reflect that, at last, there is one city in the world,
now after nineteen hundred years, that has a greater
Jewish population than even Jerusalem had in the period
immediately before its destruction, and that this modern city
is one no less significant, in commerce, finance, and education, than New York. The educated Jews the world over
also have not been slow to recognize that in very many
particulars the American Republic more resembles their
own theocratic nation of old than does any other State in
the world. Their ancient theocracy in many of its laws
was even more democratic than America has yet become;
but the newer trend of American legislation concerning
land and capital moves towards the ideal embodied in the
ancient Jewish code. But in order fully to understand the
tendency of the Jews in the United States to deify the
national spirit, we must bear in mind that the Jews are the
only people of the Western world who since the ascendency
of Christianity have identified religion with the higher
patriotism. It would seem the most natural thing in the
world, therefore, that the Jews in the United States should
be in the vanguard of those who recognize the divinity and
the redemptive grace of the Soul of America.

It is not enough, however, to remember the Jewish
identification of patriotism and religion if we are fully to
explain the incident which Mr. Wells narrates; we must
also remember the workings of human nature when a man
transfers his allegiance, spiritual and political, from one
country or one ideal nationality to another. It is the
greatest error in social psychology to believe that a man,
in becoming the citizen or subject of a new State and nation,
empties his soul, or ought to empty his soul, of the love and

gratitude and the stored-up traditions of the land of his birth or of his ancestry. It is one of the preposterous pedantries of the mechanical and atomistic psychology of a century ago to imagine that the highest honour and loyalty toward one's new psychic environment is to forget and deny the old. But the natural and the right thing is for an immigrant to America to preserve all that is finest and best in the tradition which he has inherited and pour these treasures of historic humanity into the new nation's common fund of mental wealth. Thin and mean, indeed, would have been the life of the United States of America if the Pilgrims and Puritans, and the Cavaliers who went to Virginia had not brought with them and contributed to colonial life all that they thought good in the old life of England. It would have been as great a loss to them and the nation they were creating to have left behind the human values which they had inherited as it would have been to forget the English language and, like primitive savages, to begin with rudimentary babblings and attempt out of these to construct a new speech. Nobody will deny the truth of what I am saying as regards the original settlers; and happily some will agree with me, that all the immigrants who have come to the United States since 1828 have also been Pilgrims, and that they should have been taught that their chief contribution to the vital wealth of America must be the highest tradition which they received from ancient Palestine or directly from the social life of modern Bulgaria, Lithuania, Greece and Armenia, Poland, Italy and Spain, Norway, Sweden and Ireland. We should know, if we were not historically and poetically blind, that all the immigrants come into America trailing clouds of glory from whatever nations were their homes, and contributing a softness of beauty, a pathos and tenderness, a dignity and depth to this still early dawn of American democracy.

2. *Subsidiary Patriotisms*

Mr. Arthur Balfour, in speaking of the Scotch in England, calls attention to the fact that there is such a thing as patriotism and subsidiary patriotism. I want to urge that patriotism is the richer for all the subsidiary patriotisms it can contain. I want further to urge, as concerns the Jew, that the alternative before him in the United States is not whether he shall be a Jew or an American in religion. The alternative is not whether he shall regard America as existing in order to advance the Jews throughout the world, or the Jews in America as called upon to use their religious tradition in the service of the United States, bringing it as a thank-offering to the altar of the God of America.

The Jews living in America see, as I have said, an astonishing likeness between that Moral Genius of their own race which they have worshipped and the Moral Genius that is revealing itself in American institutions and history. They feel that they are in America now not from any adverse necessity, but by supreme good fortune; they would not go back to Palestine, even if the powers of the world conceded to the people of this race an independent political state there. A Jew, in adopting such an attitude of mind, becomes a better Jew and a better American than he would be if he felt any incompatibility between Judaism and Americanism.

As a native-born American, with thirteen generations of New England Puritan ancestry behind me, and as one who has transferred his political and spiritual allegiance to England, I wish to give my own testimony that the longer I have lived abroad and the more I have become English in my tastes and judgments, the more deeply and consciously American have I become at the same time. My very loyalty of sworn allegiance to Great Britain assumes the form of contributing something to Britain's life and thought which I feel she needs, but which only those of her subjects can contribute who have inherited the American tradition.

I therefore can understand that Americans of Hebrew descent and tradition are faced by no such unqualified alternative as that between Jew and American; but there is confronting them only the choice indicated by the young Jewish philosopher, whom Mr. Zimmern quotes in a passage I have already cited, — the choice between an American Jew and a Jewish American. Surely, however, the choice, if it be rational and disinterested, must be to become a Jewish American. The assertion that a Jewish American is a mere amateur Gentile, doomed to be a parasite forever, is simply malicious libel and grossly untrue. In the venom secreted with the words and poured out upon the Hebrew American I seem to detect the disappointment of some antisemitic Jew whose personal effort to enter into Gentile society had failed. I am not unacquainted with a number of the leading Jews of America and, irrespective of whatever label they may give themselves, or others may attach to them, I make bold to affirm that they are all Americans and not a single one is an American Jew. Neither is a single one of them in any degree whatever an amateur Gentile or a parasite even for an instant. It is a cruel prejudice, fostered by some sinister and malignant motive of a selfish nature, which would stigmatize the Jewish American as a counterfeit. The man whom Mr. Zimmern quotes may have been a philosopher; but many a man's philosophy is an exudation of his own pettiness.

For years I have studied the character of the Jews in America, and all whom I have met were thoroughly Americans, and not simply those who had discarded their religious allegiance to Judaism. Those who still remain most loyal to the sufferers of their own race and in outward conformity to synagogue or temple are in culture and spirit Americans first and Jews only by virtue of subsidiary patriotism. My valuation of the Jews is the very opposite to that presented in Mr. Houston Chamberlain's chapter on "The Entrance of the Jews into Western Civilization," in his popular book called, "The Foundations of the Nineteenth Century." There is no psychological impossibility in a man's becoming the better American, the more he remains a Jew; just as the more a man is loyal and devoted to his own family, the more he may love and serve the city in which he and they live. An American of Hebrew descent can, in this way, be true to the people of his own race the world over, and in proportion as he lifts them out of poverty and oppression he knows he is illustrating in his life the organic laws of American citizenship.

3. *Two Voices in the Old Testament*

Men like Mr. Houston Chamberlain, who have become obsessed by antisemitic hatred, can present a plausible historical argument for their interpretation of the Jews; but the argument is only specious, not genuine. If one goes back to the Old Testament, one finds two distinct voices: the one, that of race-egoism and self-conceit; and the other, that of race-humility and reverence for the moral genius of other nations as well as for that of Israel. In short, the Hebrew scriptures reveal both a vulgar jingoism and what I have in these pages often spoken of as "the higher patriotism," — that which is identical with a sense of national responsibility towards its own members and the world at large. It is in the Hebrew scriptures exactly as it is in English literature. There are the same two voices in English poetry and prose — the voice of the national egoist and the voice, as that of Edmund Burke, of the national idealist. If one judges the English by their vulgar jingoists, England is as race-proud and domineering in temper and

purpose as was ever Israel. But no one who has studied
England in the great historic manifestations of her moral
genius will deny that the voice of the idealist is the real
voice of England; and the other is that of pretenders and
climbers. Now, when I turn to the Jews of to-day in Germany, England, or America and ask them which voice in
the Old Testament is the true voice of the Hebrew people,
they all, without exception, declare that no Jew of to-day
thinks for a moment that the Jewish people have ever been
the only chosen people of God. None of them, I find,
believes that the Jews ever had any spiritual monopoly of
moral insight and creative energy. One Jewish Englishman has expressed the sentiment prevalent among Jews
to-day in these words: "In the later Rabbinic days it has
never been contended that Jews alone make for spiritual
regeneration. May I remind you of the Rabbinic saying:
'The good of all creeds have an equal share in the world
to come'? Could there be a more exquisite recognition
that there are people of other faiths who act for the benefit
of mankind?"

The two voices in the Old Testament are not equally
frequent nor equally loud; that of the baser jingoism is
far more insistent and frequent. The same thing is true
in English literature. The other voice in Hebrew writings
is a very still small voice and it speaks in clear tones and
with unequivocal articulation perhaps only once. Hundreds of passages might be cited to prove that the Jews
claimed a monopoly of the spiritual resources of humanity.
I shall not quote them; for I hate them as I hate the similar
voices in England or in Germany; but the still small
voice which is of infinite prophetic significance when it
speaks with perfect distinctness is that which is heard
in the 19th chapter of Isaiah, verses 24 and 25: "In
that day shall Israel be the third with Egypt and Assyria,
even a blessing in the midst of the land: Whom the

Lord of Hosts shall bless, saying: Blessed be Egypt my people, and Assyria the work of my hands, and Israel my inheritance." This the Jews of to-day, the world over, recognize as the essential spirit of Prophetic Judaism towards the rest of the world. It should be noted that here there is no cosmopolitanism of the kind that overlooks or obliterates national distinctions. Here is true and vital internationalism, the recognition of all nations as coequal, coördinate, but separate spiritual entities. The Lord, here, is the Lord of Nations, not simply of individuals. Israel is still a Holy Nation; but only the third with Egypt and Syria. The Socializing Spirit of humanity has formed Israel; but the prophet here knows that to that Spirit Egypt its people is equally blessed, and equally blessed is Assyria the work of its hands.

I have said that Mr. Houston Chamberlain can present a plausible defence of his charge of spiritual arrogance against the Jews. But his argument is only specious; for, after all, the one and final question is: What is the sentiment of representative Jews throughout the world to-day? So far as I have been able to receive answers, and I have not been without adequate opportunity, I am certain that no educated Jew to-day denies that Israel is only one with England, America, China, Japan, and some fifty other nations; and that the same Holy Spirit which calls Israel its inheritance blesses America also as its people and China as the work of its hand. If I am wrong in saying that every educated Jew in America is a Jewish American, I am sure that before long after the publication of this book my error will be brought to my notice by American Jews. But any Jew denying that Egypt "my people" and Assyria "the work of my hands" are equally blessed along with Israel, would prove an enemy of his own race and his own religion. He would play into the hands of the antisemites like Sombart and Chamberlain. He

would confirm their judgment that the Jew is spiritually
race-proud, a religious egoist, or a would-be monopolist of
ethical insight and redemptive energy.

4. *Jews must declare their Attitude*

Some two years ago, after reading Mr. Chamberlain's
indictment of the Jews, I preached at the Ethical Church
in London on the question: "Is the Jew a Menace to
Western Civilization?" I said that the answer wholly
depended on whether the Jews living to-day do really claim
a spiritual monopoly of moral insight and energy, or not.
If they claim such a monopoly, they *are* a menace to the
religious originality and autonomy of every nation in which
they sojourn. But if they recognize that Egypt and Assyria
are equally with themselves manifestations of God, then
they are not a menace to Western civilization. I took the
position, however, that it was for the Jews themselves to
say which of the voices in the Old Testament they followed,
and that it was not for me to declare. And I suggested
that, in the face of the strong antisemitism which boldly
expresses itself in Germany and which mutters under its
breath in some circles of America, the Jews of our day
should loudly and unequivocally demonstrate to the Gentile
communities about them what their inward attitude is
towards the spiritual equality of other nations.

I regret that there has been no adequate attempt on the
part of the Jews to make their present attitude on this
question felt throughout the world at large. But at least
for my own satisfaction, as a result of my individual inquiry, I am convinced that no educated Jews of to-day,
anywhere, lay any claim to be the only nation begotten of
God. It is not enough, however, that here and there an
individual like myself should be clear on this question;
and if the Jews themselves, from any sensitiveness or pride,

refuse to educate the Gentile world concerning their present attitude of mind, it would seem that then, on a matter of such universal importance, individual Gentiles like myself should do their best to remove the misunderstanding. It must be remembered that the Gentile world has from the beginning of the Christian era been inoculated with the idea that the Jews were the only chosen people of God. They have taken the Jews at the self-valuation of the race as appraised by the louder but now repudiated voice that speaks in the pages of the Old Testament. The Jews of to-day, therefore, cannot much blame the Gentiles for believing that the descendants of Israel are spiritually race-proud and still think that no other nation can compare with them in religious, moral, political, and economical insight; for it requires a very careful searching of the Old Testament and a close listening for its finer voice to detect any other utterance. I myself should never have heard the voice that speaks in verses 24 and 25 of the nineteenth chapter of Isaiah except for the scholarship of Canon Cheyne, who, in his notes on Isaiah, directed me to it. And if I mistake not, Canon Cheyne speaks of this passage as a very wonderful and strange utterance, which has no parallel in more than a thousand years of Prophetic utterance and of literary editorship.

If any reader is of the opinion that in devoting a chapter of "The Soul of America" to the Jews I am giving the question an altogether undue prominence, I would refer him to Mr. Houston Chamberlain's reasons for devoting upwards of two hundred pages of his " Foundations of the Nineteenth Century " to the Jews. He counts the Jews a menace, I count them a blessing, to every nation of the West; but the facts which he gives in apology for assigning them so conspicuous a position hold good with one who counts their influence salutary instead of sinister. For in any case their influence is becoming very great. The mere numbers,

2,000,000, I believe, in a population of 90,000,000, would seem to indicate that the Jews in America are a negligible quantity; but it must be remembered that 2,000,000 people who stand by one another in friendly aid, who have a common tragic past, who have inherited also mental vitality and will power without parallel, and whose intellectual genius has been specialized both by artificial selection and by social tradition in the field of finance, may be more than equal to 20,000,000 individuals unorganized in purpose and anæmic in brain power. The Soul of America, if her spiritual resources are to be conserved and developed, will need the organizing genius of the Jew as much as the *haute finance* of international capitalism has required it. It must also be remembered that the conservation of the spiritual resources of a country will require as much financiering and as large an investment of capital as would the conservation of its natural resources. But it also must not be forgotten that among the Jews there are in this day, as there were in ancient times, two types of genius, the financial and organizing type, and the ethical and spiritually quickening type. In America, unless the great misunderstanding of Judaism which has led to the ostracism of the Jews be continued, the religious type of Jew, with his prophetic passion for economic justice and domestic fidelity, will be called in to supplement the predominantly inward and transcendental idealism of the Christian tradition. Ancient Judaism stood for justice; historic Christianity has stood for love and faith; but, in the religious synthesis of the twentieth century in America, these two will unite; and a balance of the outward and inward aspects of moral experience will now be attained, such as has never before been manifested in the sentiment and practice of any nation.

5. *Mr. Zangwill not Explicit Enough*

I reiterate that in the bringing about of the required synthesis of Christianity and Judaism, the first step must consist in the removal of the notion from the Gentile mind that the Jew of to-day is spiritually arrogant. Unfortunately, in all that I have been able to read of the writings of the most humanistic and catholic Jews of our time, I have found no sufficiently unequivocal repudiation of the claim to spiritual supremacy over all the other peoples of the world. For instance, even Mr. Zangwill, whom I know to be not obsessed by any such illusion of race egoism, in his brilliant and passionate paper delivered in 1912 before the First Universal Races Congress in London, never quite meets this point. His language squints and might in some passages imply that the finer Jews still believe themselves to be the only medium and missionary of a righteous social order and an ultimate unification of mankind. In one place he says: "The soul of the Jewish race is best seen in the Bible, saturated from the first page of the Old Testament to the last page of the New with the aspiration for a righteous social order, and an ultimate unification of mankind, *of which*, in all specifically Jewish literature, *the Jewish race is to be the medium and missionary*." A critic like Mr. Houston Chamberlain would seize upon this sentence and say: "There, you see the Jew as I depict him illustrated even in a modernist like Mr. Israel Zangwill. Does not Mr. Zangwill confess without shame, if he does not even boast, that the Jewish race counts itself to be the one and only medium and missionary of the ultimate unification of mankind? He practically says the Jew thinks his race has a monopoly of spiritual power, that is, of the ability to unify the human race and establish the reign of righteousness." Now, of course, I know, and every one who is acquainted with him knows, perfectly well that in

Mr. Zangwill's judgment the Jewish people have no such spiritual monopoly. Mr. Zangwill sees, as clearly as I do, that Abraham Lincoln and George Washington were as great moral geniuses and unifiers of the human race and builders of the ultimate righteous order as were the Isaiahs, Ezekiel, Jeremiah, or the editors of the Book of Deuteronomy. But if this is so, then America is equally with Israel a medium and missionary of the unification of mankind. Yet Israel did not produce America; and the moral genius of Washington and Lincoln cannot be traced to the influence of the Old Testament upon them any more than each succeeding genius among the ancient prophets was the product of the preceding geniuses. For the essence of originality is that it is the direct and immediate mouthpiece of an excellence prevailing immediately around it and forming, as Froude says in the passage which I quote elsewhere, the environment in which it grows. America may be more like the ancient Jewish theocracy, I have said, than any nation in the interim between them; but let anybody read the Book of Deuteronomy and then read the Constitution of the United States and of the several States; and, if his judgment be impartial, he will feel that to trace America to Israel would be to convict oneself of obsession by an *idée fixe*. Nor could such an *idée fixe* obsess any one who was not the victim of racial self-deification. Yet because such self-deification has been expressed in the Bible, and ever since by the vulgar jingoists of Israel, exactly as it has been expressed by the vulgar jingoists of America and of England and of Germany, it is essential that the finer Jewish patriots should be quite unequivocal in rejecting the lower patriotism; just as every American, the moment he speaks of his country, is in duty bound to guard himself against what could be interpreted as national self-conceit and egoism. This duty which I am urging upon the Jews is one which the finer patriots of every other nationality are scrupulous in fulfilling. They should prefer to give no expression to Semitic sentiments than to be mistaken for the vulgar and rampant counterfeit. Mr. Wells says that in America patriotism is now little else than cheap flag-waving; yet the opposite to this is not a shame-faced silence, but an overt branding of it as counterfeit.

If the modernist Jew says that it is preposterous that he, whose politically independent State was annihilated some 600 years B.C., should be required to explain what sort of patriotism his loyalty to his ideal nationality is, I reply that it is by no means preposterous. The deepest insult that one nation or the survivors of one nation can give another is the denial that it, too, is a medium and missionary of the ultimate unification of mankind. A distinguished American Rabbi has recently said : "The most menacing foes of Israel are not the brutes and ruffians who inflict physical hurt upon her sons and daughters, but the more subtle and insidious creatures, such as Sombart and Chamberlain, who out of their minds evolve the creature which they call menacing Israel." In the spirit of this most discriminating utterance, I would say that the most menacing foes of America would not be the brutes and ruffians who inflict physical hurt upon her sons and daughters, but the more subtle and insidious creatures who, by claiming to be themselves the only medium and missionary of the ultimate social order, would thereby insult the Soul of America by denying the divinity of its power and of its unique spiritual task in the world.

The present-day champions of Judaism must remember, furthermore, that while every other nation in the world has been tainted with a strain of vulgar jingoism, no other nation's cruder self-deification has ever taken the form of the highest insult to other peoples — the claim to a spiritual monopoly; no other nation's jingoists have claimed a right to supremacy and the sole initiative in the unification of the human race. England pretends no such thing. Germany does not dream of that form of self-worship. Indeed, the arrogance of all other peoples has been of a far more materialistic order. But a materialistic national pride is merely that of brutes and ruffians, and does not inflict the deepest and most fatal wound.

6. *An Injury wrought by one of the Voices in the Old Testament*

I maintain that spiritual originality has been checked at its sources for two thousand years in all the nations of the West, exactly as musical creativeness in the Jews, according to Weismann, was compelled to lie absolutely dormant from the time of the destruction of Jerusalem in the first century to the beginning of the nineteenth century. The Jews hung up their harps by the waters of all the rivers of Christendom, because they were forbidden to sing. During all these centuries of terrible oppression, throughout the ghettos of Europe, they gave evidence neither of musical appreciation nor of musical creativeness. Through all this period, they were not even conscious themselves of the faculty which their artificial social environment prevented them from exercising. But, the moment the Jews were liberated in the nineteenth century and allowed to come into contact with the formative musical atmosphere of European culture, they began to manifest a keener musical appreciation than did the people of any other ancestry and also a far greater and higher average musical productivity. Christendom had breathed a blight which, as it were, atrophied these splendid psychic gifts of the Jews for two thousand years. In the same way, the idea, so often reiterated in the Old Testament by the spurious representatives of Judaism, that no other people but the Jews were spiritually elect of God has paralyzed the latent power of spiritual

F

prophecy in the soul of every Western nation for two thousand years. I have just said that Washington and Lincoln were equal in moral genius to any of the Hebrew prophets, but I did not overlook the fact that they were barred out from the sphere of religious insight and utterance by the two thousand years of Christian-Hebrew tradition, and thus their genius was compelled to work on lower planes of human interest and to minister to needs below the highest.

It should be fully conceded to the Jews that, thus far in the history of the West, they have been preëminent in the mission, on the religious and spiritual plane, of the righteous social order and the ultimate unification of mankind. But why is it that the other nations have not equalled them in the sphere of religion? I answer, without hesitation, because that spiritual arrogance of the meaner Jewish patriots, which is now dead and universally repudiated by educated Jews, has breathed a blight over all the nations of the West. These nations, having accepted the Jews at the spiritual self-valuation of their religious jingoists, have quite logically, instead of relying upon their own spiritual initiative, looked wholly for light to the Jews — to the Old and New Testament. The result is that the whole of Christendom has been thus far, in religion and in all matters spiritual, a parasite to the Jews. It is this parasitism which now every lover of every nation of the West must end, by extracting the initial falsehood that caused it, the deadly microbe that has paralyzed the highest spiritual centres of the brain of every Christian nation. And I feel that it is the duty of educated Jews to assist the idealistic patriots of all other nations in ridding their countries of the false notion that the Jews have ever had a monopoly of religious genius. Mere history must not browbeat us! The nations in religion must now become superhistorical; we must begin an era without parallel or analogy in the past.

CHAPTER V

ROMAN CATHOLICS, MARXIAN SOCIALISTS, AND SOME OTHERS

1. *The Importation of Spiritual Wares*

It would be a sin against the Holy Ghost of America that fanatics from other countries should be allowed to overrun her territory and introduce ideas, political, economic, domestic, or religious, that give the lie to her Constitution, her historic development, and the great personalities who have lived and died to save her from disruption. That she herself should feel no alarm at the moral prejudices, the vices and blindnesses, the ignorance and superstitions of the hordes she annually welcomes to her household, would be, to say the least, a short-sighted levity. As if the market value of the merely physical strength of her immigrants were to count with her, and their standards of conduct and character were to be treated as a negligible factor! As regards the importation and exportation of material commodities, free trade may at times be expedient and even necessary; but when we turn to consider spiritual wares — ideas, doctrines, disciplines, habits, moods, and purposes — we see that the only policy consistent with national autonomy must reserve the right to exclude.

What is true policy, however, for America must be equally valid for every other nation in the world. China, for instance, has a right, and it is her duty to herself, to say what religious propagandists she will admit into her territory. Often in recent history countries have been embroiled in misunderstandings and even in bloodshed, through the interference of foreigners with the religious beliefs and practices of the people of the East; and the time must soon come when Western nations will not permit their subjects to go as missionaries to foreign lands unless they are wanted there, nor to indulge in spiritual encroachments any more than in territorial aggressions.

But this question as to the moral interference of one nation with another is more intricate and involved than would seem on the surface. Often at the root of the internal unrest of a nation is a spiritual protest arising from a new vision of a higher moral order; then the conservative ruling classes, who are enemies of internal progress towards democracy and social justice, are prone to call in foreign powers. These, it is true, do not send missionaries, but soldiers; and yet they abet the spiritual violation of great masses of men by coercing them into submission and conformity. This was the case when, in the middle of the last century, the effete Manchu dynasty in China called in the British Government to suppress the Tai Ping Rebellion. Then it was that General Gordon, with his blind mystic sense of duty, lent himself as an instrument to the powers of darkness. The recent Revolution in China, which to-day all the nations of the earth respect as a manifestation of the awakening self-consciousness of an ancient people, should have come about sixty years ago. The leaders of it know and have publicly announced why it was not feasible then but has proved so now. They tell us that fortunately there is no General Gordon now to check the spiritual and political self-realization of the Chinese people.

As regards material wealth, the universal policy implied in the dictum, "America for the Americans," may or may not be a sound one. I would not even advocate "America for Americans" in respect to intellectual resources. But the inverse proposition, "Americans for America," involves a principle universally true and always applicable.

We must see the wisdom and justice of the aphorism, "The Chinese for China"; for if not for their own land, for what country would they be? We cannot say, "My country, right or wrong"; but we must admit that when our country is wrong, that is just the time when the citizens are most bound to set it right, not to separate themselves from it and leave it in the lurch. One's country being right, one may not be needed and might be excused from duty; but my country being wrong calls to me. When our private friends violate our principles and standards, we may be at liberty to drop them; but to wash our hands of our country's stain is to stain them.

The dictum, "Americans for America," does not deny the larger truth that America must exist for all humanity. It is illogical to maintain that patriotism is necessarily national egoism; for the moment you universalize the principle of patriotism, you affirm the equal inviolability of all organic units of national life.

But the advocate of universal patriotism, that is, of the virtue of loyalty towards each nation by its own subjects, is confronted in the sphere of spiritual interests by cosmopolitanism on the one side and on the other by sectarianism. Of the latter I shall speak at length in a future chapter. Here let me point out that cosmopolitanism manifests itself in five different forms, four of which are highly organized and have been directed with consummate astuteness. They are: Roman Catholicism, the lower form of Judaism, Marxian Socialism, and the International Finance-Peace movement. The fifth form of cosmopolitanism is that vague but widely diffused sentiment (rather than an integrated enterprise) which is usually spoken of as "humanitarianism." Every one of these tendencies denies the ethical right of a country to exist as an autonomous unit of spiritual life, and overlooks the patent fact that each recognized nation is practically a self-contained psychic sphere and as such deserves respect. They all aim to obliterate and paralyze the spiritual autonomy of nations. In the last chapter I have shown that the lower form of Judaism is obsolescent and no longer a menace to any nation. I therefore need not discuss it further.

2. *Individualistic Humanitarianism*

Let us here begin by considering that abstract philosophical feeling which is sympathetically summed up in the saying of Thomas Paine: "The world is my country, and to do good is my religion." Now, except in the vaguest sense, it is not true that the whole world is any man's country; for the whole world is unorganized, and it never will be unified except by a federation of nations; and if there are no nations to federate, there will be no universal country. It is not a fact, and cannot be, that a German or an Italian or a Chinaman, in his own country, is just as much to you, an American, in your own country, as your compatriots are. Undoubtedly, you wish your fellow-mortals of every nation well; but they are not interdependent members with you of the same economic, political, and spiritual organism. Try as you will, you cannot know them and feel with them and serve them, physically or morally, nor can they you, as would be possible if you were all members of one economic and psychic whole, with traditions of coöperation and with a common opportunity and destiny. The needed multiplicity of points of contact fails you in your relations with a human being who lives in another historical and social environment. Very few are the benefits, even of science and invention, that flow spontaneously from one country to another. Science is not automatically cosmopolitan, as is often declared; American scholars themselves import German science into America; or, if it is not the scholars, it is the capitalists or the statesmen that do so. Science does not pass from one country to another of itself, but moves in response to a call.

It is passing strange that, while the rank and file of sentimental humanitarians would discount nationality, and boast that every man should train himself to act without the mediation of his nation, as if he were a citizen of the world, the two greatest philosophers and prophets of the unity of the human race in the nineteenth century — Auguste Comte and Giuseppe Mazzini — were both nationalists. Both maintained that, exactly as the family is the cultural group through which a man's country plays upon him, so every man's country must be the mediator for him if there is to be any communion between him and humanity as a whole, or between him and individuals in the outlying groups of humanity. Mazzini, who preached the brotherhood of all men, preached first and foremost the brotherhood of all Italians. These, until Italy could be restored, could not perform their function in the universal fraternity of nations. Auguste Comte, who set up Humanity as the object of religious worship, had so profound a sense of deference for every nation that he looked beyond our period of empire-making tyranny to an age when each aspiring nationality, however weak and poor, would be allowed place and scope for self-development.

It might be well also in this connection to call the attention of persons who have not sojourned in foreign lands to the fact that nothing so demoralizes character and destroys individuality and the capacity and achievement of service for one's fellow-men as the cultivation of the cosmopolitan spirit — the training of one's affections and interests so as to be no more directed towards one's own country than towards any other. Of all the amorphous characters in the world, none are so disintegrated as those of the isolated individuals who feel equally at home in any land, and who,

boasting that they belong to every nation, really belong to
none. They have not the virtues of the French, nor the
Italians, nor the English, nor the Americans; but they tend
to acquire the vices of all, plus an incoherency into which
the stay-at-home workers of any people never degenerate.

The ethical law here undoubtedly is that if a man detach
himself from his own land, he must forthwith begin to
attach himself to the redemptive trends in the life of some
other nation. Wherever he be, he dare be neither pleasure-
seeker nor spectator; and in proportion as he sojourn long
in any country, he must permit his whole being to be influenced by those needs and aims of the new country which
command his reverence. And if any person move from
country to country, it shall be only when his object is self-
equipment and self-education, to be ultimately offered
at the altar of some one nation. When once we respect all
organic units of spiritual life, and understand the relation of individuals to these, we see that there is no necessity that a man shall always serve humanity only through
the land of his birth; but wherever he be, that land
shall he serve. A man may expatriate himself, intending
from the first to devote himself to another nation either
for a time or for his whole life. If it be for the latter,
then even a complete transference of political allegiance
would be inevitable and wholly consistent. The policy
in the interests of all mankind must be not retrospective
and conservative, but radical and forward-looking. A
man owes himself not necessarily to the country where
God *did* place him, but to that country "to which it
shall please God to call" him. At all times, next in
sanctity to the god of his own land, must appear to any
man the gods of the other nations of the world.

But, of course, a metaphor which implies a plurality
of gods is inadequate. The Formative Spirit in any one
nation is ultimately identical with that at the heart of

every other. It is under Humanity that the nations find scope for their individuality. Indeed, the nations are but so many forms in which Humanity fulfils herself, and without which the manifoldness of her creative energy could not be revealed.

The common-sense fact, however, must never escape us that practically and normally a shifting from nation to nation can be but a rare occurrence, and that even such immigration as America permits, and Europe takes advantage of, will in a few generations be a thing of the past. There is reason to think that humanitarian pity in the United States, instead of welcoming from Russia the poor whom the Czar casts out, will take the form of compelling the Czar to be humane, even in his own territory, to his own subjects. There will be less and less difficulty in exercising compulsion upon Russia, and it will be still easier to constrain the less powerful governments of the world. More and more, then, men will remain in the service of the land of their birth. And this will prove only a blessing. For the nation is naturally and rightfully the character-building school of the individual; and, other things being equal, a change of schools is no gain.

The sentimental humanitarian overlooks nationality not only as the character-building school of the individual, but also as the most conspicuous upward trend of human history in a thousand years. He fancies that the main current of progress has been towards the transcending of national self-consciousness, and he therefore condemns patriotism as a vice instead of extolling it as a virtue. He is apparently so little skilled in concrete thinking that to him an increase of conscious solidarity among all men as human beings argues a proportionate decrease of the spirit of nationality; and this in spite of the fact that it is by and through and because of the growth of national consciousness and the intercommunication of nations as nations that the very sense of universal humanity has itself developed. I have no space here to trace the protest of nationalities against the dominance of the Roman Empire and the Catholic Church. I must rely upon the historic information of my readers; but I would for a moment briefly call attention to the solidification of awakening nationalities during the last two decades throughout the whole world, the East as well as the West, and to the growth of general humanitarian sentiment as an accessory to this uprush of nationalism.

Recently Norway expressed by plebiscite her desire for self-government, and was permitted to dissolve her political partnership with Sweden. Portugal is another instance of the coming to consciousness of spiritual autonomy in a nation, in that she, by changing her form of government, asserted herself against the spiritual aggression both of the Church of Rome and of the royalist parties throughout Europe. Those who know the facts say that Portugal would have become a republic a generation ago, had it not been that foreign monarchies brought pressure to bear against her internal self-expression.

Indeed, that movement which began with the reawakened consciousness of the modern Greeks and led to the restoration of Greece to a place among the nations reappeared in the enthusiasm of the makers of modern Italy, and triumphed in Norway and Portugal; it is now asserting itself with magnificent poise in Finland, and is on the verge of victory in Ireland. There is no sign anywhere of a growing anti-nationalistic cosmopolitanism that can compare with the power of the national spirit evidenced in the recent awakening of Japan and Turkey, in the revolution in China, and the prophetic unrest of India.

But I have said enough to show that between the spirit of true humanitarianism and of nationality, instead of an antagonism, there is a vital and organic unity of purpose;

only in this unity the nation is the primary and creative factor, humanity the derived and dependent result. On this account, the individual men and women of the whole world have a stake in the spiritual self-realization not only of their own, but of every nation on the earth.

3. *"Five per Cent. Bonds of Peace"*

Wars may be condemned from two points of view. From the one, every individual human being is counted so holy that no institution, no social group, no principle or idea is worth shedding any one's blood for. This attitude of mind found its most influential protagonist in Count Tolstoi. Wars are wrong because they involve a sacrifice of human lives; it is nations as political units that wage war, and therefore all governments are at enmity with men.

The leaders of the so-called International Peace Movement continually defend their cause from this point of view. In so far, they condemn patriotism as a vice, and they would sacrifice the idealism of nations to the interests of peace. They are champions of that form of cosmopolitanism with which I have already dealt at length.

Here, therefore, I need only call attention to other motives which are dominant in the Peace Movement, and which masquerade as humanitarian and altruistic, but which at heart are really commercial, and emanate from and appeal to the financial greed of individuals. These self-interested supporters of cosmopolitanism oppose war in the interests of trade, and they back anti-patriotic sentiments, because national self-consciousness, if not beaten down, might sacrifice commercial interests, in order to maintain the existence and the integrity of national unities. They proclaim a new and newly discovered factor that tends powerfully to prevent war between nation and nation. That factor is the increasing international investment, during recent years, of private capital. How can England upset the commercial interests of her own subjects in Turkey or Russia or Germany by warring against these countries? So we are to find in our foreign investments a motive strong enough to prevent our injuring another people. The advocates of this Norman Angell argument cite as parallel the influence of domestic commerce in preventing civil war. But just at present this beautifully specious analogy is rudely shaken by what is going on in Mexico. The citing of Mexico, however, proves something still more to the point — a something positive as well as negative. Foreign investments in Mexico for thirty terrible years suppressed the civil war which, in the interests of justice and honour and humanity, ought to have been allowed to break out there at the very first inception of that Peace of Slavery and Fear and Shame, which Diaz established.

To prevent rebellion on the part of the oppressed of any country, in order to secure the dividends of foreign capitalists, is an idea which only a born criminal can entertain without horror. Law and order within any one land must never be judged as a good until you have looked beneath it and seen what it is that wails and mutters there. Peace for the sake of oppressors is the devil robed as an angel of light. In the same way it would seem that no one can prejudge whether international peace in any given case is relatively a good thing. We must first find out that no money power is causing some entrapped nation to be bled to death. A war of China against England, when the opium traffic was introduced, would have been infinitely more ethical than the smiling, shameless peace that prevailed, pandering to the sensual mammon of international trade.

It cannot, of course, be denied that the wide-awake self-interest of private capital invested all over the world will sometimes secure peace. The White Slave traffic, for instance, is international; it ships its goods most discreetly to foreign lands, and a war would disturb the even tenour of its ways. It, accordingly, would throw in its dead and deadly weight on to the side of peace. But some things which peace abets are worse than bloodshed. It must be proved, therefore, on other grounds, that the foreign investments of a private profit-monger are good for races, sexes, and nations before we dare give our sanction to the peace they engender. It may be wiser to cast in our influence with those who see the greatest hope of true and final peace in the awakening of the classes in every country who have no land or capital, and who maintain that every one who means to get rich without serving society by hand and brain is a dangerous enemy to those wars that ought to be, and to that peace which is not gagged despair.

It is self-evident, then, that "five per cent. bonds of peace" are not to be trusted. The motive of commercial greed will advocate peace only until war would serve its ends better; and yet if one studies the oratory of the leaders of the Peace Movement, one notes that next to sentimental humanitarianism is set up this foreign investment of private capital as an argument in favour of peace. So prominent and so closely interwoven are these two individualistic motives that an impartial observer is forced to declare that the Peace Movement, so far as it trusts to international capitalism, has no right to call itself international; it would be glad to dispense with nations altogether, so that dividend-seeking capital could flow unchecked from land to land. It would disintegrate mankind into individual atoms, because it is the mental clash of social group with social group that sometimes precipitates bloodshed. Now, such a polity is an enemy of civilization, which is identical with socialized life. In my judgment, the Peace Movement, with its eye

on foreign investments, is a counterfeit. We cannot surrender the psychic integrity of nations merely in order to
avoid wars.

There is another point of view from which war can and
should be condemned. A true Peace Movement would be
nationalistic. It would find out what organized interests
within each nation make for war; it would insist that all
Governments become champions of economic justice the
world over, because private greed is the War God. There is
not too much patriotism, but too little of the right sort.
A true Peace Movement would educate the masses of the
people, and especially the statesmen and politicians and
voters of all countries, in the higher functions of nations.
It would identify religion with the patriotism within every
nation, and beat out of existence all those commercial
private enterprises which for the sake of higher dividends
are hostile to the moral consciousness of nations. The
true inspiration to peace must be one and the same with
the motive that would lead men to die rather than permit
a foreign power to annihilate their own nation or to practise
outrage upon a neighbour. It would say with Mrs.
Browning, in her "Casa Guidi Windows": —

> I love no peace which is not fellowship,
> And which includes not mercy. I would have
> Rather the raking of the guns across
> The world. . . .
> Such things are better than a Peace that sits
> Beside a hearth in self-commended mood,
> And takes no thought how wind and rain by fits
> Are howling out of doors. . . .
> What ! your peace admits
> Of outside anguish while it keeps at home ?
> I loathe to take its name upon my tongue.
> 'Tis nowise peace. 'Tis treason, stiff with doom, —
> ' Tis gagged despair, and inarticulate wrong,

Annihilated Poland, stifled Rome,
Dazed Naples, Hungary fainting 'neath the thong,
And Austria wearing a smooth olive-leaf
On her brute forehead, while her hoofs outpress
The life from these Italian souls. . . .
O Lord of Peace, who art Lord of Righteousness,
Constrain the anguished worlds from sin and grief,
Pierce them with conscience, purge them with redress,
And give us peace which is no counterfeit !

4. *The Anti-nationalism of the Church of Rome*

The anti-Catholic feeling is spreading rapidly and deepening in intensity among the non-Catholics of America. I shall not enter into the question of the relative merits of Catholic theology, discipline, and influence, as compared with those of the various Protestant denominations. For the purposes of my argument, the whole of ultimate religious truth and goodness may be on the side of the Catholics. Even if this were so, however, their allegiance to a foreign bishop and their denial of the spiritual autonomy of America is a sociological heresy so deep and vicious as to more than offset the worth of any abstract spiritual truth of which they may be the depositary. From my point of view, at least for the purposes of my argument here, America may voluntarily adopt the whole of the Catholic system of redemption, minus the "Roman." The question is not: To what conclusions will America come in matters religious? but: Shall they not be the result of her own free, independent, and deliberate insight and reflection? She must be true to the moral genius of her own soul; but, if she is this, her Catholicism cannot possibly be Roman. Her Pope cannot possibly sit at the Vatican. Her cardinalate must consist of Americans, chosen democratically, territorially, from America alone by American Catholics. It is not at all a question of the Seven Sacraments; it is a question as to where the final seat of authority in matters spiritual for the people of America shall reside, and from what human source it shall spring. I speak not as a Protestant, but as a humanist; I speak as one who knows what a mighty curse it has been to Italy that so great a part of her organizing and moral genius has been drained off from attention to the higher needs of Italy towards the keeping up of a world-wide cosmopolitan organization. If there ever is to be a World-Church, it will not be Roman any more than American or German or British. It will have its spiritual centre in no historic territory, but will manifest a diffused sovereignty with centre everywhere. It will consist of a federation of nation-churches, coördinate and recognizing absolute local autonomy in matters spiritual.

I foresee only calamity of a direful order for America if she opposes the Roman Catholic organization on the ground that Protestantism is truer than Catholicism. The one hope for the spiritual unification of America, as regards this Roman Catholic controversy, is that all American citizens, Protestant and Catholic alike, shall be educated, drilled, and steeped in the doctrine of national idealism as the essence of true religion. The crux of the question is not what the religion of America shall be, but who shall dictate it. Were it not for the overpowering influence of America in moulding the sentiments and habits of all her citizens, I should share the alarm of the extremest anti-Catholic fanatics. But there is one Church mightier than Rome in the United States, with a still greater organizing genius and an infinitely closer opportunity; and that one Church is America herself. You can be a Catholic; but you cannot be a *Roman* Catholic and at the same time be in spiritual life a true and loyal *American*.

It is just possible that when the hierarchy of Rome realizes the situation, it will, with its consummate instinct for self-preservation, transform its whole political struc-

ture so that the Catholic Church shall cease to be cosmopolitan, and become truly international, reorganizing
herself so as to permit all the Catholics of America
to have complete local autonomy, both as regards the election of officers of the Church and as regards the choice of
forms, ceremonies, and creeds. She may become democratic; but if she does, then the final authority in the
Church will henceforth rest in an international council elected
by nations from among the Catholics of each. This, however, is a very far-off vision; no one need entertain it; but
there is occasion most energetically to condemn every
trend in the Roman Catholic policy which does not make
for the spiritual autonomy of all the Catholics of America,
in order that they may become simply one of the many
patriotic religious groups which count themselves as nothing
more than a means towards the spiritual integrity and
perfection of the United States.

So long as American schools are supported and controlled
by the various States, and so long as the Protestant denominations omit to preach the doctrine of the identity
of true religion with the higher patriotism, the Roman
Catholic propaganda in America will be a menace to the
nation; but the moment the idea spreads that America
is primarily a spiritual and not a mere political or commercial unit of social life, that moment the Roman Church
will have to deal with a Church which will tolerate no dictation from any hierarchy of which the seat is in Europe
and of which the long tradition has been predemocratic
and prescientific. The Roman Church must be placed
on the same basis as any other importer and retailer of
spiritual wares from abroad. But America's policy must
not be one of destructive attack upon the Roman hierarchy, so much as one of constructive development of her
own native insight and character. When once America
knows herself to be a church, *the* Church, she will ordain

G

a thousand priests of democratic humanity to every
emissary whom the Roman Catholic hierarchy can introduce. Then, the Roman spiritual jingoism would soon
become, as the Jewish jingoism has already become, a
thing of the past in America.

5. *The Danger of Anti-patriotic Socialism*

Marxian Socialism is a menace to the spiritual autonomy
of every nation. It must be pointed out that while it uses
the term "international," it means by it only "cosmopolitan." Its followers do not believe in nations, and therefore have no idea of an intercommunication of autonomous
nationalities, either economic or moral. The Marxian
Socialists hate patriotism. They proclaim the dangerous
falsehood that the interests of the proletariat in any one
country bind its wage-earners more closely to the proletariat of other nations than to the middle and upper
classes of their own nationality. As regards America in
particular, their notion is grotesquely unlike the truth. Their
assertion, moreover, is based upon the long-ago exploded
error that every human being is solely and purely an economic, wealth-getting, or money-grabbing animal. We
may well grant that, under the present distribution and
ownership of property, there is an antagonism of economic
interest between the wage-earners and the employing
class; and if to eat and have possessions were the whole
of life, then it might be true that wage-earners all the
world over constituted, so to speak, one nation, and the
employing classes the other. But bread and butter is not
the whole of life; it ceases to be so for any family the moment they are no longer starving. The working-men and
employing classes of America must instantly see, if they
stop to reflect, that they have a common life and ideal,
a common sentiment, education, opportunity, and out-

look, and therefore an identity of manifold interests; and that, despite economic injustices, they in fact constitute one living, organic unit of psychic life. It is therefore treason against themselves for the working-classes of America to claim a nearer kinship with those of Germany than with the middle classes of the United States; and it would be not only moral death, but economic suicide, for them to carry out such a policy. Despite every clash of material interests, and despite the injustice of capitalists, the working people and employing classes recognize increasingly their common humanity. Who preaches to the contrary either consciously falsifies facts or is blinded by some anti-nationalistic prejudice.

Two characteristics of American life furnish us with an adequate disproof of cosmopolitan Socialism. First, the American proletariat does not need and knows that it does not need the coöperation of that of Europe in order to extort — if extortion it must be — from the employing class a communal ownership and control of the sources of the wealth of the United States and a fair distribution every Saturday night of the nation's income. However feeble American working people may be in intelligence and power, they are aware that they do not require intellectual any more than material support from the working people of other countries. The second fact that exposes the lie at the heart of Marxian Socialism is that the working people of America, when they are in bitterest antagonism with their employers, are educating and moralizing their employers as well as themselves. Two men or two classes quarrelling with each other, unless their humanity be wholly obliterated, grow nearer in their sense of a common nature, and even in their moral influence upon each other, than two masses of working people sundered not only by thousands of miles of ocean, but by the whole difference between two separate historic atmospheres. What have men reared under Prussian autocracy in common with American working people, except the thinnest and abstractest, most artificial and enforced, identity of purpose?

It is significant that Marxian Socialism, with a contempt for nations similar to that of Roman Catholicism, likewise derives its policy primarily from that Jewish jingoism which among the Hebrews themselves is dying out. Karl Marx remained to the end a Jew of the lower type, in the sense that he had no respect for any Gentile nation.

It is a marvel of self-contradiction that his sort of Socialism should have incorporated into itself this ancient racial pride, inasmuch as it has everywhere made household words of the phrases, "the *nationalization* of land," "the *nationalization* of capital." At the same time that it has popularized these valuable terms, it has been insidiously undermining the whole conception of the nation as the integral unit of social life. The very idea that land and capital should be *nationalized* points to national idealism as the only possible spiritual philosophy to justify the new economics. And yet the Red Flag of Karl Marx is anti-nationalistic! Down with the Stars and Stripes, and up with the Red Flag, to symbolize the solidarity of the proletariats of all nations!

CHAPTER VI

HOW TO CONSERVE AMERICA'S SPIRITUAL RESOURCES

1. *America not merely a Unit of Material Wealth*

OF all the ways to conserve and develop the spiritual resources of America, it seems to me the first is to preach in the churches, in the schools, in the homes, and in the Press that America is primarily and essentially an organic spiritual being. The notion must be beaten out of men's minds that she is preëminently a great material and wealth-producing entity. Any one will appreciate what I mean in insisting that America shall be regarded as an organic sphere of spiritual life, who has a family — a wife and children of his own. Such a man, if he be conscious of his higher responsibilities, is aware of his home as a spiritual organism, as a psychic sphere of influences environing not only him and his wife, but especially his children. The mother and father guard with a jealous alertness the very possibility of the intrusion of any adverse moral influence, through servant or neighbour or friend, into the sanctifying sphere for which they are responsible. Their home is no doubt at the same time an economic and a biological unit; but what mother and father would not resent the insinuation that it was primarily and supremely this? My contention is that the hope of America, even as an economic and biological factor in the world's history, will be henceforth dependent upon the recognition of herself as a spiritual organism which is to be jealously and unceasingly guarded against influences from within or without that might lower her standards, corrupt the people's taste, bias their judgment, and weaken or sidetrack the General Will of the nation. I have in an earlier chapter explained the spiritual resources of a nation as meaning a sense among its citizens of the power and reality of the ideal order which the nation must embody if it is to fulfil its true destiny. But lest I shall seem to mean something very abstract and remote from the concrete fulness of life when I say that a nation is a spiritual organism or psychic sphere of creative energy, let me add here that the ideal order includes more than simply the moral character and responsibility of a people as a Puritan interprets the word moral. Besides the ethical sphere of the ideal in this sense, there are also the scientific and the æsthetic spheres. And I wish to affirm that for the American people America is the formative sphere of creative power in the domain of all forms of art and science as well as of morals. If America be not this, then Americans will have no art appreciation or originality in art creation. Or if America be a very anæmic sphere of formative art energy, then her citizens will suffer proportionately. They will be crude in æsthetic discrimination and appreciation and her cities will fail to constitute what is called an art atmosphere. As a result her artists for inspiration and illumination will go abroad; and they may possibly be tempted to remain there, lest, returning, they should suffer the anæmia prevalent among their fellow-citizens. This law of the identity of the æsthetic spirit of nationality with the creative art atmosphere that environs any individual applies not only to music, painting, sculpture, and architecture, but to manners, speech, and literature. Let us consider here the last only. It is always the nation as an organic unit of spiritual life that stamps its qualities, both content and form, upon its literature. If anything in the world be Russian, it is the books of Tolstoi and Dostoievsky. A literary artist, in proportion as he is a genius, is one sensitive to and expressive of the contemporary trends of his own nation's life. As far as the artist himself is concerned, it is only an accident if his books hold the mirror up not only to his own nation, but to the contemporary life of other peoples. Dostoievsky, in "The Idiot" and "The Brothers Karamzov," is not only Russian through and through in the kind of characters and of society he depicts, but equally in the style and structure of these books. They are Russia herself revealing her own soul. I need not multiply instances, but the law of the dependence of literature upon nationality is universal.

This fact that only the genius of a nation, streaming into the sensitive will of the individual artist, creates great art is well stated by Froude in the opening chapter of his "History of England," where he says: "We allow ourselves to think of Shakespeare or Raphael or of Phidias as having accomplished their work by the power of their own individual genius; but greatness like theirs is never more than the highest degree of an excellence which prevails widely around it, and forms the environment in which it grows. No single mind in single contact with the facts or nature could have created out of itself a Pallas, a Madonna, or a Lear; such vast conceptions are the growth of ages, the creations of a nation's spirit; and artist and poet, filled full with the power of that spirit, have but given them form, and nothing more than form." So essential is it to the literary creativeness of a people that the literature they study shall be the output of their nation's own soul, that it is almost as fatal for a people to read the literature of another country in the way America has hitherto read British prose and poetry, as it would be for them to read none at all. The same calamity that has befallen America by accident of history befell ancient Rome. The very proximity and dazzling splendour of Greek poetry and philosophy overbore whatever native genius and originality in literary expression the Roman people began with and might have developed. Happily, in another sphere of purely idealistic creation the soul of America has found original expression and has manifested her individuality — that of scientific invention. In American inventors there is a unique blend of expert knowledge in the specific sciences with originality in discovering the laws of the universe and at the same time applying that knowledge and those laws to the exigencies of material and social life. I have already cited, as men typical of this peculiar genius, Edison and Luther Burbank. Science, if anything is so, is cosmopolitan; its atmosphere more than any other transcends and overarches and unifies all the civilized nations; yet no one can be acquainted with the scientific methods and spirit of Germany, England, and America without conceding that, despite the trans-national intercommunication of science, Germany is one formative sphere of scientific incentive and fertility; England, another; while America is equally distinct from both. But I have said enough here to illustrate the fulness, scope, and reality of the truth that America is an organic unit of ethical, scientific, and æsthetic life, and that to develop her idealistic resources, she must be awakened by direct instruction and challenged into responsible consciousness of the fact that she is such a generating organism.

2. *America the Living Church of all Americans*

The second means of conserving her spiritual resources is to teach that America herself is the living church of which every citizen, whether he will or not, is an active member. He may be a bad member and the church itself may be far from perfection; but the fact that every citizen is spiritually dependent for his character and for his standards of manhood upon the psychic influence of his nation is undeniable; and the responsibility of the nation for the individual and of the individual for the nation is unescapable.   It can be avoided only by death or by expatriation;   and even this latter means of escape is not efficient.   For whithersoever he flees, he enters into another living church, another nation, and becomes of it an active member, either for weal or woe, and enters into a new sphere of duty.

To say that America is the church to which all Americans belong is something more than to say that she is the formative sphere of spiritual influence in which they all live. For the word church links up the idea of the national sphere of spiritual influence with that of religion.   The word ·church is the name of that specific kind of society the bond of which is religion and the practice of which is worship — praise and prayer.   In urging, then, that the nation herself is the living church of her citizens, I am advancing to the position that national idealism in the hearts of the citizens is in the nature of worship, of religious praise, and of that sense of spiritual communion and dependence which inform prayer.

Furthermore, when it is taught that America as the standard-bearer of her own ideal is the church of which every citizen is an active member, her citizens' eyes will be opened to the fact that she is really doing in a very full and powerful way what the various religious denominations within the land can only possibly achieve in a minor and most subordinate, although necessary, manner.   Indeed, it becomes apparent that everything which the sects themselves accomplish must somehow be assigned to the nation itself; for they are a vital and organically dependent part of the nation, even though their discipline was imported originally from abroad and although, in some instances, they continue to be manipulated and dictated to by foreign authorities.   In all the sects the moral spirit is impregnated with the genius of the nation. What is more, if we were to take even the devoutest member of the most exclusive religious denomination and trace the inmost qualities of his soul — his yearning for truth, his craving for beauty, his longing for holiness — to its social sources, we should find that for one impulse which he had received from his special denomination, he had received ninety-nine which the nation would have communicated to him even if that particular denomination to which he belonged had not existed. When we make a psychic analysis of an American's moral, intellectual, and æsthetic values, we find it difficult to discover whether he had been a Methodist instead of a Baptist, or an Episcopalian instead of a Congregationalist, or whether he had been a member of any professedly religious communion; but it is by no means difficult to discover that he is American and to detect even whether he were American-born as well as reared. But the spiritual dominance of the nationality in general is in no wise impugned by the fact that the immigrant or the child of the immigrant is not exclusively the offspring of the soul of America. For whatever in the child is not derived from America is nevertheless traceable to some other nation; it is therefore, forever and everywhere, nationality. Nations are always the formative environments from which special characteristics of the individual have been engendered. And of the things American in origin within the soul even in the sphere of religion, it will scarcely ever be found that the individual has derived more instruction and edification from the discipline of his own denomination than from those of other religious organizations. Nothing has in contrast with England struck me on recent visits to America more than the fact that through the newspapers all the ideas of the newest organizations in religion are communicated to the citizens at large. I meet no American, though he be an Episcopalian or a Calvinist, that has not been forced by the newspaper into an acquaintance with the method and message of Mrs. Eddy and been challenged to think more about the truth and falsity of Christian Science than about the tenets of his own religious communion. Equally have the ideas and sentiments of Spiritualism, through newspaper publicity, pervaded all homes and exercised an influence even when they have been rejected. America herself by her daily press mothers "freak religions"; but also in more subtle ways she foster-mothers even such historic importations from abroad as Anglicanism, Roman Catholicism, and Judaism. Whoever knows by close comparison the differences between the Episcopal Church in America and the Established Church in England knows that America has had infinitely more structural influence upon the Episcopal Church in America than the Episcopal Church, with its less than a million adherents, has had upon the soul of America; and many who are close observers of the functional life of the Protestant Episcopal Church of America think they have reasons to believe that within a decade or two it will become far more Americanized both in character and in conscious aim than it has been hitherto. Despite, also, the utmost efforts of the Vatican, the Catholic Church in America is becoming less and less Roman and more and more Americanized. Why, then, should not all the denominations wake up to the fact that the one real and living Church to which all their members belong is America herself, and that all the denominations are but so many distinct congregations attempting to interpret her and serve her?

It was recently my privilege in New York City to submit the idea that America herself is the church to which all Americans belong, to a company of liberal ministers of religion. I went on to say that America should hold the same place of preëminence in the religion of Ameri-

cans as Israel had occupied in ancient Judaism.   I argued
then, as I am doing here, that the indwelling moral genius
of the Jewish people, the will of the race as it pressed forward
in creative yearning to fulfil the nation's innate destiny,
was the reality which the Jews called Jahweh, and was
their God.   In the same way, I pleaded that the moral
destiny of America as it was foreshadowed in her history
and opportunity must be regarded by Americans as the
living and immanent presence of God.   Among my audience was a Jewish Rabbi of distinction, who in the conference following my discourse replied to this effect: "No!
Israel, we must remember, was no mere ordinary nation.
Her prophets and rabbis had from the first seen that she
was a congregation of the Most High as well as a nation;
that she was, as her own prophets expressed it, the bride
of God, the wife of God.   Her God was far more than an
indwelling socializing spirit; it was a universal God.   And
the fact that she lost her political independence, but continued as a theocracy to survive for five centuries and has
since existed as an ideal community scattered over the
face of the globe, proves that, with her, religion was something more than the spirit of nationality and God than the
indwelling genius of a race."   When my opportunity to
reply came, I met not only what the Rabbi had overtly
said, but what he had also implied.   I asked: "Who dare
suggest that America is merely an ordinary nation?   You
have begged the very question which I have raised, in implying that America is not just as much a holy people, a congregation of the Most High, as was ever Israel.   My
whole object is to induce people in the United States to
view their nation in this light and set exactly this value
upon her.   I concede that Israel was the bride of God and
that her prophets had the insight and the wisdom to think
so and say so.   But I at the same time maintain that for
an American to acknowledge Israel to have been a bride

of God and not to see that America must be *his* bride of God is an abomination.   The one unforgivable sin among the Jews was that any one of them should follow after the God of another people instead of their own.   Why, then, should it not be equally an unpardonable offence in an American to transfer the highest homage of his soul to a manifestation of God in an alien people ?   That each people should worship God primarily as the Redeeming Power among themselves is my contention.

"There is no antagonism between a universally applicable nationalism such as I advocate and a recognition of the oneness of the spirit which is socializing each of the several nations of the earth.   It is perfectly consistent ; just as it is, for instance, to say that the sunlight that actually falls on English soil and quickens vegetation there is not the same as the light that falls on the territory of the United States, and yet at the same time to affirm that it is one and the same sun that sheds its rays on all the surface of the globe.   I am not denying that God is the God of Abraham, Isaac, and Jacob ; I am only protesting that it is morally preposterous for Americans to think of him in that way instead of regarding him as the God of Washington, Jefferson, Lincoln, and Wilson.   It does make a great difference whether a nation thinks of the Power it worships as the genius of another people more than of itself and as having directed their history more than its own.   I am not denying that Israel was the chosen people of God ; but I am urging that it is high time that the citizens of the United States shall count themselves as one of some sixty peoples now suffering and struggling on the face of the earth who are as much the chosen of God as was Israel. There is no shadow of jingoism or chauvinism or appeal to national vanity in the doctrine I am setting forth ; but I maintain that the notion prevalent throughout Christendom that Israel was in some unique manner or degree the chosen people of God has acted like a blight upon the spiritual originality of all Christian nations. That blight can never in my judgment be removed until each nation counts itself equally with all others preordained, by its unique position and experience, to discover and contribute to the world moral truths, duties, and visions which no other people has had as good an opportunity to perceive and formulate. The Rabbi has further offered the fact that his nation survived the destruction of its political independence as a proof that its religion was far more than mere patriotism. To me that fact is the supreme proof of the opposite, that its religion was nothing less than patriotism. The Jewish State was destroyed; but the spirit of nationality was able to survive, because it had been regarded as the most high, the most real, the eternal."

But that the young men and women of America shall be brought up to regard her as the Church to which they belong will require a mighty reformation and transformation in all the religious denominations of the land,—a transformation, however, that will make of them the greatest factor in the nation's total life, and will coördinate and consolidate them through the unity of their ultimate aim: the service of the nation as a spiritual organism.

3. *The Denominations as Parties in the Nation-Church*

The third means, then, of conserving and developing the spiritual resources of America is that all the religious denominations throughout the land shall make themselves the centres for the propaganda of the higher patriotism, and of the principle that the nation as a standard-bearer of the ideal is the Church in which each denomination is only a party, and that the God of the Christians, the Holy Spirit of the creeds, exists and acts here incessantly, and is none other than the unifying Soul of America.

As one religious congregation after another adopts this modernist point of view, each will begin to modify its conventional phrases and ceremonies accordingly. The religious denominations will rewrite American history from the point of view of the evolution of social justice on American soil and will count American history and literature sacred. This idea will also become incorporated in their canticles, hymns, anthems, and prayers, as well as their sermons. On one occasion recently when I gave utterance to this suggestion, an American professor of theology informed me that I was mistaken in thinking that such was not already the sentiment and custom in American churches, at least in those of the Congregational order. These all, he said, recognized and expressed the identity of religion with the higher patriotism in general and, for Americans, with loyalty to their own country in particular. In proof of his contention he referred me to the Pilgrim Hymnal. And, surely, the title seemed to furnish an argument on his side. The word Pilgrim pointed to American origins; and that was wiser and more sincere than if it had pointed to the deliverance of the Jews out of their house of bondage. In high hope of finding that my view of religion was already incorporated in the active gospel of one great American denomination, I hastened to purchase the volume that had been recommended to me. But, alas, I was doomed to disappointment. Except for the inclusion of the "Battle Hymn of the Republic" and "America" and one or two other hymns with vague allusions to this country, the book did not embody the idea of the identity of patriotism and religion in any place except in the word Pilgrim on the title-page and cover. I turned to the department of the book entitled "Responsive Services." They were all taken from the Old and the New Testaments; and, so far as there was any reference to any cities, they were those of the Jews and of their enemies and neighbours. This hymn book is issued from the head-quarters of the Congregationalists on Beacon Hill in Boston — Beacon Hill, from whence in more than one dark hour for humanity a light has issued forth to cheer the suffering and the oppressed. But in the Pilgrim Hymnal there was no mention of Beacon Hill; and, where one would have expected it, the hill spoken of was Zion! Nor was there any reference to the streets and marts and slums of Boston, but only to the palaces of Jerusalem. I am by no means so much of a literalist that I cannot see and am not moved by the imaginative and poetic significance of Mount Zion and the palaces of Jerusalem, even for the citizens of Boston; but I maintain that the reason we count Jerusalem and Zion holy is because the ancient dwellers there had poetic imagination capable of discerning the divine meaning and transcendent beauty of the very ground they walked on and of the sufferings and hopes of their own fellow-citizens. I maintain that the real significance and beauty of the Hebrew poetry cannot be rightly appreciated among Bostonians until Beacon Hill is as hallowed in their public worship as Mount Zion was by the Jews.

The religious congregations of America must assume the task of educating the American public to deify the Moral Genius of the United States. It is the task of the churches to bring vividly before the imagination of the people the invisible glory and hidden meaning of their own responsibility and opportunity.

From the Pilgrim Press on Beacon Hill I chanced to pass into the State Capitol, which I had not entered for twenty-five years. Straying into the newer part of the building, I found myself in a beautiful rotunda, restful in colour, dignified in proportions, and modest in size; within niches covered with great panes of glass I saw the trophies of the Civil War, the bullet-riddled flags taken from its battlefields. Now I knew why this rotunda was called Memorial Hall, and my soul was thrilled with the deepest and most vivid memories of my childhood. While gazing at these historic battle flags of the Republic with eyes not undimmed, I observed the notice placed conspicuously on a card: "Honour the Flag by removing your hat." I obeyed gladly the command, but not without an added emotion of the sense of fellowship in my religious reverence for American history. I could not refrain, however, from asking myself, "Instead of always remaining here, why should not these sacred flags be brought into the religious fanes of the nation—into the buildings set aside for the worship of the Most High? Why should there not be in every church in the country at least once a year a great Festival of the Nation, when the congregation gathering should honour the historic flags of the Union grouped about the altar? Would not such a festival be a means of bringing vividly before the minds of the worshippers the reality of the unseen but eternal Meaning of American History? But if at the opening of such a ceremony there were to be a salutation of the flags of America, there should be before the close, lest America forget, another ceremony when the banners of all the other nations of the world would be brought in and borne to the altar and grouped about the sacred trophies of the Republic, to symbolize America's gratitude to all the other peoples of the earth for the representatives that for generations have been flocking to these shores as to the Promised Land, and to symbolize America's recognition of the equal sanctity and inviolability of all other nations."

It should be noted that the change which I propose is not that churches in addition to their religious ceremonies should become institutional and as adjuncts of religion should group about themselves various secular activities. Such undertakings never have strengthened the religion

H

of any denomination nor have they ever brought to the people whom they attract the thing they most need — the sense of the divine meaning within oneself and within the social opportunity of daily life.

What I am proposing is the introduction of that sort of a national idealism into the church services which during the last thirty years has increasingly entered into and emanated from the universities of America, so that all the world knows of the fact and talks of it. Such an influence must now proceed from the churches, from their services, from the altar, from the pulpit and the pew. If I am wrong in affirming that the churches of America are not yet the centres of idealistic patriotism, it is astonishing that I can scarcely turn to a book on America without finding the statement that her universities are centres of a new civic enthusiasm, but that I search in vain for any such reference to the churches. In Professor McCarthy's "Wisconsin Idea" is quoted the following from Professor Turner of Harvard : —

"Nothing in our educational history is more striking than the steady pressure of democracy upon its universities to adapt them to the requirements of all the people. From the State universities of the Middle West, shaped under pioneer ideals, have come the full recognition of scientific studies and especially those of applied science devoted to the conquest of nature, . . . all under the ideal of service to democracy rather than of individual advancement alone."

There is no doubt that there has been just such a steady pressure of democracy upon American universities as Professor Turner declares, but no mortal who studies Professor Carroll's book on "The Religious Forces in the United States" can discover any analogous steady pressure of democracy upon the churches to adapt them to the requirements of all the people. What strikes one is the

astonishing imperviousness relatively of all the churches
to the requirements of the people. It would seem as if
democracy had not troubled itself enough about religion
and religious organizations to bring its pressure to bear
upon them. It is only in the slightest degree true that
the religious denominations of the Middle West, for instance, have been shaped under pioneer ideals. I have
above asserted that America has more modified the churches
than the churches have modified America, but I have in no
way committed myself to the belief that America has done
anything like what she might have done in this direction.
This book itself is a cry to the churches to do what they
might for America. The churches must accept as fully,
heartily, and intelligently the whole method and spirit and
results of modern science, and especially of applied science,
as the State Universities of the Middle West have done,
and turn the conquest of nature through applied science,
to an infinitely greater degree than the University even of
Wisconsin has done or has pretended to do, to the service
of the Ideal Democracy rather than of individual advancement. But the universities have set an example towards
the founding of an American Kingdom of Heaven which
the churches would be wise to follow. As far back as
1883 President Andrew D. White of Cornell, speaking
at Yale, pointed out that the hope of America lay in the
American colleges and universities, and it was with universities in mind and their professors, not of churches and
their preachers, that he said : —

Mercantilism, necessitated at first by our circumstances
and position, has been in the main a great blessing. It has been
so under the simple law of history. How shall it be prevented
from becoming in obedience to such a law a curse? . . . I
answer simply that we must do all we can to rear greater fabrics
of religious thought, philosophic thought, literary thought,
scientific, artistic, political thought, to summon more and more

young men into these fields, not as a matter of taste or opportunity, but as a patriotic duty; to hold before them not the incentive of mere gain or of mere pleasure or mere reputation, but the ideal of a new and higher civilization. . . . I would have the idea preached early and late.

It was the new patriotism of the universities that determined the careers of both President Roosevelt and President Wilson and made them representatives of a new type of American citizenship. It was from the colleges that the great movement represented in the 400 social settlements of America emanated. I speak here from personal knowledge and reminiscence. The chief inspiration in America which I myself received in founding in 1886 the first University Settlement in the United States, came from Professor Julius Seelye, who was then president of Amherst College and who had been my teacher in philosophy.

There can be no doubt that the new conscience to which Mr. H. G. Wells so often refers in his book on "The Future in America" first became articulate in the colleges. "There is every sign," says' Mr. Wells, "that a great awakening, a great disillusionment, is going on in the American mind. The Americans have become suddenly self-critical, are hot with an unwonted fever for reform and constructive effort." Again he says, "America for the first time in her history is taking thought about herself and ridding herself of long cherished illusions." But this national repentance the country does not owe to revivals in churches; it might be said rather that American colleges have become churches, while American churches have become universities of mediæval learning.

Now, this third means for developing the spiritual resources of the United States which I am suggesting is based upon the natural inadequacy of universities as such to meet alone the nation's spiritual needs. The efforts of the colleges in this direction must be supplemented by an organized undertaking on the part of the great profession of the teaching of adults as distinct from the teaching of mere youths and maidens. There are in the United States, according to the statistics of W. D. Carroll, in his "Religious Forces in America," 110,000 professed ministers of religion! Here are 110,000 men who devote their whole time (and earn their living thereby) to teaching, presumably, the highest ideals of manhood and womanhood. It seems, therefore, an appalling indictment that no observer of social phenomena has traced the new awakening of the social conscience in politics and philanthropy to the ministers of religion. It would seem to me, however, that scarcely more would be needed to replace this sin of omission on the part of ministers by a magnificent record of service than the mere bringing home to the attention of preachers the splendid opportunity which the nation offers them. The higher patriotism requires at least 110,000 preachers who identify it with religion. Must the nation produce and subsidize another 110,000? If so, what is to become of the existing profession for the moral teaching of adults? The ministers must be converted. Will not the teachers which the new patriotism will call forth make use of the one day of rest in seven and the traditional hours for the assembling of the people in the churches? Then the churches will be opened every evening in the week for instruction, discussion, conference, and edification; and throughout every day committees and small groups be meeting in them to think out together and plan the great campaign for that development of the nation's spiritual resources which shall be able to sweep away forever the injustices and iniquities that now threaten the nation's health and life.

4. *A National Committee Needed*

But I have already anticipated a fourth (which should perhaps rather have been counted as the first) means of storing up the moral dynamic of the nation. It would seem as if some sort of a national committee should be formed for permeating the churches with that patriotism which Andrew D. White and others introduced into the universities.

In England was formed last year a Church Comprehension League, the object of which is to educate the public, but chiefly the 50,000 preachers of religion, to the idea that, while religion is the service of the universal human ideal, the nation, being the individual's spiritual environment and sphere of duty, is the living church of every Englishman, and that the various denominations are the parties in the church. This League proposes, as the first means of educating the public and the clergy to its idea, the sending out of leaflets, pamphlets, and books setting forth its principles and the appointment of special men and women to teach and preach throughout the country the identity of religion with the higher patriotism. It would seem that a similar method of propaganda would be as natural and inevitable in America. It would involve the establishment of a national committee or league in which sympathizers, on the payment of an annual subscription, would become members. Out of such subscriptions and donations the expense of the publication of literature and the sending out of missionaries could be met.

5. *The God of Personal Salvation*

I cannot pass on to the next chapter, in which I shall deal with a fifth means of conserving the spiritual resources of America, without anticipating in the reader's mind an objection which is sure to arise if he has not grasped the total bearing of the thought. The idea that religion and patriotism are one and the same thing, whenever the religion is sound and the patriotism is high, is so unfamiliar and even strange that it naturally seems as if it must involve some great heresy. I therefore wish to point out that the kind of change which would be involved in religion would not involve the denial of any of the fundamental doctrines of theology, or the discarding of any of the clauses of the great historic creeds. The teaching of this book involves only the seeing of the old ideas in new relations. It is as if I invited my readers to view the old realities of their faith from a new point of observation. I ask them to shift from the individualism of the old (eighteenth-century) Protestantism to the vantage-ground of the new social psychology, and to view the old teachings of religion in relation to the interests of organic society. Nothing that I propose involves denial of the personality of the Creator or of a life after death or the doctrine of the Trinity or of the Incarnation. To say, for instance, as I have said, that the Holy Ghost in America is the socializing spirit of the nation is not to deny the Holy Ghost nor its manifestation as reported in the New Testament or as manifested in the historic Church. To say that America is the church of Americans goes counter to no historic creed or dogma. To say that the moral genius of America is God is by no means to deny that God is an infinite person. For I have not implied that the moral genius of America is not an infinite person. For anything I have said or anything that I believe, the moral genius of America may be a self-conscious, intelligent Will, infinite, and, in some sense or other, omnipotent.

It is possible, also, that some readers, because I have not yet pointed it out, may have failed to see another side of the teaching of this book. Recently after I had been giving some arguments in favour of the identity of sound religion

and the higher patriotism, a clergyman present said that
my interpretation of religion was preposterous, in face of
the fact that to everybody else in the world except myself
religion did not refer to these externals of national life, but
to the holiest and most inward experiences in the depths of
the individual soul. He said that to most human beings
religion was a personal matter, and that in their private
griefs and temptations they went to God as the strengthener
and saviour of their own soul. Now what had such a God
as theirs, he asked, to do with the socializing Spirit of a
nation, with the Moral Genius of a people ? Let me anticipate the like objection from some of my readers by giving
here the substance of my answer to this clergyman. I
said that I, too, in my duties as the head of an Ethical
Church had been sought out as a spiritual adviser by many
persons in their hour of deepest inward anxiety. It was at
such time especially that I had found out the efficacy of
my own faith and the adequacy of the God who is identical
with the Indwelling Spirit of every social group drawn together in devotion to the Moral Ideal. I tell those who seek
my advice that they can find the power to resist temptation
and to lift themselves out of their individual and private
grief or shame or disappointment only as they identify
themselves with the Quickening Spirit of some great redemptive work for others. Let them enter into any great
Social Cause which they believe in but have neglected, and
they will find — I tell them so on the strength of my own
personal experience — that their personal wounds will be
healed, their very weakness transformed into unwonted
strength. I warn them that there is no consolation for
sorrow and no redemption from sin except as they identify
themselves with some group of fellow-workers or as they
themselves start out alone to redeem others. I tell them
that the Spirit of Social Service is God, Christ, the Holy
Ghost, or whatever they want to call it. I often give them

the version of a well-known story in the "Buddhist Scriptures" which was told to me by an Englishman who himself passed a year with the Buddhist monks in their retreats in the mountains of the East. According to this version, a woman who had lost her only son came to Buddha that he might cure her grief. He told her that this he could do if she would bring him a grain of mustard seed from any household wherein no loved one had died. She set forth on her quest. After many years the Buddha met her again and he questioned her about her grief. "What grief, Lord?" she asked, "I have no grief." She had even forgotten her former anguish; for, in her attempt to assuage the sorrow which she found in every household that she visited, she had not merely lost her own grief, but had found it transformed into some rare power to soothe the suffering of others. The Spirit of Social Service, then, is a quickening, redeeming God to the individual soul in its hour of weakness and despair. But this statement of mine is no heresy. The promise of the Spirit in the New Testament is not to the isolated soul, but only to the two or three gathered together. There, in the group — in a family, in a religious meeting, in a city, in a state, in a nation — there and there only, is the Power that keeps us from falling! Let no one, then, cast any disparagement upon the Moral Genius of a Nation as if it were subordinate to or other than the God himself of personal redemption.

CHAPTER VII

1. *As an Object Lesson and Laboratory*

THE interpretation of religion here presented may, to some readers, seem so different from Christianity as ordinarily understood, as to appear incapable of unforced adoption by the historic denominations. Those who receive such an impression may therefore be inclined to conclude that everywhere, side by side with the old churches, new organizations must be started if the new interpretation is to be incorporated into the creeds, sermons and prayers, rites and ceremonies of popular religion. But, in my judgment, the founding of a new sect upon the idea that sound religion and ethical patriotism are identical would be an error in policy fatal to the very object it wished to advance. There are already enough churches to serve the country's immediate need. In many towns and cities there is a lamentable overlapping, due to a refusal to coöperate merely on account of difference of intellectual interpretation. It is not multiplication of religious centres, so much as coördination of propaganda, that is at present required. Let us, then, have no new sect.

There is occasion, however, for having in the largest city in each State in the Union one new religious centre, where the sermons and all the items of public worship will be in harmony with the principle that America herself, as a spiritual organism, is the Church to which all Americans belong, and that God, in America, is the Historic Moral Genius, the Socializing Spirit, that would animate the nation.

One such centre in a State would be able to disseminate the idea by illustrating it. As a result of its activities, in twenty or thirty years all the other denominations would have become familiar with its principle and policy and would have decided for themselves how far to accept and incorporate the new forms and methods.

Such a new centre of religious expression would appeal not simply to persons who have discarded the old creeds and forms, and not simply to those who have severed their connection with the old religious organization. On the contrary, the modernist members, both ministers and laity, of all denominations would welcome an experiment by an organization made up of those representatives of all the churches and persons of no church who stand for the religious significance of the higher patriotism.

One of the great difficulties in the way of gradual revisions and new developments in religious forms and ceremonies is that nobody seems to have thought of making new experiments outside of all the existing church services. The result is that any preacher with new ideas has had no laboratory in which to test the effect of his new scheme. He has had first to convince his committee and possibly a majority of his members; and always with the risk of turmoil and confusion, misunderstanding and controversy which are not in harmony with the spirit of worship. Scarcely any preacher, therefore, has ever been an innovator; and those who have dared to be exceptions have generally ceased to be ministers of religion. If experiments could be well tried and tested and the ceremonial embodiments of the new thought illustrated and demonstrated to be good, without in any way disturbing the even tenour of ordinary church life, then any one congregation, having participated in the demonstration which proved the beauty, dignity, and suitability of any one given item, could adopt by majority vote one innovation after another. Even such adoption might be only tentative — for a year or six months.   Or it might be only permissive, not coercive; that is, it might allow the minister or committee the liberty, at discretion, to introduce the item.   Or some new feature whose worth had been tested elsewhere might be counted, sufficiently valuable to be introduced once a year, but not oftener, or once a month or on special occasions.

When it was clearly known that such a centre of public worship existed only as an object lesson and was of the nature of a religious experimental laboratory, it would be seen by the church-going public in general not to be a competitor, a new sect, or a rival.   As a result, all those church members who believe that evolution in religious forms, statements, and intellectual interpretations should be encouraged rather than opposed, at least those along the line of making religion of greater moral service to the nation at large, would support financially and would attend occasionally the centre of the new worship, in order that they themselves might participate in the experiment and share in the enthusiasm of aiding in any new discoveries or devices that would contribute to the spiritual deepening of humanity.

2. *Institutes for Religious Research*

I recently had the privilege of being shown over the Rockefeller Institute for Medical Research, in New York City, and of talking with each of the great investigators there retained for the benefit of mankind.   Ever since then, I have been haunted in imagination with the possibility of Institutes for Religious Research along similar lines.   The ultimate object of such an institution would be the moral cure of souls, of cities, of nations.   The methods would be those not only of experience, but of experiment, of test conditions, and of verification in religion. It is as possible to know that the effect of a religious meeting has been morally curative as to know that the effect of medical treatment has checked the disease and saved the patient. The past has preserved the testimony of thousands of patients who have had inexact experience of God; but the true believers to-day all over the world are anxious for experiment in God. God must be placed beyond all possible scepticism; he must be verified by the most rigorous methods. The time will come when to doubt his existence and beneficent activity will be a proof either of perversity of will or derangement of intellect; for no church will teach an unverified and unverifiable God.

Even the slight advances that have been made towards a scientific psychology of religion during the last twenty years have already strengthened all the churches of Christendom. Whatever elements of historic religion transcend all possible verification or go counter to the results which have been verified, it has become quite manifest that religion as a whole is well founded in human experience and can be explained, but will not be explained away, by scientific observation and test. It has become undeniable that there are certain factors in experience not of the nature of hallucination or illusion which are denoted by the words God, Christ, Heaven, Hell. It has further been proved that some elements or other in prayer, in praise and worship, private or public, and in rites and ceremonies, have most beneficent moral effects upon all who participate in them, effects which never could have issued if religion had been a figment of fancy, or a deception imposed by priests. These great positive results favourable to religion have already been attained, although as yet psychological investigators have limited their attention almost exclusively to the one phenomenon of "conversion," which is only the starting point of religious experience and is often very obscure. Another crudity of psychological investigation up to the present time is that it has studied the individual soul

in isolation, as I have criticised Professor James for doing.
The Sociology or Social Psychology of religion has scarcely
begun.   The chief results of my own investigations in this
field are presented in this book.

Now the new synthesis which will link up religion with
patriotism and God with the Spirit that quickens men into
Moral Fellowship will enormously advance the cause of
the churches, even while it induces minor modifications in
rites and ceremonies, in the phrasings of religious utterance,
and in the interpretation of ancient documents.   Especially will this reënforcing of the churches, even during any
period of changing forms, be sure to take place, provided
experimental work be done outside of the regular denominations and provided only those results which experiment
has proved valuable be adopted into the historic places
of worship.

3. *Argument rendered Superfluous*

Let it not be supposed that scientific research for the
finding of more effective forms and statements and of deeper
meanings, will require any initial discarding of the religious
experience and practice of the past.   No science, in its
beginning, is ever anything more than a development of
common sense towards greater exactitude and scope.   An
institute for religious research of a constructive order,
that is, in the interests of the moral health of the community and of its individual members, would be devoted to a
psychological and sociological search for the mental as well
as material causes of moral disease and to the creation of
ideational influences, social and personal, that would
strengthen and purify the civic and individual will.   Nor
could it conceivably fail to bear fruits for the healing of the
nation.

It is also difficult not to believe that such an institution
for religious test and verification must itself be of the nature

of a church, that is, of a place of public worship. For it must be an institution which attempts to create a sense of the immanent reality of the moral ideal. It might, of course, carry on experiments in personal and private spiritual advice and in mental therapeutics; but its chief work must be preventive and social and public. It must chiefly consider normal human beings, that they may not through adverse influences become morally abnormal. The goal of all constructive religious research must be the creation of a spiritual atmosphere, without resort to unverified ideas, which favours the growth of such character as the nations need.

In the past there has been far too much dispute and controversy concerning religion. But this has been because there has been almost no scientific experiment or test. The period of religious dispute will cease the moment that of constructive research begins. It is quite evident that mere logical arguments can lead nowhere, because we have not yet secured the facts upon which to argue. Mere argument is also inadequate, even after constructive research has attained most valuable results, to convince a person who has not himself witnessed and taken part in the experiment. Arguments based on demonstrations which one has not participated in oneself are as unsatisfying in religion as in art. But arguments not based on any one's experience are of no worth. Suppose it is a question as to whether a play, which has never been seen by any one on the stage, will delight and entrance an audience or not. How can we ever settle the point except by producing the play on a stage in the presence of an audience and noting whether as a matter of fact it does delight and entrance them or not? New forms of public worship embodying new ideas are in the same predicament. Arguments about them cannot possibly so excite the constructive imagination that it should supply details which any abstract reasoning must have omitted. We must suspend judgment until we have some basis for judgment. The testimony of others also can arouse the enthusiasm only of the very few who by precedent trains of thought and experience are already ripe. For instance, suppose my arguments, which are based on experiments in new forms of social worship, have made it seem altogether plausible that it would be possible to conduct a purely humanistic church service and preach a sermon along the lines suggested by this book, which would create in all present a powerful sense of the reality and holiness of the ideal social order. This is what all the churches now attempt to create and in great part succeed in doing; but most persons attribute the spiritual atmosphere induced to a supernatural and transcendent order of things. Suppose now that the argument of this book either has or has not opened some minds to the possibility of creating the same atmosphere without any reference to the transcendent order of things; let us further suppose, however, that the persons in question attend such a religious service as I am pleading for and observe that others are moved with a sense of the reality and redemptive grace of the moral ideal, and that even they themselves also feel its presence; such an experience will have accomplished what no argument could achieve. Indeed, a demonstration by an object lesson renders much argument superfluous. It would therefore seem that while no new sect should be founded, there should be established at suitable centres throughout the nation humanistic and nationalistic church services, so that all could see and know for themselves. Then, those ministers and congregations who found any items in the services congenial to their own thought and temper could introduce these at least tentatively.

In a generation of such trial, with final acceptance or rejection, as experience dictated, there would gradually grow up a type of service and sermon which would be expressive of the living conscience of our day.

4. *Creeds the Last Documents to be Revised*

I should like to point out that long before the ultimate creeds of any historic Church can be modified or set aside, it may be possible to revivify the whole of the sentiment embodied in hymns, anthems, readings from sacred literature and sermons. It is also further possible that there will be no occasion for either restating or discarding any of the fundamental creeds of Christianity. Possibly all that will be needed will be a frank and avowed reinterpretation of these old documents from the humanistic point of view. But I deal with this theme in Parts II and III, and therefore need not dwell upon it here. I wish instead to illustrate in this chapter how a church service, incorporating the idea here advocated, might become universally adopted in the course of one or two generations. Suppose the National Committee, which I suggested in the last chapter, for teaching the identity of Religion and Patriotism, besides issuing pamphlets and books, should establish in the chief city of every State an illustrative church service, to be held every Sunday morning and evening. The constructive idea with which they would set out would be to create in the congregation a sense of the unifying spirit which animates any group of men and women who are drawn together in devotion to the human ideal. Their first object would be to make them One in vision, in heart, and in will. There might be many devices to bring about this unity and a realizing sense of it. But the device which has been adopted in hundreds of congregations of the historic churches is that which most naturally suggests itself for the beginning of the meeting. It is that at the very opening of the service all present should rise and

I

stand and that the first word of the conductor of the service should not begin until there were perfect silence — not only an absence of noises but of restless motions. Instantly and inevitably, everybody present would be aware of one Will, one Idea animating and controlling the various individual wills and intellects. There would spring up a sense not only of the two or three hundred present in individualized bodily form, but of the "I" in the midst of them who is not only greater than each, but constitutes the inmost selfhood of each, — the social self of every one. Such an act in common, as that of each person standing in silence to listen for the opening words of the service, not only creates a sense of the Unifying and Over-arching Will but also of a mystic identity with that Will. The individual in rising contributes to it; he feels that he makes it, while he is also thrilled with the feeling that it is remaking and regenerating him. It is clear, then, that before a single word is said, so simple and natural an act has created a sense of the Presence of the Unseen Order, the Order of the Universal Will, the Will of the Social Whole, made up of individualized self-respecting units and yet greater than the arithmetical sum of them all. They are in it and it is in them, interdependent and inseparable; yet the whole is felt by every one to take precedence, in dignity and power, over each and over all severally.

5. *The Liberty of Intellectual Interpretation*

I am aware that any person may interpret this experience as an evidence of the supernatural and the transcendent realm of Spirit, and in my judgment the liberty of so interpreting it should be denied to no one. I would only claim a like liberty for all those who have no love for metaphysical theories whatever, to account for the Most High which they have experienced, and who almost regard the metaphysical habit as an impiety in the presence of the Divine Reality itself. They are quite ready to allow those fellow-mortals whose intellects crave metaphysical explanations, to indulge in them; but they resent, and rightly so (it seems to me), any spiritual or intellectual airs which the cravers for transcendent realities may assume. I would also plead for a like liberty, with that of the metaphysicians and creed-makers, for those who are not satisfied with the simple, unexplained experience of the Divine Presence, but who crave only a scientific explanation. A scientific explanation, of course, in the ultimate metaphysical sense, explains nothing; but it does coördinate the factors of one's spiritual experience and formulate the law of sequence. For instance, it is only a scientific, merely a psychological and sociological, explanation, when I trace, in part, the spiritual atmosphere of a religious meeting to the fact that all the individuals rise and stand in silence together with one direction of thought and heart and will, and when I posit the General Will of the Group as a factor, real in a scientific sense, as accounting for and justifying the belief in a Universal Self. This initial act on the part of a congregation of rising and standing in silence illustrates the effect of all other acts in common by the congregation in inducing a spiritual atmosphere, and I need not therefore dwell at length on other details.

6. *The Contents of Things Said and Sung*

Here I will dwell only briefly upon the contents of things said and sung. I will purposely select illustrations which omit the words God and Christ or any of the terms which are common in Christian theology and are generally understood as referring to realities that are more than human and natural and are therefore called superhuman and supernatural. If I selected such phrases and declared that I knew by experience and experiment that they induced a spiritual atmosphere, I should fail to prove the point for which I am contending. But if I omit all of them and use in a religious service only sentences which refer to factors within universal moral experience and which no religious scepticism has ever dreamed of denying, but if, nevertheless, everybody present experiences a still deeper intimacy of communion and feels his will enlarged by a new influx of moral power, I have gained a scientific demonstration of the adequacy of mere references to the Socializing Spirit to redeem the members of any group united in devotion to the ideal of the perfect. Suppose the words I select be these : —

Let a man be of good cheer about his soul, who has cast away the pleasures and ornaments of the body as alien to him, and has followed after the pleasures of knowledge in this life, who has adorned the soul in her own proper jewels, which are temperance, and justice, and courage, and nobility, and truth.

Immediately the great realities of the Universal Will, of which the words temperance, justice, nobility, courage, and truth are the accepted symbols, present themselves to each mind in the congregation, and begin to adorn the soul of each and, by their radiance, induce the good cheer of the spirit. Or suppose I say : —

It is not possible to enter into the nature of the Good by standing aloof from it — by merely speculating upon it. Act the Good, and you will believe in it.

Forthwith every mind present, which has come in good faith and has not with malice prepense set itself against the influence of the meeting, will move to enter into the nature of the Good and will predispose itself to act the Good. For each soul needed only to be reminded, in order to have its own moral faith reënforced. Or the sentences might consist of the following invocation to what I have called the Group Spirit : —

Thou Soul of All in the soul of each,
Blessed shall the nations be when thy glory is recognized,
When all who love thee unite to succour and raise the weak !
We praise thee in thy power, thou Soul of our Souls,
    We praise thee in thy sanctity and thy wistful hopes.
We praise thee, thou Dweller in the Innermost,
    O strength and secret nourisher !
No voice can duly proclaim thy majesty,
    No heart can comprehend thy glorious destiny,
Thou Mother of all our spirits.

A similar effect is produced when the following words are used : —

Let not Moses speak to me, but Thou, O sacred Self of my selfhood, eternal Truth ; lest I die and bring forth no fruit ; being inwardly admonished, but not enkindled within ; lest the Word, heard but not followed, known but not loved, believed but not obeyed, rise up against me in the days to come.

Or this : —

The prophets utter commandments, but Thou, Spirit of Holiness, helpest to the fulfilling of them. They show the Way, but Thou givest strength for the journey.

If all that is said in any one service be selected in relation to the dominant idea that is to be presented in the sermon for the occasion, that idea would give unity to all the items in the service. The liberty on the part of a preacher always to select for each occasion whatever items will give supreme unity to the whole of the service, is indispensable, if the service is to exercise its full power upon the minds of the congregation. No prescribed forms, even though so beautiful and great as those of the Episcopal

Church for Morning and Evening Prayer, can fit all sermons and can equally suit every occasion. It seems quite certain, therefore, that within the next thirty years in America an ever increasing right of discretion will be left to the minister even of denominations which forbid extemporaneous prayers. From hundreds of items approved by the church as a whole, the minister will be allowed to select those he thinks best fitted under the immediate circumstance. Nor can I avoid the conclusion that the illustrations which I have just given contain nothing out of harmony with the spirit and purpose of the Episcopal Church and possess some mark which would upon occasion commend them to any minister of any denomination who was alive to the needs of his congregation and to the demands of modern life. Any person, therefore, attending a service where any of these sentences were pronounced, if he had felt the power in them would, upon going away, become a propagandist of the new idea and would help create public opinion in the direction of a religion of nationalistic humanism. By his propaganda he would be hastening the day when every denomination will be ready to admit new forms and phrases expressive of the living habit of thought and of the conscience of our age.

I have no space in which to cite the contents of further items in a purely humanistic service; but I may point out the fact that every participant in such a service interprets all references to social life or to duty or to character, although expressed in universal language, in relation to the human world in which he himself immediately lives. All such utterances, therefore, have a reference to his own personal conduct, his own family, his own city and state, and, when he is an American, to the United States. It is not necessary, therefore, to be forever saying, "America, America," or "Illinois, Illinois," or "San Francisco, San Francisco." All this will be understood, as the essential

meaning of great literature always is in what it suggests
rather than in what it literally expresses.   Only occasionally
need there be a direct naming of the immediate social
group; then, the very infrequency will enhance the effective-
ness of the naming.   There is, however, often a great power
added to words, if the congregation know that the author
was one of their own nation, and his life was identified
with its history and that its history poured itself into his
prose or verse.   For instance, the congregation at the
Ethical Church in London, England, sing with keen appreciation — it is one of their favourite hymns — the poem of
Emerson's containing the stanzas : —

> Out from the heart of nature rolled
> The burdens of the Bible old;
> The Litanies of nations came,
> Like the volcano's tongue of flame,
> Up from the burning core below —
> The canticles of love and woe.
>
> O'er England's abbeys bends the sky,
> As on its friends, with kindred eye:
> For out of thought's interior sphere
> These wonders rose to upper air;
> And nature gladly gave them place,
> Adopted them into her race.

They are grateful for the exquisite reference to England's abbeys; but I cannot resist the feeling that these
words, of America's greatest philosopher and prophet of
democracy, would find their way the more readily to the
heart of an American congregation.

CHAPTER VIII

1. *A Voluntary National Church*

THE separation of Church and State in America has thus far been a political necessity; but, unfortunately, her citizens have drawn the wholly illogical conclusion that if it was necessary to separate the institutions of religion from the State, it must have been because religion has no vital connection with nationality. Colour is lent to this notion by the large part which supernaturalism has played in theology, and by the close association of religion with belief in another world. But, despite the plausibility of the inference, I have shown that religions, in their great periods of creative and beneficent energy, have always been identical with the souls of nations, and with the enduring interests of this world. At this stage of our argument it is only necessary that we bring to mind again the distinction of nation, State, and Church, and the relation subsisting between these three social entities.

The State is the nation organized and acting with sovereign power through its Government. Where a State does not undertake certain enterprises, it may be only because it believes that they can safely be left to individuals and voluntary groups of individuals. The reason, therefore, for the separation of Church and State need in no wise be that religion is not a mundane interest, and is not essential to the common weal. A nation's life is infinitely more rich and complex than that part of itself which is organized under political government. My reader must therefore concede that the mere separation of Church and State can in no wise be taken as proving a separateness of religion and nation.

Let me venture to point out, further, that the separation in America between Church and State is not so absolute as the ordinary language of Americans would lead one to suppose. I am alluding not to the indirect influence which powerful religious bodies may exert upon legislation, but to the fact that the State in America has throughout the country the whole task of education. Now, any one accustomed to resolve the religious life into its sociological factors knows that, until the last century, throughout the world, the religion of a country has always been its system of popular education, and that in Christendom the Church has, until quite recent generations, organized and controlled intellectual as well as moral instruction and discipline. We may fairly say, then, that so far as the State has adopted education as one of its functions, it has taken over the work of the Church, and is in so far a Church-State. If it be retorted that such education as the State in America gives is not religious, the answer may be hurled back, Is it then education? If it does not cultivate moral taste and direct the instincts and organize the sentiments to serve the great ends of national life, can it be anything but pseudo-education? — can it be really of ultimate benefit to the country? And, if not, why should the nation lavish money upon it? If the schools simply train the intellect to be a more efficient instrument of self-centred egoism, are they not turning the children into enemies of the State itself?

To return now to our general analysis : Whenever a State includes in its purview those activities of a nation's life which are called religious, we have a State Church. But there might be a highly developed and organized and unified national Church wholly aloof from the State. There might even be only one religious organization throughout the nation, comprehending all religious persons — and that a purely voluntary one. We should then have a national Church which was not a State Church. This would be possible where all the members of a nation were of one mind in regard to religious doctrines and methods; or, there might be nothing like unanimity of doctrinal opinion, and there might be many separate groups standing for distinct philosophies and points of view; yet still each group might see the necessity of coöperating with others for the social and national ends which religion serves. Common loyalty to the nation might override differences. Each denomination might value highly the benefits of conference with persons of opposite opinions, and even prefer to submit temporarily to adverse majorities on special issues, rather than suffer the disadvantages of isolation.

I have implied that the development of national idealism would require the organization into one voluntary Church of all the religious trends in the nation; but I must qualify this sweeping statement. It is evident from the inherent nature of allegiance to a foreign bishop, that no national Church could find place within itself for a body pledged thereto. And on the other side, no organization in allegiance to an alien hierarchy could consistently do anything but refuse to coöperate in a national Church.

But if this is true of the Roman Catholic body, it would also be true of any community which should believe itself to possess a monopoly of spiritual insight, as some Jews have believed of their race. Self-excluded from every national Church would be the few surviving Hebrew jingoists and all Roman Catholics who had not become converted to modernism.

2. *A State Church Un-American*

The further fact ought to be again recalled, that even where there is not one voluntary organization embracing all separate religious groups, nevertheless the seemingly separate sects do reciprocally influence one another. The Episcopalians of America, for example, are not the same in their teaching as they would be, had there been no such thing as the New England Unitarian Movement, blossoming in Channing, Parker, and Emerson.

We may therefore say that there always is a national Church where there is a nation containing groups of spiritually minded men and women devoted to the higher ends of humanity and not wholly uninfluenced, as groups, by one another. Just as we can speak of American architecture and American commerce, although there is neither a State nor a voluntary organization of all the architectural or commercial interests of the country, so we may speak of American religion and the American Church. In regard to architecture or commerce, however, so long as their purposes and technique and ideals are unorganized throughout the country, it is apparent that they cannot be developed to their highest degree. Any interest, if we take the point of view of the nation as a whole, must be greatly handicapped in proportion as it is left exclusively to individual effort or to scattered groups in private coöperation. Likewise, a nation's religion cannot at any period have advanced far beyond the degree to which there has been established an intercommunication of all the forces involved.

As there is always a certain national spiritual unity, we may, as I have just done, imply that there is always a national Church; for the nation is a Church. Yet because its growth is retarded by lack of organization and its energy checked by the notion that religion is not vitally bound up with national life, we may, without being misunderstood, sometimes say of any country that it has no national Church — meaning no coördination of all the religious efforts within it.

For the sake of clearness in political thinking, it is fortunate that we have the two words, *nation* and *State*, the only difference between the two realities indicated being that the nation is the whole life of a people, whether organized politically or not, whereas the State is only the nation in so far as it is organized with sovereign power, levying taxes, passing laws, and enforcing them by means of a police and of an army and a navy. But it is most adverse to clearness in religious thinking that the word *Church* has to serve both for the unorganized national spiritual life and also for the religious organization, whether under the State or voluntary, and whether national or sectarian. Despite this equivocal reference of the term, however, we can remain clear in our thinking if we bear in mind the great difference between a State Church and a National Church. There may be a National Church where there is no State Church, but also there may be a State Church which is not a National Church; that is, there may be a religious organization established and endowed by the political Government, highly organized, centralized, and powerful, and yet it may by no means embrace all, or even the greater part, of the idealistic trends in the nation. Such a State Church would undoubtedly be a part of the National Church, and yet it would incontrovertibly be one of the chief causes hindering the coming into existence either of a voluntary National Church or of a truly national State Church.

This is the present condition of affairs in England. The Established Church is not national. There is a National Church — because there is a nation — but it is still rudimentary; and perhaps the chief reason why the Nation as a Church is in such a backward stage of development is that the Establishment retards the coöperation of all the national religious forces.   This condition of affairs can be denied by no one; even those who believe in the existing Establishment deplore that in attempting to unify the nation it has disrupted it spiritually.   They admit that it offends one-third of the population and never touches another third.   Likewise, many Englishmen who advocate disestablishment of the present State Church do so chiefly because they see that it militates against England's becoming an organic unit of spiritual life.

Happily for America it has no State Church professing to be national when it is not, and so preventing the advent of at least a voluntary National Church.

Whether America will ever organize her spiritual life under the sovereign power of the State is a question which we need not here discuss, because every one who knows her genius and tradition must agree that a national State Church, if it is ever to be established, ought not to be founded until after there had grown up a voluntary organization of all the religious groups in the nation.   Moreover, even those who would bitterly oppose a State establishment of religion need feel no alarm at the voluntary unification of all voluntary churches; for there is nothing inherent in a truly national voluntary church that would incline it to become a State Church.   The only vital question, then, for America is the relation of the nation as an organic unit of spiritual life to the various religious denominations already in existence.

3. *Religious Parties versus Sects*

The theory that a nation, in so far as it reverences ideals and aims at their realization, is a Church does not in the least overlook the fact that there may be violent party strife among various religious groups.   Nor does it even

involve a disparagement or condemnation of such strife.
A nation does not lose its unity in religion because of theological controversies any more than it ceases to be a unit
in civil life because of the antagonism of various political
parties. On the contrary, the idea of a nation as a Church,
far from favouring the suppression of religious differences or
opposing discussion and the continual creation of new
groups to advance new ideas, recognizes that ultimate harmony, real uniformity of belief, and deep inward identity
of insight and aspiration can never arise throughout a
nation except by way of the freest and boldest expression
and propaganda of every fresh sentiment. It is only by
means of a struggle for existence among competing standards and principles of personal and social life — it is only
by experience and experiment, by trial and test — that a
people can ever become able to select those ideas and
standards which will really best serve the spiritual life of a
nation. In our day, so patent has become the beneficial
effect of religious freedom and of liberty to proselytize by
moral suasion that before many decades priests and
preachers will, I believe, accept discussion and democratic
ballots on the first principles of religion as legitimate instruments of spiritual advancement. They will count
these devices equally sacred with private prayer and with
meetings for worship and praise. Only by continual fric-
tion of sincere intellect with intellect and by clash of devout
character with character, can a whole nation ever come to
see and rightly value righteousness, duty, and truth, and
the means to the actualization thereof in life. When once
the idea of the nation as a quickening sphere of spiritual
power becomes prevalent, sectarian aloofness must fall
away. Sects will cease to be sects; each one of them will
become a recognized party among the many within the
nation as the Church.

Our argument has now brought us face to face with a

national danger — the idea which every voluntary religious group now entertains of itself, that it is a self-contained unit of spiritual life.   This is the principle of sectarianism, in antagonism to which I wish to plead for such a reinterpretation of the various religious denominations that they shall look upon themselves not as self-contained churches, but as parties in the one spiritual life of the nation.

The doctrine of sectarianism stands seemingly at the opposite pole of thought to cosmopolitanism; and yet the two are mutually compatible outgrowths of one and the same philosophy. Cosmopolitanism, as we have seen, denies that the nation is the spiritual unit of mankind; but it carries with it no objection to the voluntary organization of private individuals into religious groups. On the contrary, inasmuch as such groups, if they set themselves up as whole churches, deny that the nation is the living Church of all citizens, cosmopolitanism encourages them. Every advance in the organization of sects constitutes a corresponding decline in the spiritual self-consciousness of the nation. An American who thinks that the Methodist or the Baptist society is the real organic being from which his soul derives its sustenance, is naturally as jealous of the new philosophy which holds the nation itself to be his living Church as are the sentimental cosmopolitan, the individualistic champion of peace, the Marxian Socialist, the old-fashioned Hebrew jingoist, and the anti-modernist Roman Catholic.

But while the sectarian looks with jealous antagonism upon the doctrine of religious nationalism, it must be noted that the attitude of national idealism towards sectarianism does not consist in the demand that private-enterprise churches should be disbanded. On the contrary, it is inconceivable how national idealism could propagate itself except through the instrumentality of voluntary bodies of religious enthusiasts. All that the national idealist would ask of the various sects is that they should link themselves up in thought and purpose with the spiritual life of the nation as a whole, and become its glad servants. In other words, its demand is that the sects should cease to look upon themselves as sects — that is, as self-contained spheres of spiritual energy, underived from any larger whole — and that they should regard themselves rather as so many participants, both dependent and determinant, in the life of the nation as the one true Church.

The distinction between a religious sect and a religious party has been almost wholly overlooked. Yet this distinction is vital to the adoption of a policy that will lead to the spiritual unification of a nation. The peculiarity of a party as distinct from a sect is that it never withdraws and stands aloof from its antagonists. It knows that it is not self-feeding, nor is it ever self-centred. It knows that for it to hold aloof would be its death. A party always sallies forth and presses forward in order to grapple and wrestle with opposing parties. The policy and the philosophy of parties is to meet face to face and contend — bitterly if you will, but always with the hope of changing the antagonist into an ally.

The truth is, antagonistic parties are, in the nature of their relation, not enemies, but friends disagreeing. They aim at the same goal, and serve the same interest. They are always understood to be but sections of a larger whole. They seek intimacy of contact in struggle, in order that they may win over opponents. Indeed, the whole method of government by majority is based upon the evident fact that one party modifies another, and that each is influenced by the forces of opposition, as well as by its own doctrines and its own leaders. The philosophy of government by majority is due to the experience that what was a majority yesterday may become to-morrow a minority, and *vice versa*.

These facts in civil polity are familiar enough, but it sounds strange to suggest that, in the same way, religious sects should be forced, or should force themselves, to enter into coöperative antagonism. Sects as sects hold aloof from one another. Each considers that it is spiritually self-contained and self-feeding, and when it ventures forth it attempts only to convert individuals — not other religious groups as such — to its own point of view. As yet, unfortunately, there is no such thing as a meeting of Baptists with Methodists, or of both with Episcopalians, in organized conference and discussion, for the purpose of beating out some larger, wiser formula of ultimate religious truth than each in the past has been able to express. It is true that there are interdenominational meetings, but only for the discussion of matters unrelated to fundamental principles.

When once the members of the various religious denominations of America become imbued with the principle of national idealism as the essence of religion, it is hard to believe that they will not adopt it. Then they will cease to be sects. They will voluntarily and spontaneously coöperate as so many parties in one spiritual community. The first result may be an embitterment of antagonism, but this effect cannot last long. Inevitably and quickly there must ensue a *rapprochement* of all the denominations, drawn together by their common effort to conserve, strengthen, and purify the soul of the nation.

Let me cite as analogous to ecclesiastical, the case of political parties. The latter meet face to face in the legislative halls of the State. They are professedly dominated by the desire to serve their country. They differ only as to the means to be adopted and as to the philosophy of society. So long as the State is in no great danger, opposition may run high; but the moment any menace to the country becomes evident to all, and in proportion as it

K

seems imminent, party strifes and differences are overborne. What a boon if among religious bodies theological
hatred always ceased the moment the spiritual life of the
nation was in danger of disruption! — and it would always
cease at this point if religious denominations met as parties
instead of holding aloof as sects.

From the point of view of America's spiritual destiny,
sectarianism is the sin of sins; aloofness is a denial of the
one organic being of which they are incontrovertibly members. For any religious body this is schism — to remain
aloof from other spiritual groups within the same nation.

4. *Sectarianism Anti-democratic*

Private-enterprise organizations in religion are, if self-
centred and if assuming to be independent units of spiritual
life, by their very nature undemocratic in method, in machinery and principle; and if it be true that America
is fundamentally democratic, then sectarianism is anti-
American. The notion is prevalent and almost universal
that a little group of persons may segregate themselves out
of the general community in which they live, and yet still
remain democratic in character, provided they practise
self-government by majority vote among themselves. But
surely a self-selected group of persons, as compared with a
whole nation, is always but a few; and government of a
few by that few, in the interests of the same few, can never
constitute democracy. Nor can a nation which is democratic on a territorial basis, and governs all the people
within its area by all for all, tolerate for a moment the
notion that little voluntary groups of picked individuals
are democratic simply because they imitate the national
machinery of democracy. A little group, however democratically governed, is always but a clique. What is more,
it never has the character of democracy on a national ter-

ritorial basis, because the clique is always vitally in touch with, and absolutely dependent upon, the whole nation in which it lives; whereas the nation is dependent upon no corresponding larger whole. If a religious clique counts itself an organic unit of spiritual life, it is blind to the most patent of all facts — the dependence of each of its members, and even of itself as a whole, upon the enveloping life of the nation. It is against the very spirit of democracy in religion — and therefore of America — that the religious elements of the nation should be segregated into mutually isolated private-enterprise churches. Such groups generally betray the vanities of petty aristocracies. Indeed, the more fully they imitate democratic forms and methods, the more grotesque and preposterous a counterfeit they become.

It is a fact generally overlooked, but one which can never be denied, after attention has once been called to it, that there never can be real democracy except where the privilege of coöperation is extended to all the individuals living in any geographical area. That area may be only a small section of the territory of a whole nation, for democracy may be decentralized; but the moment the privilege of coöperation is denied to any of the inhabitants, there is a discarding of the territorial basis, which is the essence of democracy.

Now, every religious denomination, whether acting as a sect or as a party, by its very nature excludes from its membership persons who do not accept its distinctive tenets. Such exclusion is inevitable, and is wholly commendable. The disbelievers in Methodism are not found inside of Wesley's organization, nor is it conceivable that they should be found there, for their presence would destroy the very character of the body upon which they had intruded. It will be noticed that I am not pleading that denominations should surrender their distinctive tenets when I advise that they transform themselves from sects to parties. My thought is that they should continue to reject heretics, but at the same time meet heretics in a larger organization devoted to the spiritual unification of the nation. I am not proposing that every Christian body should become simply an ethical society, and then as such coöperate with all others. I am not proposing that before they organize nationally, they should drop any of their present conditions of membership; I am only pleading that they should rid themselves of their prejudice of sectarianism. In future generations every denomination may be ready to discard any tenet which is found to be not essential to the highest service of the nation; but such a change within any one religious denomination may well be left to the reaction upon its members of contact with other religious groups, under the inspiration of a national ideal.

It may further be noticed that what I am advocating in no wise involves the necessity that any religious denomination should in its own government be representative. Just as such a denomination does not become democratic by adopting for itself the machinery of government by majority vote, so, on the other hand, it does not cease to be so because it is episcopalian in its government. It becomes democratic, whatever its own form of government, the moment it seeks to coöperate in a national organization for the spiritual uplift of the world, and it does not cease to be so until it becomes self-centred in its interest, and denies its moral dependence upon the psychic reservoir of the whole people.

In the spiritual interests of America, sectarianism must be stamped out of existence; then every denomination, becoming a party, will assume a new life and virility. All the defects of the various denominations in Christianity may be traced ultimately to sectarianism. Because they have counted themselves as autonomous churches, they have outlived by centuries the times which originally caused them and needed them. How unlike in this respect are they to the life of a whole nation, either as a Church or as a civic body !

One of the differences between a sect and a true democracy is that the latter does not attempt to exclude or suppress geniuses for promulgating new opinions. Geniuses, remaining within the nation, whatever turmoil they stir up for a time, in the end react upon the nation's life, and are recognized of it. Religious denominations, however, not regarding themselves as parties, are noted for being founded by men of rare originality, but are notorious for never afterwards providing scope for prophets of fresh insight. In other words, the fundamental difference between a sect and a democratic religious party is that in the latter, by meeting with the members of other parties, every individual is stimulated to independent judgment; and parties are compelled in self-defence to modify their formulas and change their point of view.

Organized contact with the life of other religious groups being thus vivifying, any one sect transforming itself into a national party would become sensitively solicitous for the nation's half-conscious needs and groping trends. It would illuminate these and turn them into conscious demands and self-directing principles. By virtue of such contact and of such service, it would deserve to be recognized as a democratic body.

The preposterous notion that a sect holding aloof from coöperation with other religious denominations is democratic, has evidently sprung out of the individualistic psychology of the eighteenth century. This regarded each individual person as originally the real unit of spiritual life, and any society as but a voluntary aggregate of separate atoms. Such a philosophy, however, cannot, by the very make-up of the word democracy, be rightfully designated by this term. From the point of view of history, etymology, and sociology, the real unit of democracy, as I have already pointed out, is always ultimately either a whole nation or some geographical section of its inhabitants, and not a voluntary group of selected individuals. Or, if the term cannot be thus limited after its long use in a vaguer sense, we must discriminate between individualistic democracy and social democracy. No one will deny that a sectarian denomination is not an instance of social democracy.

The aloofness of one sect from another has been the curse not only of the nation as a whole, but of the religious bodies themselves. We find throughout America that organized religious life, as compared with other forms of social activity, is weak and ineffectual. Its thoughts and methods are petrified. The preachers are not the dominant factors in the intellectual and moral enlightenment of the nation that religious teachers ought to be. If the people are being led forward to new heights of self-control and vision, it is not the churches which are leading. They are timid, apologetic, alarmed, and cautious. Why is it so? Why are other social agencies more progressive, valiant, confident, and beneficent? It is because they are in democratic contact with one another and with groups with which they disagree. Such contact is the great vitalizing agent; but the churches have not yet learned the wisdom of seeking it.

CHAPTER IX

THE SOCIOLOGICAL FUNCTION OF THE CHURCHES

1. *Religion not merely a Private Concern*

OUR age is turning more and more away from the old-time habit of trusting to intelligent beings other than man. The help we once expected from invisible and incorporeal agencies we are now demanding, with the enthusiasm of a new faith, from our fellow-mortals. Although each of us be weak and blind, we feel that infinite is the help, spiritual as well as material, which Man collectively can yield to men individually.

Among the morally intelligent, religion is accordingly ceasing to be regarded as a merely private concernment. The individual is looking to society to deliver him from sin and suffering; and the society he looks to is nothing less than the nation to which he belongs.

Until the last decade of the nineteenth century, those who had discarded communion with supernatural beings inclined to the belief that adequate consolation could be drawn by each person from the inner recesses of his own soul. The profounder life of the human spirit was supposed to be of such a nature that to attempt to communicate it was to expose it to degradation. "We descend to meet," said Emerson. To crave religious communion with one's fellow-mortals was thought to be a denial of the sufficiency of one's own inner store of spiritual wealth. Solitude and the vastness of isolation were the only immensities befitting the self-contained soul. Thus those who discarded communion with supernatural beings withdrew into themselves.

Even within the churches, the discipline, except in special centres, had been more and more falling into disrepute. Whole classes in the community, although they retained a belief in a personal Creator and in the traditional teachings of the Church, inclined to count coöperation with other human beings in religious practices as superfluous. The very fact that they found the consolations of fellowship in communion with personal agencies outside of the social organism made them the more ready to dispense with religious communion with other men.

Many observers interpreted this tendency as indicating a decline of religious conviction. But such an interpretation is incorrect. The religious life became less social, but there was not anything like a corresponding decrease of belief in the existence of a personal Creator or in the divinity of Jesus Christ, or of reverence for the Bible.

The whole fact is that the doctrine of an individualistic psychology, while on the one hand injuring church life, had on the other hand been temporarily intensifying the religious devotion of those who already had attained a spiritual consciousness of their own. It had injured church life in the same way that in politics it had been working against the full functioning of the State. By the year 1860, the theory of *laissez-faire* had caused the Government of England to restrict itself almost entirely to police duties. In the previous century, the Constitution of America had in similar manner been framed under such distrust of political regulation that the Federal Government was not given full powers of sovereignty. No wonder that the Church was severed from the State, and that finally the identity of religion with the spirit of nationality was wholly forgotten. Nor is it a wonder that individuals preëminently religious by nature, accepting the doctrine of individualism, interpreted religion as a merely private concern.

2. *Professor William James's Error*

The individualistic interpretation of the inner life so possessed the mind of the late Professor William James that in his "Varieties of Religious Experience" he begins his investigation of "personal religion" with a deliberate setting aside of churches and all their works as worse than irrelevant. He justifies this procedure on the ground that ecclesiastical organization emanates from individual geniuses, but that individual genius is not quickened by contact with church organization.

A survey of history [he says] shows us that as a rule religious geniuses attract disciples, and produce groups of sympathizers. When these groups get strong enough to "organize" themselves, they become ecclesiastical institutions with corporate ambitions of their own. The spirit of politics and the lust of dogmatic rule are then apt to enter and to contaminate the originally innocent thing; so that when we hear the word "religion" nowadays, we think inevitably of some "church" or other; . . . but in this course of lectures ecclesiastical institutions hardly concern us at all. The religious experience which we are studying is that which lives itself out within the private breast. First-hand individual experience of this kind has always appeared as a heretical sort of innovation to those who witnessed its birth. Naked comes it into the world and lonely; and it has always, for a time at least, driven him who had it into the wilderness, often into the literal wilderness out of doors, where the Buddha, Jesus, Mohammed, St. Francis, George Fox, and so many others had to go.

Now, in the name of history, I protest that all conclusions drawn from this premise are rendered worthless by the initial blunder of imagining that ecclesiastical institutions have no significant and helpful bearing upon the inmost religious experience. It is the very opposite of truth to say that such experience comes into the world "lonely."

There never was a great religious innovator who was not nourished and fostered, as it were, at the bosom and in the very heart of an ecclesiastical organization. Jesus was conceived in the womb of Judaism; Savonarola and Luther, of Catholicism; Wesley, of Anglicanism. They all loved their spiritual mother, the Church. Their very innovations were for her sake. Their sacrifice was for her. Not one single religious genius known to history discovered and brought forth, in isolation and by direct unmediated communion with the Infinite, "the originally innocent thing" which the Church at first perhaps failed to appreciate but afterwards adopted. Nor has any religious genius known to history ever been the product of what is called "the world" as distinct from the Church. Even the withdrawing into the wilderness on the part of innovators was a taking with them of the precious secret of the ecclesiastical organization, that they might penetrate deeper into its spirit.

It is psychologically unwarrantable, therefore, to imagine that a man's mind is isolated from social institutions simply because he has withdrawn for a period to meditate. Even George Fox did not get by isolation the new truth he uttered; he got it by contact with the quickening social life of his time, when all England was a church, and religious controversy filled every nook and corner of the nation. Thousands were feeling what they could not express. In him, exquisitely sensitive as he was to the needs of the social organism about him, these feelings became conscious, articulate, and effective.

If it were impossible for Professor James to see the whole truth, that personal experience comes from church organization as much as church organization grows out of some one's personal experience — if he could only see half of this truth — it is a great pity that he should have seen the less significant half, and devoted his rare gifts to that side of it which of itself alone can never bear fruit unto life. The world's need is to know under what controllable conditions geniuses with fresh religious experience appear in society. If the world knew these conditions, it would bring forth a thousand where now, by haphazard, it produces only one.

3. *The Quickening Influence of Churches*

If we are ever to deepen personal religious experience, it will be by intensifying, developing, and systematizing church discipline. Only ecclesiastical institutions quicken religious emotion and clarify insight to the degree that drives men, stung with the splendour of new vision, into the desert, and then back again into the slums of the city, with plans thought out and purposes and policy fixed and matured. If we want a Jesus to appear on earth, some nation like America must do what the Jewish theocracy for five whole centuries did — focus the attention and desire of men and women, by means of national Temple services, in expectation of faith, upon the necessity of a deliverer.

As regards Savonarola, if we remember that the Catholic Church consisted not only of the immediate phase which dominated in Italy in his day, but of the whole reach back to the time of Jesus, and even, through Judaism, to Isaiah, we cannot deny that all that was new and most characteristic in Savonarola was old and most distinctive of the Church. The same is true of Luther. Had he not been a monk, he never could have made Germany. And in the case of Wesley, it was no accident that such unique first-hand experience of religion as his came to one whose father and mother both had been preachers and even fanatics of church discipline, as were also his remoter ancestors, and that he was bred in Oxford, the hotbed of ecclesiasticism.

How could any one, in the face of these well-known facts,

hope to account for personal religious experience from the point of view that ecclesiastical institutions hardly concern it at all? Even Emerson, with his fresh democratic American gospel of self-trust, never could have gained his unparalleled penetration and insight had he not been trained to be a preacher of an organized religious body, had he not studied at a university founded to equip preachers, and had he not sprung from generations of ministers of religion. The truth which a study of the historic facts brings to light is that great heretics, as well as the most powerful defenders of the old order, are formed only at the heart of ecclesiastical institutions. Heresies are but vital manifestations of the spirit of the old order, as it adapts itself to changes in the intellectual and social environment, to meet for the Church's sake the exigencies of the coming hour. The spirit of orthodoxy and the spirit of heresy are one; the opposite of both is worldly indifference. Let heretics remember their kinship with orthodox enthusiasts. Let them beware; for if they destroy instead of transforming ecclesiastical institutions, they will involve their own inspiration in a common ruin. Instead of living humanistic idealism there will remain only the dead matter of selfish conventionality. It is as unscientific to think that fresh spiritual insight can be gained in isolation from organized religious bodies as to imagine that scientific discoveries and inventions like those of radium and wireless telegraphy will come to men and women who have been kept all their lives aloof from chemical and physical laboratories and from the great educational institutions of technical research.

This error is the more astonishing at the beginning of an era when at last the law of cause and effect and the idea of the spiritual interdependence of mankind have taken practical hold of all the great thinkers of the world. The truth is, Professor James was the victim of a false individualism. His psychology was blind to the fact that those whose minds are most self-reliant, intuitive, and creative are the ones most sensitively receptive to the higher tendencies of the age and society in which they live. When they were least aware of drawing spiritual vitality from the community about them, then most was the common life streaming into them and invigorating them.

During the last fifteen years, not only has the main trend of enlightenment been away from communion with superhuman agencies, but the religious geniuses of our day have at the same time become acutely conscious that they have no ethical life apart from the men and women who constitute the world about them. They know that if from these they cannot derive the inspiration which men in former times undoubtedly did receive under the discipline of the old religious practices, their souls must wither at the root. But they are beginning to realize that a man may be all the time absorbing spiritual sustenance from his fellow-mortals, although he be under the illusion that he is drawing the waters of life wholly from some inner well unfed from social sources. They are becoming convinced that those who attribute their salvation to supernatural agents, and to the belief in such, are, in fact, deriving their power and enthusiasm not ultimately from within any more than from above, but from round about — from the spiritual reservoir of their nation, their city, their church, and, through literature and history, from the past of human society carried over and flowing on into the present time.

4. *The Self-made Man in Religion*

Now, it may be contended that a man can be spiritually in touch with the religious life of his times although he be not a member of any church. He may go from one religious meeting to another and hear all the preachers of his town. In periodical literature and books he may follow the great controversies of the hour on theology. Through the daily Press he may become aware of all the currents and cross-currents, the main stream and the eddies and back-waters of the spiritual consciousness of the time. What, therefore, it may be asked, is the need of his entering into the routine and the dogmatism of active membership in any one church organization? Let him spare himself such trammels, and in the freedom of independence let him draw vitality from all the sources round about him. It may be maintained that by thus holding aloof and yet remaining receptive he would avoid all the pettinesses and corruptions which inevitably manifest themselves in the life of any organized body of human beings, and yet gain that which is highest and of enduring worth in them all.

In answer to this contention, I would reply: A person who is outside of all religious organizations is less likely to gain an expert intimacy with religion. However much he tries, he will remain veritably an outsider, and all those who are under the discipline of the organization will realize that he has missed something that is essential to a correct understanding. Experience does not justify the notion that a man quite aloof from the religious life and thought of others will possess any highly developed spiritual life of his own. The very organs of religion in his spirit will become atrophied. After twenty years of isolation he may become a fanatic, but he will be one whom every member of organized life will know to pity rather than respect. He will have no message for his age or any other age, because messages come from that source from which he has cut himself off.

Would Professor James have maintained, in regard to scientific insight and enthusiasm, that it also lives itself out within the private breast, unrelated to the organized scientific life of the community? If a man makes great discoveries in chemistry or physics, it is due, at least in our age of more than primitive knowledge, to his discipleship and discipline in scientific organizations. In withdrawing for greater concentration on some special problem, he takes with him the whole tradition and apparatus of scientific investigation. Further, if in his isolated investigation he remains long aloof and drops out of touch with what other men are doing in the privacy of scientific organizations but have not yet published to the lay world, he will be overtaken and left behind.

Now, what is the difference between the insight and enthusiasm of religion and the insight and enthusiasm of science that would make any one cast something like contempt upon ecclesiastical organizations? In science, art, and literature, the idea of the self-made man has been forever exploded. But religion being still more complicated and its tradition still longer and more involved than the scientific or artistic interest, the self-made man in religion must be more grotesque and impossible than in other domains of human effort. One may trace almost all the follies and vanities of religious men to their notion that in religion one need not take counsel of one's fellow-men either for warning or example, but may open up in isolation infinite inner sources of light and life. It is the self-made prophets and prophetesses who bring forth such "abortive, monstrous, and unkindly mixed" fanaticisms as Mormonism and Eddyism.

Lest I seem to exaggerate the radical significance of Professor James's individualism, it must be remembered that the sentences which I have quoted from him contain no merely passing observation, but are introduced to justify the entire omission from his whole volume of any tracing of spiritual conversions and illuminations to the influence of churches upon the innermost centre of men's souls.

It may be true that ecclesiastical organizations begin

to develop corporate ambitions of their own, and that the spirit of politics and the lust of dogmatic rule enter and contaminate the originally innocent thing. But is not this imperfection equally to be noted in schools, in universities, in cities, in states, in families, in business organizations? Yet would anybody expect a man to become richer or more learned or more civic by standing outside these imperfect institutions than by entering into them? Furthermore, does a historic knowledge of churches lead us to think that they are any more corrupt than other social bodies? And does not a knowledge of others lead us to think that their ambitions, their politics, and their lust of domination are often more than offset by a still greater development of their true ends and methods? Harvard University, if one knew intimately its inside workings, would no doubt show its fair proportion of frailties and corruptions; yet in the eyes of the world it stands not for these, but as the foster-mother of such geniuses as the writer of " The Varieties of Religious Experience."

5. "*Omne Vivum ex Vivo*"

Again I would meet religious individualism by pointing out the fact that even innovators and heretics in religion derive their followers not from "the world," but from among those who have long undergone the discipline of church communion. Those who have withdrawn into temporary isolation gladly turn to some new prophet who is voicing their living convictions. The men who have always been outside of churches may care for music or painting or the drama or athletics or wealth; but they have been too much occupied with these concerns to have attended intimately to the new religious promptings of the age.

It is to be feared that as a result of the wide popularity of Professor James's book, the impression has arisen and

become fixed that on account of something in the nature
of the religious life, religion is necessarily individualistic;
whereas the truth is that the psychological study of religious
experience must trace it to the nutrition and stimulus which
the ecclesiastical organizations give to the growing soul, just
as biology traces the embryonic life of a child to the environing and vitalizing organism of the mother. When
the new organism has become severed, its vitality cannot
again become dependent upon that of the parent; yet this
very independence is undeniably the result of its prior
vital dependence; so although a church may be the cause
of new insight and of religious energy, yet the innermost
experience of the soul, when fully ripe, may be vitally self-
sufficient. Nevertheless, it is so because within the church
organization a long period of gestation had been taking
place. So patent are these facts that one wonders whether
Professor James was not rendered blind to them by some
unconscious bias. It would almost seem as if he had approached his investigation of personal religion on the presupposition that its phenomena are the manifestation of
occult powers in the soul, which are not derived from the
environing social organism of mankind, but which emanate
directly from a transcendent and supersensible world of
spirits. A person holding such a belief might naturally
become oblivious to the historic social causes of inner experiences. How else could any one overlook the obtrusive
fact that personal conversions to religion are nearly always
special instances of religious epidemic, and that such
epidemic spreads not wholly unintentionally and unplanned
from those centres of organized life called ecclesiastical
institutions?

The high value I place upon the spiritual discipline of
ecclesiastical organization arises from my recognition of
the perfectly patent connection of cause and effect existing
between moral fellowship and personal enthusiasm. My

L

protest, on the other hand, against the tracing of conversions to supernatural or occult causes is due to my acceptance of the fundamental presupposition of all psychological reasoning — that no special mental phenomenon shall ever be traced either to occult or supernatural sources if it can be accounted for by the action of specific social influences and stimuli. Professor James, although he does not commit himself overtly to a spiritistic source of inward illumination, nevertheless seems to favour it At the same time he traces conversion to subconscious and unconscious processes, which, in turn, by the very limitation which he prescribes for himself at the outset of his investigation, he refuses to trace to definite social circumstances and to the influences and organized efforts of other human beings.

6. *The Social Genesis of Conversion*

Now what is it that actually takes place during a revival? We can easily discover the essential nature of what goes on if we remember that religious folk have "lumped together as the grace of God" — to use the late W. T. Stead's expression — all the diffused and disseminated influences and agencies throughout the community that are beneficent and ethical. A revival is an organization of these good influences and agencies so as to bring them to bear with their full force upon the character of individual members of the community. Conversion is the surrender of the individual to these influences. He may not be a member of any ecclesiastical organization, but it is such an institution which directs the influences, and by concentrating them intensifies their power.

If we assume that conversion is an advantage to the man converted, we can but regret the tendency to trace it to supernatural or occult causes; for no one except a believer in magic would presume to be able to constrain the supernatural and the occult in the same manner in which he would expect to control purely human and natural forces. It is a pity that an effect like conversion, which is capable of being wrought in millions of men by the society in which they live, should be generally declared to be beyond direct human control. It is especially a pity, because ever-increasing numbers of men refuse to believe in the supernatural and the occult, and yet are told that the sudden transition from badness to goodness is a supernatural event. They accordingly are bewildered and hardened, they are distracted from entertaining and absorbing that holy influence which the revival irradiates, merely because it is labelled miraculous. Indeed, the majority of organizers of revivalistic movements require of every convert, not simply that he shall renounce the evil and turn to the good, but that he shall also accept supernaturalism with its accompanying occultism. They brand as counterfeit every transition from badness to goodness not effected under their peculiar interpretation.

There are thousands whom the churches do not convert because the old theory offends the modern scientific spirit. Countless numbers would be wakened up to their own higher selfhood who now remain spiritually dead, if only Christian teachers would but drop their supernaturalism and their individualistic psychology with its naïve moral trust in the subconscious and the occult. These theories are antagonistic to the complete and thorough control by the community of the good influences latent within itself.

7. *Spiritual Environment deliberately Prepared*

The pernicious effects of individualistic psychology and of supernaturalistic theology are seen in the preference given by most people to whatever is purely spontaneous in the religious life, and their dislike for whatever has been planned

and worked up with deliberate intention. Many persons
entertain this prejudice against conscious and systematic
effort without being aware that it is the off-shoot of supernaturalism and occultism. Such persons might readily
admit that individual conversion was due to the spiritual
state for the time being of the community at large, but they
would shrink from the idea that this spiritual state might
have come otherwise than spontaneously. They could
scarcely believe that it really was holy and sacred if it
had been planned months ahead and if definite means
of propaganda and organization had brought it into existence.

Although those who dislike the conscious efforts of
ecclesiastical institutions, as somehow incompatible with
true spirituality, may not be aware of it themselves, this
sentiment of theirs is essentially opposed to a belief in the
spiritual organism of society as the source of redemptive
energy. They maintain that a revival is more genuine
and more holy if it comes quite spontaneously. But why
should man's purposes, his reason and foresight have a
polluting effect? Have they in science, art, politics, or
domestic life? Are not consciousness and self-consciousness
the highest manifestations of humanity, and the chief
blessings which society engenders in its individual members?
Why, again, is an event in the individual soul, if induced by
occult and mysterious forces or by unembodied spirits,
any more beautiful or beneficent than if occasioned by
human purpose and foresight? Such a sentiment can only
arise from a preference for the superhuman, which casts
discredit upon and so paralyzes the efficiency of the human.
Why is the conscious less to be treasured than the subconscious? Why is effort less holy than spontaneity?
And if it be not less holy, why is a revival systematically
planned and controlled less sacred and beneficent than an
unpremeditated outburst? Those who discourage the

effort of others in bringing about a man's conversion cast a slur upon conscious human effort altogether.

Now, there is urgent need that the beneficent influences and ethical agencies latent within the nation should be wisely directed and applied for the healing of the people. So far as these influences are uncontrolled and unorganized, and not even recognized as existing and as controllable, they are practically non-existent. So frequently do they remain latent and unperceived that whenever by any chance, or by the half-unconscious efforts of supernatural-ists, they begin to operate, they are so unusual and unfamil-iar that they seem to the unreflecting mind to emanate from some source outside of our accustomed universe. Society itself thus gets no credit for the best that is in it. Only the evil is attributed to human beings and their social organization. All this beautiful freshness of the spirit, this wonderful influx of energy, insight, and joyous, unselfish life are laid to the credit of some transcendent world. What is good in society has brought it about that men who were morally dead have become alive; yet society, rightly blamed for their death, is not rightly praised for their resurrection. Society has saved them; they lacked motive to live, and the power to live aright was beyond them; but now it is as difficult for them to sink to their former level as it was before for them to rise to their present height. Yet society, which has lifted them, is the very being from whose clutches they imagine that they have now at last happily escaped. Such is the mental confusion of our day that churches do not see that the only philosophy which fully appreciates their function is what I may venture to call social mysticism or mystical socialism. The supernaturalism and the individualistic occultism with which the churches are now saturated weaken enormously their vitality and their power to quicken individuals into original centres of spiritual insight and enthusiasm. Mystical socialism or social mysticism is the only philosophy which fully realizes that when a man is converted, it is because into his central personality have rushed those higher social influences and agencies hitherto latent, and perhaps undiscerned, which before scarcely touched him. Now they have become his very self; and not only that, but he himself has become a creative point of ethical energy.

8. *The Power that Saves*

What takes place at every revival is exactly analogous to the physical phenomenon which is witnessed when a burning-glass is so held between the sun and a piece of wood that first there is a bright spot of focussed light, and then a charring and smoking, till finally the wood itself bursts into a blaze shining back to its parent sun. It becomes a flame, with power to communicate its own heat and light to other objects of like nature with itself. Now the organization of ethical agencies by ecclesiastical institutions forms a burning-glass which gathers and directs the love of men and the love of duty, hitherto diffused and therefore weak, upon individual human beings who have never before felt the good in overmastering strength. Lonely isolated souls, timid and shy natures, the cynical, the violent, the envious, the jealous, the malicious, self-indulgent victims of vicious habit, now for the first time experience the quickening intensity and wholesome joy of being cared for, respected, and sought out as of infinite worth. Divinely tender is the message with which every ecclesiastical institution heralds its revival — that the lowest and most degraded sinner is precious beyond all price. This message is coupled with the announcement of the infinite worth of purity, justice, and all personal and civic virtues.

If conversions ever took place unrelated to revivals, either undesigned or prearranged, there might be some ground for the individualistic or the supernaturalistic theory of the origin of personal religious insight and enthusiasm. But in the face of the undeniable connection of institutional life with the conversions, one is forced by all the canons of logical inference to believe that religious genius is made luminous through the action of society upon it.

Where there is no concentration upon individuals of the redemptive influences and agencies which are already stored up within society, there are no conversions. There must be at least a few persons actively united in devotion to the higher life, else others who are spiritually cold and dead do not experience a new birth. It is quite true that there may be no actual prearrangement to bring about a revival; also, the persons converted may not have been attending religious meetings of any kind. In such cases, however, the spiritual energy overflows the accustomed centres, where it has been preserved in the community from past experiences. By some happy chance it lodges, like a flake of fire, in the soul of some isolated individual and sets it aglow. Always — unless the methods of inference universally acknowledged as valid cannot be applied here — conversion is due to social forces of a moral order impinging upon the rational will of an individual.

The more one investigates religious experience, the more one is led to the conviction that there never has been a conversion where such social forces were not, at least accidentally, impinging upon the individual's mind. And wherever the forces reach a certain degree of power and persistence, conversion is inevitable, even against the set determination of the individual himself. Thus it happens that what is called the working of the Holy Ghost in the inmost spirit of a man can always be brought about by the right sort of social organization, and it will always be prevented by unfavourable social environment. Given the conditions, the Holy Ghost is always manifested. This is not surprising if the divine Spirit be identical with the informing will of society as a spiritual organism. By psychologists who have no individualistic bias, the Holy Ghost is readily identified with the Higher Will, the deeper selfhood, of some social group bound together in devotion to the moral ideal. It is true that the Holy Ghost cannot be arbitrarily and dictatorially summoned; but one may be certain that it can be induced whenever any ecclesiastical institution is devoutly and wisely bent upon a manifestation of its presence and power. The Holy Ghost is a visitant that always comes, either in response to a given summons, or whenever by unpremeditated circumstance the avenues into which it is forever pressing are opened. This simply means that the moral influences and agencies within the community have been so gathered together and directed that no one upon whom they are brought to bear can prevent himself from being lifted to and borne along on a higher plane than he would otherwise have reached. If social mysticism discloses the secret of personal religion, it is evident that the real religious interests of the nation are not only assailed by the old-fashioned supernaturalism, but are also being undermined by the new-fashioned individualistic occultism. It is essential to religious development that we should check the social heresy that religious conversion is a merely private or subjective change, effected by subconscious incubation within the individual's own mind, unrelated to society round about him.

It well may be that the soul's own energies have been secretly developing like a folded bud, and that now in the fulness of time the blossom bursts of itself into an expanded flower. But what are the forces which have been warming and moistening the subsoil of the individual's conscious mind? These, I maintain, are social influences; new moral vitality from the community round about is passing quietly but effectively through the normal channels of

PART II

CHRISTIANITY TO BE REINTERPRETED IN THE LIGHT OF SCIENCE AND AMERICAN IDEALISM

PART II

CHAPTER X

CHRISTIANITY MINUS MIRACLE

THE reinterpretation of religion and the revision of its rites and teachings which I have been recommending consist in the elimination of every trace of trust in moral intelligences who are not members of human society, and in a corresponding expression of faith in combined human effort under natural law. Before considering the moral justification of this principle and before applying it to current religious formulæ, it would be well for any one to bring fully before his mind which those factors are, in the ordinary orthodox scheme of religious instruction, that must be rejected as coming under the head of "intelligent agencies who are not members of human society." For this phrase may be so vague to many that they will not otherwise realize exactly its specific applications. At the outset it must be noticed that all events in being traced to supernatural intelligences are thereby regarded as miracles, and that a Christianity no longer tracing events to such sources would be Christianity minus miracles.

1. *No Guidance from the Dead*

Let it then be observed that in setting aside supernatural agencies as a source of redemption we give up the possibility of any help from any human being after he has died, except such as he had set into operation before his death. We close the spirit world as distinct from the human, and refuse direct assistance from human beings after they cease to be responsible members of society, excepting always such wisdom and character as they left behind them when they died.   But we lose nothing hereby.

This general principle permits intimate communion with our personal friends after their death through the work they did and the character they revealed when on earth, and thus prolongs to us their redemptive influence; but it shuts us off from any trust in them as agents operating directly upon and within human souls.

The rejection of this kind of intercourse with human beings after their death, however, in no wise involves a denial of their continued individualized existence. For of all the things which we may or may not say of death, only this is undeniably a moral fact: when a man dies, whether he live again or not, he must by universal consent and law cease to be any longer a constituent member of organized society.   After death he may still be living, but, although he may communicate with us, he ought not to be allowed to vote; he may still be living, but he must not be permitted to amend the last will and testament he made before dying; he shall inherit no property; he shall not stand for election to any political office; he shall not marry; we must refuse to accredit him with the paternity of any children except those he begot before death.   Otherwise, human society becomes a madman's last dream! Whatever else death is or is not, it is certainly a moral removal of that individual agent from within the pale of the political and biological fellowship of human society. In thus refusing to trust to the departed as agents in the scheme of human activity, we are only acting along the line of common sense as it has embodied itself increasingly in the laws and customs of all civilized peoples, and we are attempting to bring into the sphere of religious economy what is already the principle of all other departments of social utility.

2. *Help from the Historical Christ*

The chief application of this principle to the dead which I wish here to insist upon is that concerning Jesus Christ. The historic Christ is ours, to use us and to be used by us; but we know that the transcendent Christ is beyond our sphere of right and duty, even though we may not doubt his continued existence. He shall be no exception. That social righteousness with which the Christian religion primarily concerns itself is made up of the very tissue of the political, economic, and physiological life of human society. To preserve the integrity of this, society must concede no powers to any human being after his death and can accept no benefits from such a source. It is in the name of righteousness and not simply for the material and intellectual interests of mankind, that the moral judgment of the world can give no place to the post-mortem activity of any spirit. When religion is brought into line with ethical realism it will, I believe, give greater prominence than before to the earth-life of Jesus Christ, and to the wisdom and moral power still issuing from it; but for the very sake of that sublime heritage it will refuse to attribute to him any operation or render him gratitude for any benefit which he may be conferring upon society since his death.

It should be noticed, in passing, that the exclusion of any effect which Jesus Christ may have been causing since his death is in no wise to be traced to a denial of him as the incarnate Creator of the universe. Although he were that, we must cling exclusively to his historic existence. Morally we dare not give him place except in his humanity while he lived on earth and as the bequeather of an earthly record. Even if he were, while on earth, the personal Creator of the universe incarnate, we could not be at liberty to recognize the transcendent aspect of his nature. All that was ethically valuable and, therefore, all that is humanly to be recognized was his natural humanity. Such was the right attitude towards him even while he was living on earth; how much less can it be permissible to depend upon him after death has emptied him of human accountabilities!

So far as I am aware, the current Christian theology has never been designated as "Christian Spiritism," but such a phrase may not seem an unwarrantable combination of terms, as it well indicates the practice, still permeating all the historical churches, of direct communion with the transcendent Christ; that is to say, a personal agent still consciously loving mankind and working for its redemption. This practice is one of trust in an intelligence energizing not as a member of human society, and therefore super-human and supernatural.

3. *The Communion of Saints*

In the same way, reverence and gratitude to the Virgin Mary for what she was before she died are entirely legiti-mate; but the moment she is regarded as a conscious being still interceding for us with her son and attending to our human woes, the practice of supplication to her becomes spiritistic; it is anti-social, because it attempts to draw moral strength from beyond the spiritual organism of society; it is therefore ethically illicit. As of the Virgin Mary, so of all the other saints of the Church. There is a purely ethical and natural communion with them. But the moment they are trusted as intelligent agents still operating in the manner in which they worked before their death, the communion cannot be morally tolerated. The spiritual power within society is a jealous God and will allow none other.

Besides personal friends departed in death, besides Jesus Christ, the Virgin Mary, and other historic saints, the Christian scheme of redemption, in a subordinate degree, recognizes the intervention of angels and of the devil. These also, however, must be denied, not as non-existent, but as outside the morally recognizable pale of human causation.

4. *Against Demonism*

Happily, there is in official Christianity no recognition of that class of spirits which in the orient are believed to inhabit natural objects and specific places and to control outward events. Yet, now that Christian nations have come into reciprocal contact with the East, where such belief is rampant, it is well that this form of spiritism should be stigmatized along with the distinctly Christian kinds, in order that the Churches, in the revision of their rites and teachings, may make provision against the possible spread among us of oriental demonism.

If the principle of discarding trust in supernatural agents were to be applied to any of the other great religions of the world, it would effect changes in them more drastic than those which it would bring about in Christianity. For all the other great religions, even Buddhism as it is actually practised in Thibet and China, are still more worm-eaten with spiritism than is Christianity. Our canon, therefore, for the revision of Christian formulæ is no petty rule animated by a specific antagonism to the particular supernaturalism found in the Christian scheme of redemption. It is a universal principle, based upon the fact that righteousness is vitally dependent upon the belief in redemption wholly from within the social organism of mankind.

5. *Against Monistic Spiritism*

There is current throughout Christendom, however, one other form of trust in invisible agents which seems not to have been recognized as being spiritistic. For some

M

reason which I cannot explain, spiritism has seemed to refer exclusively to a belief in *many* spirits, and Christian theologians have assumed that if you have ceased to believe in any but one, and that an infinite spirit, you have ceased to be a spiritist. But surely in the conception that there exists one all-wise and omnipotent personal Creator who interposes directly in human affairs, we have spiritism *par excellence*. If the churches are to turn from trust in invisible agencies outside of society and look for redemption only from within its own actual and latent resources, they can no more tolerate the idea of ONE outside will, although omnipotent and omniscient, than of a multitude of finite wills. The only God consistent with the integrity of mankind as a spiritual organism is one who is identical with the universal human spirit acting from within man, identical with his constitution, and under natural law. Inasmuch as an intelligent Creator of the universe cannot be treated as a responsible member of human society, he must be excluded from our scheme of salvation on the same grounds as those on which we would exclude any other superhuman intelligence. Human salvation would not be salvation if it were not wrought *by* men as well as *for* them.

There is no occasion of a practical order for denying the existence of a Creator or for doubting it; but the moral sanity of society compels us to insist that he must not be made either an object or a subject of human rights or duties. His majesty and power can be of no avail, for they would obliterate our initiative and responsibility. If he were to come among us in unmistakable bodily presence, even if only to advise, political society would be at an end. His will, in so far as it is not identical with the general good of the community and the organic bent of individual men, must be overlooked. Despite all this, however, we may at the same time acknowledge that all the uniformities and regularities of natural law are embodiments of his will. These uniformities fortunately manifest themselves to the moral judgment of man not as purposes of transcendent intelligence, but as conditions, inevitable and inexorable, under which and within which our kingdom of ideal ends is to actualize itself. Every rule of righteousness is a condition laid down in the sequence of nature — in the objective order of things — for the attainment of the ideal ends of humanity. Happily, the order is never broken and the beneficence of the sequence of things is bound up with its inexorability. In a scheme of moral redemption, therefore, the cosmic order, the laws of nature, the uniformities of cause and effect, must be revered not as themselves animated with a purpose of their own, but because they are our opportunity for fulfilling the human ends of social justice. The moment transcendent intelligence is approached for help, that moment there is a shirking of human responsibility, a denial of God as our Cosmic Opportunity and as the Immanent Source of Redemption.

6. *A Presupposition of All Moral Judgments*

If any one will consider the universal practice of men, where their ideas have not been warped from common sense by priests of the supernatural, he will see that they refuse to attribute any event in human experience to intelligent agencies beyond human society. He will see that this refusal is well founded; for the tracing of human events to superhuman agents is socially and morally suicidal. Suppose you were suddenly to come across the dead body of a man who had been evidently killed by the bullet of a pistol. You see the pistol lying near the body and it is obvious that the man has bled to death. Could it enter your mind, as a sane human being, to entertain for an instant the thought that some supernatural agent had fired the shot? It could not. The extremest spiritist would not so far wander from the common-sense belief that all events are caused either by purely physical forces alone or by these together with human volition, as to think for a moment that a man had been murdered by an unembodied spirit. The presupposition that underlies all moral reasoning is that no supernatural agent ever commits the deeds which we call crimes. And what I am pleading for is that this presupposition of all sanity, of all thinking upon moral conduct, should now at last be extended so as to cover all our holiest deeds and all our most inward aspirations and inspirations, and should enter into and control religious practices and teaching. It must now become the principle for the revision of public worship. If spiritism is not to be driven out from the realm of religious practice as it has been driven out from other spheres of human thought and action, it should be reinstated throughout the whole domain of experience. Such a reinstatement, however, is too preposterous to be entertained even in jest.

7. No Mediumship

If it be conceded that no incorporeal spirit has ever directly and unaided by a human being committed any crime, it might still be maintained as a possibility that some supernatural agent might take possession of a human being and make him the instrument of its will. But is this supposition any more tenable than the notion of unmediated agency? If it be true that a human being may suddenly, against his will, and possibly even without his knowledge, be transformed into the medium of some bodiless intelligent agency, is not the attribution of deeds to human doers forthwith and forever at an end? How can we nail any deed to any human doer, if we concede the shadow of a possibility of truth to the suggestion that some other invisible being than himself is instigating from within him the crime which his body commits? It is of course possible that a man may suddenly become insane; but then there is no longer any question as to our assigning his deed to any personal agency. His act itself then ceases to be a moral deed, and becomes a meaningless accident. But the moment we assign the motions of a man's body to some supernatural agency within himself, we are landed into a state of mental anarchy fatal to moral judgment. If all events without exception are not to be traced either to unconscious nature or to nature animated by some human self-direction, where are we? If the doer be not the same person in whose present consciousness the memory of his past deeds lives on as his own, how can we approve or disapprove of any human being?

Let me then once more state that presupposition of all moral judgments, in accordance with which I plead that the religions of the world should be reconstructed: No crime nor evil thought and no good deed nor holy desire of ours should ever be traced to any other spiritual agencies than those actually inhabiting our human bodies, and recognizable by all other human beings as fitting subjects of human rights and privileges. Let me also point again to the most important application of this principle. To attribute the highest impulses of our hearts to Jesus Christ as directly operating upon us from some celestial sphere of his present existence is morally and religiously a mistake. Whatever influence of his we now experience must be traced back to what he did and said while living on earth, and to persons who since then have transmitted to us his quickening spirit. This new interpretation in no wise tends to overlook the power of his spirit; and under it the influence of his example will undoubtedly grow. Those are not wise disciples of his who are not ready to attribute all his present power to his actual short life on earth. They unwittingly sin against him in undermining the fundamental presupposition of all social life.

8. *Naturalism*

Before we consider the changes which this new idea will work in religious forms and expressions, we must pause to guard it from being grossly misconceived. The principle which I am setting up is generally spoken of as naturalism. This is the term which even Sir John Seeley selects as the most fitting, and he calls the type of religion which is in harmony with it "natural religion." Yet the term naturalism has become increasingly associated with the materialistic and atomistic theory of existence. It is generally supposed to imply that the ultimate reality of things consists of atoms of matter. Yet such a notion has absolutely nothing whatever of kinship with the principle which I have been advocating, and which is the presupposition of all of Sir John Seeley's thinking. That presupposition does not trace all events to material atoms or to physical forces, for it assigns many happenings to personal agencies. It is true that it assigns none to spirits who are not members of human communities; but the recognition of one single finite person in a human body as the cause of any event is incompatible with the theory that the ultimate substance of all things is physical energy. Naturalism, therefore, as it is held by many physicists, and as it is censured by the philosophical idealists, — such as Professor James Ward, in his book on "Naturalism and Agnosticism," — is not at all the naturalism which Sir John Seeley respected and defended. Nor is it in any sense the naturalism which is opposed to religious supernaturalism.

In the literature of religious controversy, supernaturalism means nothing more nor less than the attribution of certain events in human experience to personal agencies who are not members of human society. But after we have excluded superhuman we may fall back upon human agency as a cause of events, and if we trace any event to the human will, we are still recognizing spiritual causation. Naturalism, then, if it is used to describe the philosophy of this book, means the recognition of only such spiritual agencies as are within the organism of human society, and the doctrine it opposes is only that supernaturalism which insists on recognizing the intervention in human affairs of intelligences beyond the pale of humanity. But how clumsy and awkward are both these words to convey such meanings! For this reason, I have occasionally presumed to adopt the term "spiritism" and avoid the word "supernaturalism."

But even the word "spiritism" is very inadequate. It is generally limited to the theories of those who call themselves modern spiritualists, and it has never been made to cover the spiritistic implications in ordinary Christian theology. I have, therefore, qualified the word and spoken of "Christian spiritism." But there is a still deeper objection to the term. The word "spirit" ought by right to be applied as much to a personal agency living in a human body as to one that is bodiless. The latter is no more spirit than the former. To designate by the word only those agencies beyond the pale of political society is to rob human agencies of a useful epithet and is to imply unjustly and illogically that a moral agent in a human body is somehow more akin in its nature to mere matter and blind force than is an unembodied agent; whereas it is easy to see that a spirit is no less spiritual when it animates a body than when denied a tenement of clay. I hope I have said enough to prevent any critic from confusing the naturalism of the religion for which I plead with materialism of any kind whatever.

For the word "naturalism" must be retained, even at the risk of its being misunderstood by persons lacking in acuteness of discrimination and logical rigour.   There is no other word that indicates the inexorable uniformity of the sequences of mental as well as of physical phenomena. Like John Stuart Mill, one may resolve all physical phenomena into sensations, and the whole reality of the physical universe into a system of permanent possibilities of sensation.   One then abandons completely the materialistic dogma ; but one retains the validity of the law of uniformity.   This law constitutes nature ; for nature, whatever else it is, is at least a system of permanent possibilities of sensation.   Such an interpretation is, in fact, idealistic, for it declares that the physical universe has no existence except in so far as it is or may be perceived.   Thus one may hold to the theory that TO BE PERCEIVED and TO BE are the same thing, and still one may remain a naturalist.   Indeed, all disciples of Immanuel Kant affirm the universal and necessary validity of the law of cause and effect.   They believe in the integrity of nature ; and yet they do not believe that nature has any existence except as it is perceived by the observing mind.   The teaching, therefore, which I have been advocating may equally well be called idealistic or humanistic realism.   But the best name for it might be idealistic humanism, for that term does not commit one to the philosophic crudity of believing that the physical universe exists independently of its being perceived.

9. *Man a Spirit*

When we cease to believe in the intervention of psychic agencies from beyond human society, it may be because we have a deeper insight into the nature of living human beings as spirits.   Whatever trust we have withdrawn from the unembodied, we may have reason to transfer to embodied spirits.   When we reject spiritism, we still have left both man as a moral agent and physical nature ; and man by no means becomes reduced to a phenomenon or an epiphenomenon of physical nature. We may regard him wholly from the point of view that his mind is real and is a positive cause not only of events which take place within the realm of his own mind, but also of changes in his own body and in the physical world round about him. Ethical idealism, although it restricts itself absolutely to the study of the hearts and wills of living human beings, deals essentially with Will as a creative cause. It recognizes the effect of mind upon outward nature through the human body. But no one could confuse it with atomism, materialism, or a merely mechanical view of cause and effect. It is well nigh an imbecility to attempt to resolve human purposes, affections and thoughts, human ideals and visions, and the distinctions between right and wrong, into differences in the arrangement of atoms of matter. Although atomism may never for a moment be denied in the domain of physics and chemistry, it is an utter irrelevance in a scheme for the moral redemption of mankind; for ethics treats of realities wholly disparate from, although possibly always accompanying, material atoms.

Professor Höffding's book on "The Philosophy of Religion" very clearly sets forth a distinction now widely recognized between science as a presentation of the relations of cause and effect in events, and ethics as a presentation of a scale of values or goods. Höffding recognizes the validity of the law of uniformity in all mental events, but he maintains that the hierarchy of values is in no wise touched by the scientific arrangement of sequences. Even the scientific arrangement does not involve the acceptance of physical force or the atom as the ultimate and independent reality. But much less does the scale of values involve such an acceptance. Ethics starts with human purposes and ideals, with the human will and the human heart, in the same way in which physics and chemistry begin with sensations of the senses. It is, accordingly, no more shaken by any doubt as to the reality of the factors with which it starts than physics by any doubt as to the reality of time and space.

While it has accorded with my argument to give here a succinct elucidation and defence of the principle by which I wish to test the rites and teaching of current religion, it is inconsistent with my purpose to present now in detail the various applications of that principle to religious experiences in general. To do so would require a volume by itself. My intention now is simply to try to justify the idea which I think should be concretely embodied in a nation's manuals of religious services. The idea I am sure will appeal to thousands and will find ready acceptance in the moral reason and emotional experience of many. It is already widely current and is the regulative principle of conduct with many American idealists. It is the inspiration and consolation of those who in my judgment represent most truly the spirit of our age and the characteristic trend of American life. This book, therefore, is in the first instance not written for those to whom its presuppositions will not appeal; it seeks rather to win the coöperation of those already ripe for the thought it starts with. It hopes to convince them of the necessity of revising the language and forms of devotion prevalent in all the churches and of organizing public opinion so as to hasten the adoption of rites and ceremonies, of sermons, hymns, anthems, meditations, and lessons which shall be expressive of the living inheritance and purpose of national life to-day.

CHAPTER XI

THE HUMANISTIC MEANING OF THEOLOGICAL LANGUAGE

1. *The Rethinking of the Old Realities*

THE supreme need of our day is not so much revision of statements as a rethinking of the realities to which the statements refer. Reinterpretation of terms has always been the chief method of progress in thought. A study of the evolution of religion exposes to view not so much a restatement of old truths as an attachment of new insight to the old words. The discovery of new religious truth has not been a discovery of another universe; it has been only a better understanding of the same, a fresh insight into the relations of the factors which were always there, but veiled.

Accordingly it is as it should be, that throughout the ages the words used have not changed even where there has been a complete revolution of the understanding of the realities to which they pointed. Nor has the retention of the old words ever produced any confusion or misunderstanding. Indeed, to have introduced new terms, when one had only gained new light on an old factor, would have produced chaos and confusion.

Let us not forget that the sun used to be thought of in a manner totally different from that in which we to-day perceive it and conceive it. To us it is an enormous sphere of light and heat, moving at a certain pace, possessing certain chemical properties, and so on. Such, of course, was always its reality. But our truth about it is new and scarcely has a point in common with the primitive con-

ception of it.   Yet with the new interpretation we have not
discarded the word " sun."   We have continued its use,
and we read the new truths into the old term.   Old words
are never worn-out wineskins.   Our justification for pouring new meanings into the word "sun" is that the reality
for which the term stood is still the same reality that it
was when savages first named it.   So with the stars.   They
are not to us what they were to men of primitive tribes;
but we need not on that account discard the word and
invent a new term.   I cite the case of the sun and stars
as typical of all the factors in the physical universe.   Our
view of that universe is new, but the words to designate
its factors and phenomena are, as they ought to be, the
same old words.   If we turn from the physical universe
to the human world, we find the same law: the growth of
new ideas and the retention of old words with changes of
meaning corresponding to that growth.   Woman, in the
twentieth century after Christ, is beginning to be looked
upon as a being essentially different in nature and powers,
rights and privileges from what she has hitherto been
understood to be.   Yet it were the merest folly on account
of any such evolution and revolution of our understanding
of her to drop the term "woman" and invent a new sign
in speech to stand for our new conception of her.   Likewise with the word "child."   Children, like women and
like the physical universe, are newly revealed to our understanding; but there is no occasion for not calling them
children.   No embarrassment or misunderstanding will
arise.

The same situation holds concerning religious terminology and the new conceptions of the factors in our deeper
moral experience.   When we discard supernaturalism, we
do not discard any of those elements of fact in experience
which were the occasion that induced our primitive ancestors to adopt a supernaturalistic interpretation of the

inner moral life. If we follow the analogy of the evolution of language in all other departments of experience, we shall retain the word "God" and all the rest of the nomenclature of religion, to denote the factors in our present experience which perform the same functions that were designated under the supernaturalistic terminology.

2. *Theological Terms Indispensable*

Many times in the foregoing pages I have used theological terms to indicate factors and relationships in a naturalistic scheme for the moral training of the human race. So entirely do the reinterpretation and revision of the forms of public worship which I advocate depend upon the justifiability and expediency of such a use, that it may not be amiss to examine here, with some degree of thoroughness, the general question of terminology. Without reintroducing arguments set forth incidentally in the preceding chapters, I shall attempt to deal with questions which have not been directly considered.

In the first place, let me point out that what are called theological terms are also the only specifically religious expressions. If we discard them, we deprive ourselves altogether of the language of religious life and practice. Even the word " religion " itself is a theological term, inasmuch as theology is always a theory which justifies religion. This being the nature of theology, one may fairly say that if the word " religion " be not a theological term, then there is no such term. Or take the word " God." Of all language, there is no expression more essentially of the nature of religion. Yet theology is, as the very word implies, a doctrine of God. If, then, the word "God" be not a theological term, theology has no term of its own. The word "prayer" designates the distinctive act of religion; yet whoever has studied theology knows that theology on that

very account is chiefly a theory of prayer. Of course the
words "religion," "God," and "prayer" are first religious
and then theological. But this is true of the whole language of theology. It possesses no terms which are not
first religious. Its nomenclature is wholly borrowed from
religion. Such being the case, it becomes self-evident, as
I stated above, that if we discard all theological terms, we
rob religion of its own language. This result would not
seem a calamity to one who had abandoned religion altogether, but one who means to retain it must feel the
necessity of retaining its verbal notation. And the fact
that that notation is also the language of theology will not
for an instant tempt him to discard it — at least, if he has
a full grip of the situation. Unhappily there are many
persons who have not.

3. *Religion and Theology*

Many imagine that if we retain theological terms, we
commit ourselves to some existing system or other of
theology. But this is a mistake which our foregoing analysis clearly exposes to view. The language was religious
before it became theological, and it may return to its original state of innocency. A man may use the words "God,"
"prayer," and "religion," and recognize them as elements
in a possible system of theology, and yet temporarily have
suspended judgment as to whether any system so far pro-
pounded is or is not true.

But I wish to plead for the retention of religious terminology not simply to indicate factors and relations in
the religious life, but also as elements in a new system of
theology. Many persons who think for themselves have
grown to loathe theology and all its works; and yet they
cling to religion. They respect the religious man; but
they turn the cold shoulder upon the professed theologian.

They will not listen to him.   Religion, they say, is a life, an attitude of mind, a thing of the heart and the will, which is good.   But theology, they say, is only theory, and it is the theory of religion which philosophic criticism and scientific research have discredited.   So, they urge, let us away with theology in the very name of religion.

Now, in my judgment, this off-hand method of renouncing theology and all its works is suicidal.   To discard all theory of religion is to play into the hands of those who are experts in manipulating the emotions and the will, without appealing to human intelligence.   There is no more fit victim for the religious demagogue than the person who protests against theology altogether, and yet attempts to be religious and to respect religion in others.   What finer subject for the priest who assumes to control other men's souls, than the man who boasts that it is well to have a God, but folly to attempt to have a theory of God?   A religion which bars out all theology is a religion minus theory; and religion minus theory is religion minus intellect.   And that, in turn, is exactly what the enemies of human reason have always commended in the laity.

If any sort of religious discipline is to be preserved, we must set out in search of a new theory the moment we put aside the current systems of dogma.   We must analyze religion afresh, and its relations to the rest of life and of experience in general.   We must bring also our constructive faculties to bear, for although we may never attain an absolutely rational system, we must hold tentatively as consistent a theory of religion as we can attain, to serve us as a working hypothesis for religious practice.   The new theory may contradict every point in the current systems of dogma, and, when applied to life, it may overthrow the rites and ceremonies of existing cults; but it will be a new theology pitted against the old.

The   notion   prevalent   amongst   so-called   advanced

thinkers, that theology is necessarily based upon authority and opposed to reason, is wholly false. It is certainly conceivable that a tentative theory favourable to religion might be constructed without contradicting or transcending experience, and without violating the method and spirit of science.

4. *The Word "Theology"*

Theology, then, is the first theological term which we must retain if any sort of rational religion is to be preserved. We must retain it in the name of reason and science. If we are to have religion, we must have a theory of religion, and to have a theory of religion is to have a theology. Inconceivable is it that persons should refuse, in the name of science, to seek for a theory of God, and yet retain a belief in him.

It is easy to see the consistency of those who, in discarding religion, discard theology; the one act necessitates the other. When they abandoned the hope of a theory about God, they did so because they had abandoned God. He had become to them nothing. But the reverse process is by no means a necessity. One may discard every known theory of God, yet retain God, and make him the starting-point, the element of fact, from which to construct a new theory. It is evident that we must discriminate between theology and every or any special system of theology. As one may reject the sociology of Comte and Spencer and every other sociologist and yet not abandon sociology as a task and an ideal goal of scientific effort, so also one may reject the current theologies and cling the more tenaciously to theology as a theory yet incomplete. Making this discrimination, we may say that if theology must go, religion must go; and that if religion is to stay, theology must stay. If we are to retain a belief in anything which we call God, or which performs the same function in the economy of experience as that performed by what other people call God, it is a primal necessity of critical thought to construct the best possible doctrine of God.

There are some who imagine that a new scientific and rational theory to justify a scientific and rational religion should not be called theology, but should be described as ethics. But an acquaintance with the history of religion shows that no theory of ethics or of the moral life can possibly cover all the facts of the religious life of man. In the first place, there have been hundreds of religions which have not been essentially or even perceptibly ethical. Religions have only gradually become ethical. The best historical judgment also sanctions the statement that morality is by no means essentially religious. The moral experience and the moral judgments of men have developed out of commerce, politics, and other spheres of experience which the religious consciousness scarcely touched at all, or, at most, only incidentally. Only after the moral life and the theory of morals were considerably advanced did they enter into, give colour, and dictate the shape to the rites and dogmas of religion. It is altogether uncritical and unscientific, therefore, to set up any theory of morals as a theory of religion. It is almost as unscholarly as it would be to set up religion to account for morality.

We may approach this question of the relation of ethics to theology from another point of view. Ethics is a theory of right and wrong, of human ends, and of standards of human conduct. If one turns to the books which have been written by ethical thinkers, one sees that they treat of the questions: what is right, what is wrong, what is the essential characteristic of right conduct as distinct from wrong, what peculiar activities of the human mind are involved in arriving at the dis-

N

tinction between right and wrong, how do men's moral
judgments vary with their varying experiences, is there an
absolute and universal standard of right? These are the
problems which ethics covers. There is another question,
however, which ethics never has been made to cover, and
nobody who understands the subject-matter has ever yet
suggested that it should now be made to cover. That
question is, Is the universe favourable or unfavourable
to the realization of our moral ideals? Granting that
we have standards of conduct and of character, granting
that there be certain ends of human life which we sanction as great and good and worthy of our devotion, what
are the chances that we can ever fulfil these standards
and attain these ends? This question involves in itself,
as is quite plain, the problem of man's moral weakness,
incapacity, and perversity. Put in another way, the
question is, Are men bad? If they are, is it in the
nature of things possible that they may become good?
If they can become good, what are the instrumentalities
by which the cure is to be effected? And even of men
whom we call good, are they absolutely good? If not,
what is the cause of the deficiency?

This problem of evil in life and therefore in the
universe — how is it to be solved? If even good men
have a touch of badness in them, how are they to become
absolutely good? Here are questions most intimately
and vitally connected with ethics; and still, by the consensus of all philosophers, they are outside of ethics
proper. They deal not with what is right and wrong
and how we come to know what is right and wrong;
they deal with the existence of evil, and how we are to
put an end to evil and establish a reign of righteousness
on earth. The relation of life or the universe to the
moral ideal, the degree in which the universe is favourable or adverse — this is not a problem of ethics. Even

as I have been stating it, my readers must have realized that it is the question of ethical religion and of the theory of ethical religion. Theology as the theory of religion and of God is quite clearly a theory as to the relation of the universe to human ends and ideals; and the relation of the universe to ethical ideals becomes the specific problem of theology the moment religion has become ethical. Then the question as to the existence of God is whether there be any great power, tendency, or Being favourable to the actualization of our standards of duty. Within us has grown up a terrific sense of personal responsibility, an overwhelming feeling that we are under obligations to walk certain paths and to set our eyes on certain goals. But is it possible in this universe, with our human nature, to fulfil the task that we feel in our inmost heart must be done or we fail and forfeit self-respect?

No one, even of those who reject both theology and religion, can deny that this, philosophically stated, is the import and significance of both. Persons may reject every theory as to the favourableness or unfavourableness of conditions to the realization of our moral ideals, but then they are face to face with a further problem. They must decide whether they will reject not only the theoretical, but also the moral, problem before them. Will they drive out of mind, in their daily business and in the midst of all their aspirations and sufferings, the whole question as to whether it is feasible to lead what they regard to be the right life? If they reject not only the theory as to the relation of the universe to the feasibility of the right life, but also the practical problem it involves, they reject not only theology, but religion. And if they reject this practical problem of religion, it would seem as if they must somehow suffer in their moral life. They would still retain the distinction between right and wrong; but, granting that there is such a thing as wrong, they would shirk the difficulty of finding means within the universe of overcoming it.

We have now arrived at a point where in the very interests of the good life itself it would seem that we must resort to religion. For the religious life, when once moral judgments have coloured and outlined it, deals almost exclusively with the practical problem of toning up the motive to do right by finding circumstances favourable to morality. Thus we have come out again to the conclusion that theology must stand if morality as a life is to stand. It would seem that those persons who, in the name of the ethical life, reject every particular system of theology which has prevailed in the past must do so on account of the beginnings of some counter-theory of religion which has begun to crystallize itself in their reason. For righteousness' sake they must find some sort of a theory of the relation of the universe to the human ideal. Otherwise it is almost inconceivable that morality as a life could flourish. Therefore I would rescue the term theology from the clutch of those who wish to limit it to their own peculiar theory of religion.

It argues a lack of philosophical knowledge and training to imagine that there is no theology except there be a belief in superhuman agencies. Discard that belief, and still the universe remains, the moral ideal remains, and the question is to be solved as to the adverseness or favourableness of the universe to the ideal. If one holds, as I do, that the moral ideal is itself a part of the universe and that the idealistic trend in human life is natural, the problem becomes one as to the relation of the whole of the universe to a part of it. And it would seem that one who has discarded the supernaturalistic hypothesis would not only be more keenly interested than before in the problem of theology, but would have a surer basis for the expectation that the problem can be solved. Whether the solution would be more favourable to the right life than were the dogmas which he had rejected is another matter. But no one can deny that in and of itself the quality of being verifiable would be a factor in the new theory favourable to morality. We should know how we stood. We should know how to reckon with the universe; and this of itself would be an incalculable moral gain. For if there be anything that weakens moral purpose it is the twilight of uncertainty, the moving about in the half dark, not knowing whether or not our efforts may not be arbitrarily or at least incalculably thwarted. To know the worst is always better than not to know certainly. But the only point for which I am contending here is that what we shall come to know about the relation of the universe to the human ideal must be called a theology. It will be an enormous stride towards the settling of religious controversies and the clearing up of the problems of religion, when scientifically trained men turn to the problem of the relation of the universe to human ideals and ends, and when so turning they know, and they make the public know, that they are theologians.

5. *The Word "Theism"*

The word "theism," like "theology," has been monopolized by the supernaturalists. But any doctrine concerning that factor in experience to which religion points when it speaks of God should be called theism. If a naturalistic theory could explain better the elementary factor to which the word God points and throw more light upon the task which religion sets itself than supernaturalism does, its claim to the word "theism" would be established. It might be impossible to prove that the real factor was a personal self-conscious agent. But what of that?

The word "monotheism" has also been unjustifiably monopolized by those who say that God is a personal agent over and above the personal agencies who are living human beings. If we can fix the factor which is pointed to by the word God, and if we find that there is only one such reality, then there is but one God. Our knowledge, systematized, would accordingly be monotheism — the science of the One God. Still greater would be the claim of such a doctrine to the term, if we found that our moral judgment backed the intuition of religious men and declared that there *ought* to be but one God and that the real factor which is pointed to in positive religions is that which all men *ought* to worship.

6. *The Word "Atheist"*

Some object that the terms "theism" and "monotheism" are exclusively theological, and not at the same time religious, like God and prayer. This stricture I am willing to accept; but I have devoted a few sentences to them in order to lead up to the word "atheism," which, by derivation, is akin to "theism" and "monotheism," and yet is by no means limited to theoretical use or associated with the coolness of temper and the calm love of truth supposed to be characteristic of philosophical discussion. The word "atheism" has been venom on the tongue, when it darts out like a fang. One cannot deny that it is a religious term, although the religiousness be turned bitter and cruel. It is, moreover, an altogether indispensable word; in proportion as one loves one's God and is jealous of his honour, one is in need of a term of utmost contempt and horror, to apply to those who deny or blaspheme or mock him. Men should not stand by and, without crying shame, allow others to insult that Being which is to them most real, to which they owe everything, and which they believe to be the only power that saves men. They must at least utter a word of moral censure. Nor may that word be mild. Under humanity, short of cruelty, indeed for the sake of humanity and with as much cruelty as is needed to be kind to those who reject that which one believes to be their best friend, the term of reproach must be the strongest which language affords. The word " atheist" has always emanated from such senti- ments of moral horror. There is thus nothing the matter with the word itself. It is wise and good. It is needed as an expression of a feeling which is inevitable in propor- tion as one reveres any reality as God. The only objection to it is that in the past it may have been hurled at the wrong persons. The question is, Who is the atheist and what is atheism? I answer, not without a touch of the emotion which those always feel whose God has been denied, that the prevalent notion about atheism is altogether erroneous and inhumanly unjust. The root of the error and injustice is the age-long fallacy that a god must be a supernatural personal agency, and that one who trusts to no personal agents except those who are living human beings is an atheist.

The tables ought to be turned. This word of anathema should be hurled, as I think, against those who believe there is no God this side of the outer limits of man and nature. Such deny the good in man and nature to be God. They do not believe in the moral law itself as divine and yet as immanent in human personality. They insult human nature by a most polluting suspicion. I will not again attempt at this point to argue the respective merits of naturalistic and supernaturalistic religion. I here wish to restrict myself logically to the question of religious terminology. As a matter of language, I assert it to be proper that everybody should brand as an atheist every one else who denies his God. Only those who have no God or having a God are unfaithful or indifferent to him should never presume to cast this epithet at others. In proportion as a man is filled and chilled with horror by the denial or ridicule of what he counts most sacred, in that proportion he has the right to hurl this term of censure.

I remember once, many years ago, sitting in a public meeting and listening to a political demagogue. He aroused uncontrollable merriment in his audience. Sitting near me was a clergyman, who entered into the rough but innocent fun. Suddenly, however, the demagogue quoted, in a flippant if not ribald manner, some saying of Jesus. Instantly the clergyman's face turned ashen white, and he sat throughout the rest of the meeting as one dead. Now any man, I maintain, to whom anything whatsoever is as sacred as Jesus Christ was to that clergyman, has a God. That man is religious; and he cannot help shrinking in horror from those who speak lightly of what to him is all-holy. They to him are atheists. And has he not a right to name them so? It would be a moral impoverishment of speech, were the word atheist to cease to be a term of reproach. It is a word which in the struggle of humanistic religion to establish itself there will be much need for.

7. *The Word "Religion"*

Let us now turn to the word "religion." It is a very common error to think that there are innumerable definitions of it, and that there exists some peculiar difficulty in finding out just what religion is. During the last twenty years, however, a line of investigation has been pursued assiduously by students in various countries, which is gradually clearing away whatever difficulty existed. So long as people turned simply to the etymology of the word, they got no further than two rival Latin origins; and even when they attained the primary meanings of these two words, no light was thrown on the problem in hand. Likewise, the attempt to evolve out of certain fundamental principles what religion must be only led to hopeless pedantry and subtlety. During the last score of years, however, empirical psychologists have said: "We will not go back to logic and abstract definition, nor to the origin of the word; we will go straight to the lives of those men and women who the world over have been conspicuous for the attitudes of will and states of heart and acts and lines of conduct which are called religious. We will compare them and their lives with persons who are indifferent to religion, and then again with those who are conspicuous as being positively irreligious." Now this is a truly scientific method of investigation. What religion is, is not a question of words and is not primarily a question of logic. It is a question as to what lines of conduct, what qualities of heart, what dispositions of the will have struck the minds of observers as being distinctive, and have induced them to designate these qualities as religious.

During recent years another cause of confusion has also been removed. In trying to find out what religion is, persons are often seeking to discover not what it is, but what it ought to be, what it would be if it were morally perfect. When they have found that, they have got not a definition, but a standard by which to gauge the moral worth of religious practices. Mistaking this standard for a definition, they generally end by declaring that there is only one religion, and that is their own. But in seeking to know what religion is, we ought to keep clear of the problem of what it should be morally. In seeking a definition of it we must look only for that peculiarity which marks all its varieties and distinguishes it from everything else.

If we keep in mind what we are looking for, we shall avoid another error into which many investigators have fallen. I refer to that which was committed by Mr. Herbert Spencer. He argued that if you collect the religious opinions of all men, and then, striking out all differences, retain only those beliefs and practices which are common to all, you get the universal religion. Educationists in England during the last thirty-five years have fallen into a similar blunder. They have thought that they could find the essence of Christianity by dropping out the tenets peculiar to each sect and to the Church, and retaining what they taught in common. This they called undenominational religion, and they sought to make it the bond of union among all Christians. Now the trained psychologist would have known that often a man himself is not conscious of that which is his own peculiar characteristic. Likewise, two persons working together may not themselves be aware of their points of identity. They may be altogether lacking in self-criticism. Their opinions may by no means be an index to what they are. The psychologist might discover it to be the peculiarity common to all persons so far as they are religious, that they focus their attention steadfastly and reverently upon some source from which they believe that they derive the greatest benefits, and from which they believe that they will derive still further benefits by this focussing of the attention. Yet it is quite possible that ninety per cent. of the persons whose religious life is scrutinized are totally unaware that they are exercising attention in practising religion. They may never have heard of such a thing. They may not know what the word "attention" means; they may never have observed the mental process, and be quite unacquainted with its peculiarities and its place in the economy of religious discipline. But because a man does not know that he is focussing his attention is not the slightest proof against the assertion that he is. Thus, reverent attention to the source of life's chief blessings may be the distinguishing mark of religion, and yet no religious person be aware of it as such.

As a matter of fact, this is what psychologists have discovered in regard to religion. *Religion is the focussing of men's attention steadfastly and reverently upon some Source from which they believe that they have derived the greatest benefits, in order to derive still further benefits.* "Benefits," it should be observed, are not limited to external advantages to oneself. At least, I use the word here so broadly as to include the advantages to one's country or to the world which one desires. Whatever we long to see actualized as a blessing to others, we cannot but count as a benefit to ourselves. Hence, let no reader interpret the term in a lower sense, and think the man necessarily selfish who prays for benefits.

This focussing of the attention may be more or less systematized. The more systematized it is, the more highly developed is the religion. This systematization may consist in an elaboration of thoughts, of disciplines, and of forms and ceremonies.

What makes a form or ceremony religious is that it is an instrumentality for thus focussing the attention steadfastly and reverently. What makes a thought or doctrine or dogma religious is the same. So, too, with any discipline like fasting or prayer. It is religious when it is an aid to what is the essential psychological peculiarity of religion.

The differences in religions never consist in the total presence or absence of this peculiarity, but in the degree to which it is present and in differences as to the object to which attention is steadfastly and reverently turned. It follows inevitably that those who thus look to the sun will be different in their religion from those who turn their attention, in order to receive further benefits, to some domestic animal like the ox or elephant, or to the lightning, or to a fountain of water welling up in the desert, or to nature-demons, or to trees. Religions, however, do not differ merely because the objects attended to are not the same. They are felt by us to vary in worth according to the ethical effects of attending reverently to the objects they set up.

Religions differ also in their rational value. If the object to which attention is turned is a pure figment of the mind, a creation of the fantasy, if it be something which to the scientific judgment does not exist, the religion is an error, and hence a superstition. Religions also vary in general practical value as well as moral and intellectual worth. The object set up for reverent attention may be either one to which it is a waste of time to turn, or one to which it pays to turn. For instance, attention to the stars was not primarily an ethical religion, but for shepherds and nomads in general it paid. By such attention, they came to know the regularities of the heavenly bodies at night, and so learnt when it was safe to move and when discreet to wait where they were.

We have found, then, a strictly scientific definition of religion. It covers every case and includes nothing which is not religion. It is true that there are some practices in the least-developed forms of religion which seem to contradict the qualification that in religion there is a turning of the attention *reverently* to some supposed source of blessings. The case is cited of savages who get out of patience with the objects they worship, and beat them, to punish them. But it becomes quite clear that in proportion as human beings beat their gods, in that proportion their religion ceases. If these feelings of contempt became habitual and constant, it is evident that the being so maltreated would cease to be a god. On the whole, the fetich-worshipper respects the Being from which he thinks to derive benefits. He, of all religious persons, pays the respect in order to secure further favours. The respect may be external, but then his whole life lacks inwardness. It is, moreover, only in the most rudimentary stages of religion, *i.e.* when it can scarcely be detected as a religion at all, that we see such deviations from reverence.

The same comment holds good in regard to the qualification of steadfastness. In proportion as a man is not steadfast in his attention to the source of his greatest benefits, he is not religious. He has religious moments or days or seasons only, but these are all marked by the qualities I have specified.

It will be further noticed that I have limited the benefits derived by implying that they are only the greatest. For one would not turn one's attention steadfastly and reverently to the source of benefits which were not highly prized.

A man may err fatally as to what object it is worth while to attend to. The benefits which he derives may prove, in the issue, to be things not worth making life's chief concern. There have been many religions, the object of which was to increase pleasures of special kinds, and the result has been the downfall of the men and the nations who cultivated attention to the means towards such ends. It must have become quite clear, then, that religion is a term which should not be used as if it always stood for a wise mental practice. Religion is not always beneficent in its effects. Those persons err in judgment who say that any religion is better than none. The simple innocence of no religion is better than the focussing of the attention steadfastly and reverently upon the means towards ends the pursuit of which leads to effeminacy, disease, and the extinction of a race. Accordingly it is a regrettable use of current speech which identifies the word religion with what one regards to be the only true and right religion, for all sorts of illogical inferences are made.

But the chief advantage, for our purpose here, of a sound definition of religion is that it exposes the absurdity of those who declare that religion always has to do with the supernatural and with belief in personal agencies who are not living members of human society. It is perfectly true that many religions have been the focussing of attention steadfastly and reverently upon such agencies. But to say that all religions have to do with the supernatural is mere blindness to the facts of religious life. It must, however, be pointed out that naturalism in a religion is only one characteristic in its favour. Natural beings vary in dignity and worth. It is worse than a waste of time to attend devoutly to some of them. It must also be noted that an object might be conceived of as purely naturalistic and yet be wholly imaginary. One might believe that there was a Mahatma in Thibet and attend to him as a source of spiritual benefits. He might be conceived of as a living human being; but if he did not exist, religion, so far as it trusted to him, would be worse than futile.

8. *The Word "God"*

Let us now turn to consider the significance of the word "god." May it or may it not justly be used as a term to designate a natural object? It must be quite clear that in our definition of religion is already involved the definition of the word "god." If religion be as I have defined it, then any object towards which steadfast and reverent attention is turned, in order to derive the greatest blessings, is a god. Any object, natural or supernatural, moral, immoral or non-moral, actual or imaginary, mental or physical, abstract or concrete, powerful or weak, becomes a god the instant steadfast and reverent attention is focussed upon it for the purpose of gaining the supreme blessings. Our definition immediately exposes to view the fact that a being is not a god by virtue of any inherent quality in itself, but only by virtue of a relationship established towards it by a human being.   To bear this fact in mind throws a helpful light upon the use of religious terms in general and the fundamental problems of religion. People ask : What is God? but they forget or have never realized the import of the question they put. They mean : *What is that real being which men ought to focus their steadfast and reverent attention upon in order to derive from it those benefits which are really the greatest blessings to mankind?*   They are asking a moral and a scientific question.   In its scientific aspect the search is for a real, as distinct from an imaginary, being.   They want the true God, for nothing can be more terrible than the suspicion and scepticism that, after all, the being one has been reverently attending to may not exist at all.   The question in its moral aspect, assuming that the being is real, inquires whether it actually is the source of the highest good.   But all the while it is clear that the word god does not refer to an inherent quality of the object itself, but to the fact or the moral requirement that men turn, or ought to turn, their reverent attention towards it.

Akin to the question, What is God? is the often-heard inquiry, Is there a God?   Again, light is thrown upon the nature of this question by substituting for the word god the definition of it.   To ask, Is there a God? is to ask whether there be in very fact any source from which supreme blessings will be gained if one attends steadfastly and reverently to it.

It will be seen, in pointing out that there are many different beings or supposed beings which people attend to, that there are, as an actual fact of human experience, many gods.   It will further be clear, however, that there can be only one true and living God, only one Being whom we could speak of not simply as a god, or as the god, but as God. God must be the real Being from whom the highest conceivable good is derived if we attend to him. In the light of these explanations, how foolish is the contention of the majority of persons that a god is not a god unless he be a personal agency who is not a human being! If there be a supreme good and that supreme good be attainable by any natural and human means, then that natural and human means surely is the real and all-worthy source of the highest conceivable blessing!

Now, there are those who contend that a naturalistic humanist should altogether drop the word god. Yet these same persons may agree that it is necessary for the humanist to focus his attention reverently and steadfastly upon the natural source from which the greatest benefits of life come. But, in the name of common sense and literary usage, of accuracy and of the need of making oneself understood, I ask them why should we drop the word god if it is a term which is always applied to anything whenever it is treated in the manner in which these persons concede we ought to treat a certain verifiable source of human blessings? Because some other person's gods are supernatural does not make the object we attend to any the less a god. One might as well refuse to call one's clothes "clothes," because the garments of beggars are repulsively unclean and torn. Clothes do not simply mean good and expensive clothes; so, gods are not simply those which we approve. When once we have cleared up this question of religious terminology, we find that the question of naturalism or supernaturalism does not touch the essence of religion and the problem as to the existence of God.

One who bears clearly in mind that the word god is a purely relational term, applicable to any object to which men steadfastly and devoutly attend, will see that, the moment a thing is so attended to, it is necessary not only to call that object by its own name, but also to call it a god; for its own name does not indicate that it is an object of worship, but the word god indicates exactly this. Suppose, then, that, following Matthew Arnold, we should teach that Goodness is God, there would be a lack of judgment displayed if any one should say: "Why not simply call Goodness, Goodness? What is the use of saying Goodness is God?" Of course the answer is that when you say Goodness is Goodness, you have made no advance in thought; but when you say Goodness is God, if what you say is true, you have added the statement of a relationship in which some person stands or ought to stand to Goodness. You have said that Goodness either is or ought to be the reality worshipped. To feel that the word god becomes superfluous because we know what the object is which is worshipped would be as if a man, knowing his wife's name to be Mary, should imagine that there were no occasion for calling her his wife. But when he says, "Mary is my wife," he says very much more than "Mary is Mary." Likewise it would be an astonishing proposal that we should never speak of Mr. Woodrow Wilson as the President, but simply as Mr. Wilson. One might ask, How should we ever communicate the fact that Mr. Woodrow Wilson is President if we never called him the President? The only way would be a circumlocution, by which in place of the word we should introduce the definition of "President." And so, as the word god is a relational term, we must use it if we wish to designate the relation. Nor let any one imagine that this defence of my use of the word god as applying to Goodness, which I think is the object worthy of supreme worship, is altogether superfluous. During the last twenty years I have been reiterating in ethical societies that as an actual fact Goodness and all living tendencies that make for its realiza-

o

tion constitute the God of those who are sincere and clear-thinking members of such societies. The result has been that many a time the criticism has been offered, "Even if we do reverence whatever makes for Goodness as the supreme necessity and reality of life, why need we call it God? Why not simply say that Goodness is Goodness?" The answer is that to many a person Goodness may be Goodness, and yet not be that person's God. The general use of relational terms justifies, and the need of communicating our thought necessitates, our calling Goodness our God.

In connection with the naturalistic use of these two terms god and religion, I would have my readers clearly understand that in declaring that Goodness is God, I do not imply that goodness has always been everybody's god. Even implicitly and unconsciously men have not by any means always been worshipping goodness. But I do contend that ancient Judaism was an ethical religion, and that the Jews were worshipping Righteousness as a Real Power in the world, and that Righteousness therefore was their God. I declare the same in regard to the founders of Christianity and the Christian theologians of all ages. In spite of themselves, despite their metaphysical theories and their growing insistence upon the supernatural character of the being they worshipped, they nevertheless were devoutly ethical. Moral attributes, moral acts were the power which they saw and felt to be the source of the highest blessings to mankind. Their religion and their God may not have been exclusively, but were supremely, ethical and naturalistic. The fact must not be overlooked that supernaturalism does not exclude the natural in the sense that naturalism excludes the supernatural. Persons who believe in the supernatural also believe in the natural, while the naturalist excludes every factor which one cannot believe in except on the supposition that there exist personal agencies who are not living members of human society.

CHAPTER XII

HUMANISTIC MEANINGS (*continued*)

1. *The God of the Bible*

It is sometimes difficult to understand how Christian theologians dare stake their reputation as educated men upon the statement that it is a misuse of the word God to apply it to anything but a supernatural being. The comparative study of religions has been going on for a hundred years, and it is inexcusable for a person to speak as if he had never heard of any religion except those which set up a personal Creator of the universe as the object of attention.

It is also growing difficult to understand how theologians can any longer assert that the doctrine of a personal Creator of the universe is the essential presupposition and the message of the Old and New Testament teaching. For half a century scholars have unearthed the truth, which Matthew Arnold and Sir John Seeley so ably set forth, that the Bible is not a book concerned chiefly with a life after death or a speculative doctrine about an infinite personal Creator and Governor of the universe. It is becoming an illiteracy of a kind that one ought to be ashamed of, so to misunderstand the Bible. And, as I believe, we shall find the current forms of public worship, if we analyze them, essentially naturalistic; their supreme interest is the moral perfection of men on earth, and their supreme means are those which are verifiable, are at hand in human experience and equally at the disposal of those who totally reject all supernaturalism.

When we turn from mere definition to literary usage, we find not only that those poets and prose writers who have been endowed with the finest sense for the differences between words employ the word god exactly in the ways which our definition would justify and establish; we further find that poets, somehow instinctively, in their better and higher moods designate as God Human Goodness itself. Take even so unlikely a writer as Swinburne, and you will find such stanzas as this : —

> A creed is a rod,
> 　And a crown is of night;
> But this thing is God,
> 　To be man with thy might,
> To grow straight in the strength of thy spirit,
> 　　and live out thy life as the light.

If God can never refer to anything but the personal Creator of the universe, this sentence makes no sense. Who could say that the personal intelligent First Cause of the universe is "to be man with thy might"? If, again, it be maintained that this is only a poetic and literary use, it must be answered that that is nothing against it. It is poetic and literary, but it is absolutely exact and precise. Let us substitute in Swinburne's sentence for the word god the definition of God which we have arrived at above, and it will read : This thing is that which is supremely worthy of being attended to steadfastly and reverently in order to get the greatest blessings possible to man — to be man with thy might. Manliness, in short, is the thing which should be reverently attended to.

Or let us turn to the use of the word god found in a poem written by a former Secretary of the English Rationalist Press Association. Mr. Hooper is a professed Rationalist. Yet we find that he does not discard the word god. On the contrary, he applies it not only in a naturalistic, but in a purely ethical, sense. The poem to which I refer is entitled "The Spirit of Man," and it begins, "Spirit of Man, ascend thy throne." Still addressing the Spirit of Man, the poet continues : —

> That path where saints and prophets trod
> To one supreme confession leads:
> The god in man — for man — is God.
>
> Be thou that God enthroned below,
>   With calm-eyed Truth at thy right hand,
> Who bids us dare all doubts, to know
>   What men can fitly understand.
> Be Knowledge linked to Love and Peace,
>   Break down the barriers of pride,
> That self, self-centred, may decrease,
>   And thou, the boundless Self, abide !

Again applying our definition, we find the absolute exactitude of the poet's terminology. He wishes that the spirit of man should be the power to which men turn their attention steadfastly and reverently in order to receive the highest blessings. What could make more fitting sense ? What greater proof of the accuracy of a definition can one find than that one can substitute the definition for the word wherever the word is used by the best writers and the sense will not only be preserved but elucidated ?

2. *The Personality of God*

As the personification of certain factors in moral experience is involved in the very form of prayer, it may be well here to call attention to what personification is.

We personify when we attribute in speech the qualities of personal agencies to factors which we do not believe to be self-conscious. Now, the question that arises is this : Is personification an exaggeration ? Do we feel less intimate

spiritually with impersonal than with personal beings?
Towards that which cannot consciously love us do we in
fact feel a less absolute and glad sense of inward union
than we experience with conscious beings?   If we do,
then to personify is to exaggerate the facts.   If we do
not, personification is legitimate, expedient, and truly
poetic.   If you feel nearer to America than you have ever
felt towards any individual living person, if you have found
more peace or more of love's solicitude in the thought of
her, more inspiration in her history, and have been more
ready to die for her than for any one human being, then to
personify America is still for you to fall short of the truth
that is in you.   For you to personify America is to come
nearer to the reality of your relationship towards her than
if you did not, but it is not to reach the full truth.   Thus
personification becomes a necessity of expression.

If, then, Emerson be filled with the sense of the absolute
reality of Virtue, Emerson must personify Virtue.   In so
doing he will not go beyond the literal truth; he will not
even reach it.   The mystics have always personified the
ethical realities.   But, in proportion as their vision was
clear, they have never dogmatically or metaphysically or
literally attributed personality to the great tendencies of
which they find and feel themselves to be an essential part.
To do so would have been to lose grip of the facts which
inspired the personification.

There is another peculiarity in the language of poetic
personification which in the judgment of some renders its
use impossible for naturalists in religion.   This is the
application of the masculine pronoun to the factor which
is called God.   How can virtue be called "He"?   And
why "He" instead of "She"?   But why either?   Why
not "It"?   The answer is that if "It" be used, the personification is lost.   We human beings are acquainted with no
personal agents that are not either masculine or feminine.

Our speech has no pronouns to apply to a personal agent or to a being personified, except those which are either masculine or feminine. Like Mr. William Watson, we may all lament that we

> must use a speech so poor
> It narrows the Supreme with sex.

So the fault, if it be a fault, of calling goodness "He" when it is personified, is a fault inherent primarily in the limitations of human experience. But when we personify, we know perfectly well, unless we have lost our reason, that the object personified is neither masculine nor feminine, and has no attributes of sex. It is therefore childish to protest against the use of the masculine pronoun to designate the object we worship.

Or, if there be occasion for protest against calling God "He," it is only because we ought perhaps to use the feminine pronoun.

In speaking of the personification of virtues and of such social groups as America, I have implied that these are impersonal entities. But it is only the poverty of language which makes us divide all things into personal and impersonal, and then use the word "personal" as a term of praise and "impersonal" as one of disparagement, as if personal entities were always higher than impersonal. Now, it is true that they are higher than stocks and stones. If speech, however, were quite exact and adequate, and if our analysis and classification were complete, we should include under "personal" all the attributes, functions, structures, and growths which emanate from personal agents. Virtue, love, mercy, pity are attributes of personality. They are of the nature of mentality; they have no existence apart from persons. Is it not, then, an error of classification and of speech to call these "impersonal"? The word "impersonal" ought to be used to indicate only non-personal entities or the attributes of non-personal entities. Now, my contention is that a quality which inheres exclusively in a personal agent must of its very nature be personal, and therefore should be comprehended under the terms "personal" and "personality." So that if a man worships Virtue as his God, it is wholly misleading to declare that he worships something impersonal. The high dignity and value which we ascribe to personal agents must surely cover and embrace all the attributes peculiar to personality. No one, then, who worships the Moral Law or Duty or the Moral Sentiment ought to concede for a moment that his God is an impersonal one. Instantly by so doing he plays into the hands of some wily opponent, who knows that if he can only brand these abstract qualities as "impersonal," he attaches to them the disparagement which that term carries with it.

Instead of an abstract quality like Virtue, let us consider for a moment a concrete unity like the historic Christian Church, or like America. Is the Christian Church an impersonal thing? It is made up of millions of personal agents, interacting and interdependent. It has no existence apart from these. Its very tissue is personality. Also its form and structure and functions are derived exclusively from the nature of personal agents. The Church is nothing more nor less than an organism consisting of persons. We ought not to say, then, that the Church, or America, is an impersonal entity.

If we are not to be allowed to apply the word "personal" to abstract moral qualities, then, to be quite exact, we ought to call them interpersonal. But we must remember that what is interpersonal cannot be classed as impersonal; for the relationship between persons must be of the nature of personality.

If concrete realities like the Christian Church or America

cannot be fairly called personal, yet they are more than interpersonal. They are not so much the bond between persons as the comprehensive unities overspanning a plurality of persons. In very fact, we have no experience of individual personal agencies who do not derive their existence from a social organism into which they were born. It is equally true that there are no social organisms where there are no personal agents. A social organism, then, if it is not to be called personal, might very well be designated superpersonal.

Thus, any one who worships either a concrete social group or an abstract moral quality may justly protest against the charge that his God is impersonal; he may insist that it is either superpersonal or interpersonal, or both.

In order to offset the supersubtleties of his enemies, a man is sometimes compelled to cultivate an equally keen dialectic. But having once indicated the interpersonal and superpersonal character of Virtue and of organic groups of persons, he may well proceed confidently to declare that *his* God too is personal.

It may further elucidate the factors which an analysis of prayer brings to view, if it be pointed out that the word spiritual preëminently applies to such realities as Virtue and social groups. No one could for a moment deny that that which is interpersonal and superpersonal is spiritual, even if he protested that it was not personal. The University of Cambridge is not, as the idealistic philosophers who live there have pointed out, a material thing; it is a spiritual entity. If, then, a man worships America, or Humanity, or the Moral Ideal, or all of them, his God is undeniably spiritual. But how strange it sounds to follow up such a concession by declaring that it is impersonal! We never associate the word impersonal with the spiritual.

3. "Worship," "Prayer," "Church"

If our definition of religion is correct, it will not only provide us with a definition of the word "god," but also of the word "worship." For worship is used to describe the distinctively religious mental act. Now what, in fact, is worship but, as our definition would lead us to think, the turning of the attention steadfastly and reverently to a source of supreme blessings? The word worship then would strictly apply to the turning of reverent attention to human goodness, as the chief source of the supreme blessings of life.

And is not this same turning of attention called prayer, when one's mind is especially focussed upon the blessings which one wishes to receive? It is the same act as worship, with emphasis thrown on the things desired.

The word "church" is a theological and a religious term, the use of which cannot be discontinued with the adoption of a scientific view of the universe. A church is a society for the worship of a being whom its members believe to be the source of the supreme blessings of life. The churches differ if the beings differ which are worshipped. A naturalistic church would be one for the worship of a being which was a verifiable factor in human experience. If it be true, as I believe, that the Christian Churches have always essentially worshipped human goodness as the real redemptive power, then they have always been naturalistic, even if their champions thought and said to the contrary. We students of the psychology of religion may understand them better than they have ever understood themselves in the past. A naturalistic church, therefore, need not count itself as essentially different from the great Christian Church. It is the Church at last awake and understanding itself better than before. We may, then, speak of the Church, meaning what it will ultimately be in its forms and dogmas, as well as what it has been in the unconscious principle vitally controlling its life from the first.

4. " Repentance," " Saint," " Holiness "

The essentially religious acts of worship and prayer may be deeply coloured by the consciousness that one has neglected one's religious duty. Then the religious act, instead of being wholly joyous, is tinged with a feeling of sorrow for the past neglect. The person is glad and sad at once, and we call him repentant.

The forgiveness of sins is the inrushing of new confidence and strength and hope, due to the reëstablished relation between the worshipper and his God. Forgiveness is a characteristic experienced in every religion, although it rises in the scale from the most superstitious to the wholly verifiable, and from the non-moral and immoral to the purely ethical types of religion.

The word "saint" must be retained in a naturalistic scheme of religion to indicate the person in whom the union of the worshipper and the worshipped is habitual and for the most part dominant, so that any wayward impulses of his nature submit without protest to the spiritual discipline. And the word "holiness" must be kept as a term to designate the saint's ability to do right effortlessly. Some one has defined ethical religiousness as glad conscientiousness. The sense of duty is to most the sense of a burden and of a task that is heavy; the saint is one whose burden, strangely enough, lifts him instead of his having any longer to lift it.

5. The Word "Christ"

Most persons who have discarded the traditional theology have felt themselves called upon, in speaking of the Founder of Christianity, to drop the word "Christ" and restrict themselves to the name "Jesus." But such a procedure on their part is again due to lack of constructive insight and imagination. When we discard the supernatural offices of Christ, he does not become for us simply a private person. He remains still official as a Saviour of the world. Just as King George is both George and King even when the kingship to us implies no supernatural grace, or as President Wilson is both Wilson and President, irrespective of our theory of government, so Jesus Christ is both the individual and private person Jesus, and also the organizer, the point of departure, of a new movement, the representative of an objective and universal principle in man. Christ is the anointed one in that he is the embodiment, the illustration, and supreme instance of the Saviour and Redeemer of the world. The more one knows of the special mission of Socrates, the more one sees that Socrates is the philosopher and not the moral saviour of the world. The more one knows even of Buddha, the more one realizes that he is not the principle of progressive manhood among nations, not the founder of a kingdom of righteous men on earth. Forever and ever Buddhism, by its denial of time and space and individual progressive existence as a good, has shut itself out, except for an Eastern people in their period of stationary suspension of ethical development, from rivalry with Christianity. Buddhism will not redeem the world, whereas Christianity, if it be true to what the new criticism and the new knowledge of evolution reveal to our gaze, will establish a world-wide kingdom of righteousness for nations and individuals. Whether it ceases to call itself Christianity is a matter of indifference. The Redeemer-principle, the Christ-principle, came to consciousness in the man Jesus, and he is therefore in the highest degree what the rest of us may in part attain. Even should any one ever in the future transcend him, still it will only be by him and in glad acknowledgment of the debt to him. There never can in the future be a dividing of the world into Christianity and not-Christianity. It will only be a new and more Christian Christianity, compatible with liberty and reason. Thus it seems that not only the word Christ as the epithet of Jesus must be retained, but also the term Christianity must be applied to a civilization which has discarded all supernaturalism and miracle and has ingrafted social democracy and science upon the tree that has now grown from the grain of mustard-seed which Christ planted.

From another point of view, also, the word Christ is preferable for a naturalist to the word Jesus, to indicate the Founder of Christianity. The authenticity of the personal life of Jesus, as narrated in the New Testament, has been questioned, so that, in the judgment of some whose scholarship and impartiality are to be respected, to speak of Jesus is to speak of a purely mythological or imaginary personage. But nobody (except Nietzsche), so far as I am aware, has ever denied the fact that in the New Testament there is figured forth an ideal or type of manhood worthy of our respect and admiration. Nor has any one ever doubted that this ideal has been the mighty power of the New Testament; and many would go so far as to say that, the ideal being there and commanding our spontaneous but rational admiration, it makes very little difference whether the person Jesus was a myth or not. It would seem to me that the word Christ may well designate the ideal which the Gospels shadow forth. For in the case of every individual person, whether mythical or historical, the ideal he suggests is the universal in the particular, is prior to it, is not fully realized in it, and will last independently of it when once it has dawned as an ideal upon the imagination of men.

There is much discussion among supernaturalists as to

the nature of the Incarnation of God in Christ; while persons who have discarded the supernaturalism seem to have lost all use for the word incarnation. Yet it must not be overlooked that this word is a very common one in everyday, non-religious speech and in general literature. We say that a man is the very incarnation of selfishness or of loving-kindness; we sometimes even say that a man is the devil incarnate. And so there are a hundred phrases of this kind which are perfectly clear and legitimate. In all of them, however, it will be found that what is referred to as being incarnate is a principle, an idea, an abstract quality, a great tendency. Surely, then, of all human beings it must be said that in this sense Jesus was an incarnation; and few will deny that he was an incarnation of the Moral Ideal of Manhood. The principle of the beneficent service of mankind was incarnate in him. It is because he was an incarnation of this principle that thousands have lived by him and will to the end of time. The incarnation then must forever remain a fundamental conception of religion. No science, no social democracy can render to any degree superfluous this notion of incarnation. Incarnation is always the actualization of a universal principle in a particular moral agent. Until all men are incarnations of the principle of constructive moral beneficence, and to a higher degree, Jesus will remain preeminent, and, as I have indicated above, it is quite possible that, in proportion as he is approached or excelled, gratitude to him will increase rather than diminish.

6. *Matthew Arnold's Insight into Christian Meanings*

The presupposition which constitutes the working hypothesis proposed here for the revision of church services is one which has already received some acceptance. Even the application of it to the historic language of religion has been well begun. One of the chief pioneers in this undertaking was Matthew Arnold. In his "Literature and Dogma" and his "God and the Bible," with inexorable logic and dazzling brilliancy of insight he applied to the literature of the Old and New Testaments the principle of society as a self-feeding spiritual organism. As the result of his investigation, he became convinced that the great writers of the Bible were purely and profoundly humanistic and naturalistic in the sense in which I have used these terms. He maintains that a man of disciplined mind and adequate scholarship, if unbiassed, cannot escape the conviction that all the Bible terms which are used to describe God refer to verifiable factors in universal human experience. He goes even further, and would sanction a continuation of the use of the Church's favourite formula for the Trinity in a naturalistic sense. On this least likely subject, he arrives at profound and beautiful meanings for words and phrases which have been understood for centuries in other ways. In the chapter in "Literature and Dogma," entitled "Our Masses and the Bible," he says:

"Suppose the Bible is discovered, when its expressions are rightly understood, to start with an assertion which *can* be verified: the assertion, namely, not of 'a Great Personal First Cause,' but of 'an enduring Power, not ourselves, that makes for righteousness.' Then by the light of that discovery we read and understand all the expressions that follow. Jesus comes forth from this enduring Power that makes for righteousness, is sent by this Power, is this Power's Son; the Holy Spirit proceeds from this same Power, and so on.

"Now, from the innumerable minor difficulties which attend the story of the three supernatural men, this right construction, put on what the Bible says of Jesus, of the Father, and of the Holy Spirit, is free. But it is free from the major difficulty also; for it neither depends upon what is unverifiable, nor is it unverifiable itself. That Jesus *is* the Son of a Great Personal First Cause is itself unverifiable; and that there *is* a Great Personal First Cause is unverifiable too. But that there *is* an enduring Power, not ourselves, which makes for righteousness, is verifiable, as we have seen, by experience; and that Jesus *is* the offspring of this Power is verifiable from experience also. For God is the author of righteousness; now, Jesus is the Son of God because he gives the method and secret by which alone is righteousness possible. And that he *does* give this, we can verify again from experience. It *is* so! Try, and you will find it to be so! Try all the ways to righteousness you can think of, and you will find that no way brings you to it except the way of Jesus, but that this way does bring you to it! And, therefore, as we found we could say to the masses: 'Attempt to do without Israel's God that makes for righteousness, and you will find out your mistake!' so we find we can now proceed farther and say: 'Attempt to reach righteousness by any way except that of Jesus, and you will find out your mistake!' This is a thing that *can* prove itself, if it is so; and it *will* prove itself, because it is so.

"Thus, we have the authority of both Old and New Testaments placed on just the same solid basis as the authority of the injunction to take food and rest; namely, that experience proves we cannot do without them. And we have neglect of the Bible punished just as putting one's hand in the fire is punished; namely, by finding we are the worse for it. Only, to *attend* to this experience about the Bible, needs more steadiness than to attend to the momentary impressions of hunger, fatigue and pain; therefore, it is called *faith*, and counted a virtue. But the appeal is to experience in this case just as much as in the other; only to experience of a far deeper and greater kind."

If even the epithets descriptive of the Trinity are applicable to factors in the religion of humanistic idealism, and not only are applicable, but become freshly beautiful and inspiring, it is likely that all the language of the Bible may be appropriated. But even if certain passages could not be used without an unnatural forcing of the text, that would not invalidate the worth of passages which required no forcing. Equally appropriate is much of the current language of religious worship, which is not directly taken over from the Bible. It may be the outcome of the metaphysical thinking of the theologians of the Middle Ages. But the question is whether their metaphysics has necessarily distorted the factors and the relations of factors in universal moral experience. If the metaphysical language of the creeds is found to have some exact appropriateness in a naturalistic scheme of redemption, it too should be embodied in a nation's ritual. It should be reinterpreted; that is, our new insight should disclose a truer meaning and then the language should be preserved. My own study of the creeds leads me to see that the metaphysicians also were among the poets, and that while their doctrines are bad science, they are admirably constructed products of imaginative thinking.

Many of the theological terms which were inflexible and absolute on the lips of the supernaturalists will become relative and assume the plasticity common to words in general literature. As Arnold says, the language of the New Testament is not that of science; and the person who uses its phrases as if they were rigid terms in a technical notation simply rules himself out of court as one incapable of judging. But although Matthew Arnold insists upon the ethical meaning of the fundamental message of the Bible, he does not for a moment deny that interblended with that message is a belief in miracles and in supernatural agencies. These, however, are altogether subordinate features. Likewise, the Bible can never again lay claim to a monopoly of our religious reverence. Henceforth the revisers of religious services will find occasion to appropriate from the literature of all nations whatever commends itself as morally true and inspiring.

P

7. *The Words "Sin" and "Devil"*

The word "sin," next to the word god itself, is exclusively a religious term. Transgression is never sin except it be against that which is counted a god — *i.e.*, against a being to which steadfast and reverent devotion is turned as to the source of life's supreme blessings. It follows inevitably that worship of the Moral Ideal and all the Powers that make for its actualization would transform all violations of the moral law into sins.

Of all theological terms, possibly none has fallen into more utter disrepute than the word "devil." Even persons who are still professed theologians avoid the word, and are generally ready to confess that they have ceased to believe in the thing. This is the more strange, for there has been no corresponding disbelief in the existence of evil, nor has the sense of horror of iniquity diminished. On the contrary, one of the striking characteristics of our age is the deepening of the sense not only of one's own sin, but of the reality of sin stamping itself on laws of property and on politics, and manifesting itself in domestic institutions. Indeed, the very institutions which once seemed to us almost perfect are now discovered in great part to be unjust and untrue. Many are beginning to feel that it is a dishonour to be rich, despite the legality of one's ownership of property.

The devil may not exist as a personal agent beyond man; but it is strange that at the very moment when we have discovered his non-existence, we have a new and appalling sense that all the attributes which constituted his supposed personality are more rampant in the world than we in our former ignorance had ever dreamt. We are also awakening to a new realization of the unity in all the various forms of evil. Things seemingly so different as lying and murder and stealing and licentiousness and love of display, and their effects on mind and body — disease, poverty, pain, insanity, despair, and early death — all these things seem to be one in nature. They are evil because they are identical in their tendency — deathward. They make for the destruction of joyous life, not only in the individual, but in the race. Furthermore, we discover not only the identity in the essential trend, but the organic unity, the cohesive affinity, among all forms and elements of evil. If Plato was right in saying that all virtue is one, we are right in saying that all vice is one, not only in its abstract definition, but as a consolidated army. It is an organized enemy against health, gladness, long life, mutual confidence, and trust and hope among men. And all evils tend to coöperate. There is an evolution of evil as well as of good. Following Spencer's definition of evolution, we may say that evil tends to develop from the incoherent, indefinite, and homogeneous to the coherent, definite, and heterogeneous. It is glaringly true that prostitution has become capitalized, systematized, coördinated, and elaborated. If virtue is health, evil is a disease like cancer; it has a virility like that of quickening life and a power of growth as intense and rapid as it is monstrous.

In proportion as one is conscious of this unifying, growing, begetting power among the various forms of evil, one is led naturally and irresistibly to do what is called personifying evil. But this personifying of evil is grossly misrepresented, if it is understood as literally attributing self-conscious intelligence to all evil, as if it actually possessed a memory and senses and purposes and plans over and above the memories and senses and purposes and plans of individual men and women. The personification is simply to indicate the organic unity which springs up among all evilly minded persons, unifying all evil tendencies in institutions and traditions and drawing to itself all the evil propensities which exist even in comparatively good men and women. Although in the literal sense we cannot attribute a unified personality or ego to the evil in the world, we can still less declare that evil is impersonal. It consists of a plurality of persons — of living men and women who are bad and plot mischief, who feed cancerously upon the organism of society. We all see that the good people of the world tend to become a unified spiritual organism. But we are beginning to detect that the evil people of the world, and all people in so far as they are evil, in a similar manner, although under cover of darkness, tend to become a unified spiritual organism. Evil not only exists—it is alive. It is not only alive, but transmits life; and all the elements of its life tend to become organized. The intense, vivid sense of this organizing principle of unity among the elements of evil forces one to personify evil. If one does not do so, one falls short of a concrete, full and alert realization of its nature. One needs a name for all forms of evil as constituting a power which begets after its own kind in the world. Now the literary name for evil thus thought of is devil.

We may not believe in a personal devil, but we must believe in a devil who acts very like a person. All spiritual organisms so act. A political party acts like a person; the Roman Catholic Church, and every nation, in proportion as we have imagination, seem to us to act like persons and to have individuality, although we are perfectly aware that they do not possess a self-consciousness distinct from the consciousness of the individual human beings who constitute them.

It is greatly to be deplored that the belief in the devil and the use of the word devil have gone out of fashion. Only one other possible decline of faith and of use of a word could be worse. The decline of belief in God and the disuse of the word god would be a greater calamity; for God must stand for Goodness as a unifying and unified power in the world. But goodness until it has triumphed is in a terrible conflict with badness. It is not only that the idea of the good suggests the idea of the bad and that these are correlative terms. It is that the good and the bad both exist and both have vitalizing strength; accordingly, it is a danger to the cause of the good if by dropping the word devil we undervalue the quickening capacity of evil. Evil may spring up in a day, in a night, almost before one knows it, in dark places, in disguised forms, in beautiful shapes; and to make light of it, to think that the forces of evil are only a chaotic mob, is the devil's chance. The forces of evil, if scattered, have been scattered by the organized efforts of the good. The moment they have a chance and the moment the capitalists and statesmen of evil give the word, they will fall into line as an armed battalion. Witness the growth of private capitalism into antisocial and antihuman trusts.

Although the devil be not a person, we must not imagine that evil is a thing dead, inanimate, and material. Evil, as much as good, is of the nature of mind; it is spiritual. It is interpersonal and superpersonal. Then let this old theological term be reinstated in the literature of religion, and let us educate the people to know exactly what is meant by it, and why and how we use it.

8. *The Word "Hell"*

In "National Idealism and the Book of Common Prayer," I dwell at length upon the naturalistic and ethical use of the word "heaven," in treating of the phrase, "Our Father who art in heaven." I therefore here only mention the word that my reader shall not imagine that it may not have a place in the nomenclature of men who insist that religion must become scientific. But the word hell must not be allowed to pass unnoticed. As we find that the word heaven is the religious term for a perfect society, so the word hell is one which the religious consciousness has put forth to designate any society where evil is triumphant, and where the consequences of sin — disease, insanity, hate — are rampant. The word God points to an individual, to persons, and to interpersonal and superpersonal relationships and factors. Likewise the word devil. But the words heaven and hell designate the opposite moral extremes of types of society. Shelley illustrates this notion in his famous line, "Hell is a city much like London." Hell is thought of as a company of agents in whom moral insight has faded to darkness, and enthusiasm has burnt to ashes; hardly a memory remains of the early dream of heaven as the fellowship of the good. In the New Testament and in the Prayer-book hell is a kind of society rather than a place and a time. We may accordingly cease to believe in a life after death and a place in which the vicious will then congregate and plot. Still we need a word to designate the fellowship of evil. There are plague-spots on earth and times in human history and even in the obscure proceedings of groups of nobodies, which are hell. By our using the word in this manner no one would be misled into thinking that we believe in a life of torment after death, and the vocabulary of humanistic religion would be the richer.

When I was considering the word devil, I dwelt upon our growing sense of the reality and power of evil in modern life. It would be very strange if, during the break-up of the old interpretations of religion, and while the consciousness of sin and the chill of moral isolation are casting us down, we should have no more use for a word to designate a society of the wayward and cynical.

The word hell will again point to a physical torment of

the damned, as well as a purely mental horror. As men advance in refinement of nervous organization and in the capacity and leisure for reflection and self-criticism, hell on earth will become more and more dreaded as the abomination of horrors. Preachers will, more and more, teach a doctrine of hell-fire. Out of kindness they will terrify by presenting the evil effects, indirect and remote, of selfish thoughts and dispositions. We must frighten people away from the edge of the abyss which yawns this side of death. It is the duty of the more experienced to warn the inexperienced and the unwary of the awful consequences of certain thoughts and deeds upon mind and body, not only to themselves, but to wife, child, neighbour, and nation. Those are probably not far from the truth who maintain that no sane being would yield to moral sin if in the moment of temptation there stood out in his imagination all the terrible consequences to everybody concerned as do the momentary and immediate pleasures to himself accompanying the deed of transgression. Many a wrong deed bears no perceptibly bitter fruit for ten, twenty, or forty years in the life of the individual; then only does it blossom into dishonour, disease, and despair. A deed may never come back to its doer, but it will to his child, to the wife, the neighbour, the casual comrade, and to the nation. With the nation it may be only in a hundred years or five hundred that the germinating seed of misery will spring up to choke the goodness, happiness, and efficiency of a people. We must preach hell-fire, and by that name. It is an effeminacy akin to the indifference altogether of our day to questions of religious discipline which has made us dwell more upon the tender mercy of God, and less upon the inexorable rigour with which evil deeds beget sin, misery, and early death. We hear much of heaven and little of hell, because preachers have not yet gripped the effects of mischievous deeds in this world. The discarding of the old belief in a supernatural hell has led them to the foolish conclusion that all the consequences of sin are relatively slight.

9. *" Redemption," " Salvation," " Eternal," " Infinite "*

The word "redemption" likewise describes a certain experience and a certain purpose in humanistic religion. Man's very constitution, his organic structure as a whole, is moral; and wickedness is always the excess or deficiency of some special impulse of his nature. Every person who sins falls away from his normal state. That state, however, despite every deviation from it, is still prefigured in man's constitution. In wrong-doing, the delinquent feels that he is sacrificing his entire being in the long run to some special or transient interest. In such a case, the wrong-doer can be set right only at a cost, only by suffering. The metaphor, therefore, involved in the word "redemption" is a fitting figure to suggest this fact. A price must be paid for restoration to the rightful owner, and this price may be the happiness and self-realization of others.

"Salvation" is a word commonly used in general literature in a non-theological and non-religious sense. It means "rescue from any sort of danger, calamity, or destruction." In a naturalistic religion it must be retained in the distinctive religious sense of deliverance from the power and penalty of sin.

The word "eternal" has plainly two meanings, that of ordinary literature and that of current theology. In the latter it signifies literally unending existence, but in literature it means the kind of life lived by one who is more interested in the remotest and most public issues than in momentary and private concerns. It means moral

superiority to transient troubles. In addition to this, it
signifies in literature the relatively lasting, as when one
speaks of the climate of the tropics as eternal summer,
or when one speaks of an eternal round of duties. The
word, in this sense, is justifiable. It is pedantry that
would restrict it to the rigid sense given it by the old
fashioned theologians. In the literary sense the word
eternal must be preserved as a distinctively religious term.
For whether human interests be literally everlasting,
continuing on after death, or not, there is a striking difference between living for pomp and vanities and living in
the real service of all men for all time. The ethical life
is therefore an eternal life, in that the individual himself,
although he has but an hour of continued existence before him, is interested in concerns that will abide practically
forever. He is not only interested, but is himself contributing to this unending life. His character and his conduct are means to enduring ends.

There is still another justification of the use of the
word eternal in naturalistic religion. The qualities which
distinguish the higher life, as reinterpreted, are the same
which were characteristic of the eternal life as described
by the older theologians. The finer spirits of Christianity
have always noted that the word eternal points not so
much to continued existence after death as to a quality
of heart and soul attainable here and now as well as hereafter. As Schleiermacher said, we may be eternal in each
moment of time — superior to personal disappointments.

Likewise with the word "infinite." It will be a great
gain to religion and to life when the grotesque subtleties
which certain schools of metaphysicians have woven about
this word have been stripped away. Infinite is a term
for the emotions; it should treat of values instead of limits
in space and time. When one's sentiments rise above a
certain intensity, differences of degree cannot be discerned

or felt; one experiences a distinct and peculiar emotional sensation of limitlessness and vastness. Wherever this emotion is experienced, it is justifiable to speak of "the infinite," describing as such that which causes the emotion. Now, it happens that the great principles and ends of the moral life and the presence of persons devoted to these ends awaken in us a degree of awe and admiration so intense and profound that exact distinctions of measured difference become impossible. That which produces this emotion seems to be without limit and without bounds. With this interpretation, the word infinite ceases to offend our scientifically disciplined judgment.

The word "almighty," as an epithet of God, like the words eternal and infinite, should be rescued from the falsely rigid and pedantic use of the supernaturalists. For the emotions, that power which exceeds measure is practically almighty; in this literary usage the word means mightier than one can measure. Such an epithet fits most congruously the notion of the active good in the world. The more we study the good as a power, the more we are conscious of its immeasurable might. But, what is still more significant, when we look to the future we see that that might will be augmented by leaps and bounds and more quickly than it has ever been in the past. In proportion as the physical universe comes under the control of nations, the power of the good in the world will be increased.

CHAPTER XIII

PRAYER TO THE GOD IN MAN

1. *The Efficacy of Petition*

THE notion prevails that praises, expressions of gratitude, and petitions addressed to some Higher Power must be dropped out of religious practices when once the trust in superhuman agencies is abandoned. Who remains, it is asked, to be thanked for blessings received? What is left to praise? Could there be any sense in appealing to a Being not conscious and therefore incapable of knowing what we asked?

Less extreme are other conclusions as to the practical consequences of limiting our moral trust to human beings under natural law. It is declared that prayer, when we give up the supernatural, can have efficacy only by reflex action. Mere aspiration, it is said, is a prayer; and it does us good to aspire. The practice of asking, praising, and expressing gratitude, although no one hears us, is wholesome for us. Sweeping is good for the broom, even if the floor be made no cleaner. It is said that, after all, the essence of prayer was not the asking for anything of any one, but the inward meditation, the serene contemplation; and that such reflection is involved in all communion with a superhuman deity and yet is independent of it. Thus prayer, even the form of address, may be preserved on account of the mental exercise it entails.

These conclusions seem to me to have been reached before making any analysis of the mental processes involved in prayer and without any comparison of attitudes of mind towards natural factors of experience analogous to attitudes towards supernatural agents. They seem to have been reached without a preliminary study of the general custom of petitioning, praising, and expressing gratitude to one's fellow-men and to natural beings, as practised by all great imaginative writers both of poetry and prose — with no shadow of reference to belief in supernaturalism.

If we approach the question of the use of prayer in naturalistic religion from the point of view of literature and psychology, we find that prayer — not simply mental but spoken, not simply private but social and public — will be more than justified. Such prayer is efficacious not only on account of its reflex action within the suppliant, but also because it is positively answered by outside beings and powers. This efficacy of prayer will also be found to concern not simply inward and spiritual states, but material possessions and outward circumstances — health, wealth, and success in life. Nor will it consist simply in passive contemplation of great realities and ends, nor in any imaginary communion with these. On the contrary, prayer will retain as its essence petition to an outside Being, and the nature of the answer to prayer will be the actual response of a Higher Power. These responses will be such that they are veritably dependent upon the petition. Had the suppliant not asked, he would not have got what he asked for.

2. *Human Beings who answer Prayers to God*

Now to our analysis, psychological and literary. When we give up supernatural personal agencies who might answer petitions, we have not altogether lost out of our lives personal agencies who may hear and answer supplications. Human beings, close at hand and powerful to help, still remain in countless numbers round about us. Only on the notion that supernaturalism is essential to religion can it be maintained that a supplication to a personal agent for help is religious so long as the agent is supernatural and superhuman but ceases to be religious the moment the agent appealed to is human and natural. The fundamental contention of naturalistic religion is that if a practice is religious when done in relation to beings outside of man and nature, it must be equally so in relation to beings within the universe of our social experience.

Apply this principle to the Lord's Prayer. If the petition "Give us our daily bread" is religious when addressed to a personal Creator conceived of as hearing and caring and able to provide for us, it is none the less so if addressed to fellow-mortals round about us. Likewise with the supplications "Lead us not into temptation" and "Deliver us from evil." Suppose any one should utter these petitions to men and women round about him, believing that they could give him the bread and the moral protection he needs, and would do it if petitioned. Suppose he were filled with a profound sense of his dependence upon them and upon their willingness. Suppose he were in dire necessity — not only he, but his family. Then all the elements of religious intensity and yearning and humility and hope would be manifested in him. Also there would be the powers at hand, mighty to save, ready to help, needing only to be asked in sincerity and with good cause. How, then, at least as regards these three clauses of the Lord's Prayer, can it be said that the moment our belief in a supernatural personal agency vanishes, that instant we must perforce cease to cry out, "Give us this day our daily bread," "Lead us not into temptation, but deliver us from evil"?

Or take the clause, "Forgive us our sins, for we also forgive those who are indebted to us." If this supplication be an act of religion in the soul and on the lips when addressed to an invisible agency, our contention is that it is equally so — equally a prayer, equally a petition to an outside Personal Power, to a source of redemption and consolation — when addressed to one's fellow-men. They can forgive. Morally, they must forgive. The imperative is absolute; and there can be no hint of superstition or presumption in asking fellow-mortals to forgive us in proportion as we have forgiven other fellow-mortals. No scepticism, no materialism, no agnosticism can in any degree undermine the foundations of this prayer when addressed to fellow-mortals. The occasion for both thinking and uttering it remains as great after we have discarded supernaturalism as it was before. Nay, the consciousness of the need for forgiveness from one's fellow-men becomes intensified. It becomes exalted into a higher degree of religious fervour and passion than it ever could have been when the chief anxiety of religion was to appease a supernatural agent. No stronger vindication of a naturalistic faith and practice could be conceived than this heightening of the significance of the forgiveness of sins between man and man.

We have, then, already justified prayer as a form of petition to an outside Being under a naturalistic scheme of human redemption. Nobody ever dreamed of denying that it is perfectly rational to pray in the manner here indicated. Furthermore, it is quite plain that the efficacy of prayer when directed to personal agencies within nature is not merely subjective; it is objective and real. The answer is dependent upon the asking. Let it further be noted that prayer of this kind is not limited to asking for spiritual blessings. It secures material help as well as outside spiritual safeguards and spiritual reconciliations.

3. *Outward Expressions of Prayer*

Further, how self-evident it has become that prayer within the limits here under consideration need not be merely mental; nay, must be spoken as well. Not only speech, but the very bodily attitudes of prayer should remain intact. It is fully justifiable to bow the head, to stretch forth the hands, and on occasion to fall upon the knees. Such practices are not only justifiable, but are actually carried out by everybody. Who can deny that the use of these towards supernatural agents is simply borrowed from the universal and everyday practice of falling on the knees, stretching forth the hands, and bowing the head towards fellow-mortals, when, in great need and dependence, men and women cry out for help, either physical or spiritual? After analysis of the case, then, instead of conceding that religious petitions to an outside Being for help must cease when supernaturalism is discarded, one rather is astonished at the presumption and audacity, or else the lack of reflection, of those who declare that men must cease to pray in a religious sense when the supernatural is given up.

For, whatever else must be abandoned, certainly petition to outside beings in whose visible presence one stands or kneels, and within range of whose hearing one's words are uttered, will forever be its own justification. The only change with the decay of supernaturalistic creeds will be that such petition, which before had been counted secular or profane or what not, will rise now into the dignity of religious ceremonial. This asking from a fellow-mortal within earshot for help is the eternal and indestructible nucleus of the substance of prayer.

4. *Prayer to the Absent*

But we have not surveyed the whole range of the practice which naturalism in religion must inculcate. We are by no means limited, in our requests, to persons within earshot. There are countless channels for communicating petitions to those absent or remote. A prayer may be written, it may be printed. Yet not even these direct means of conveying a supplication to the Being implored exhaust the possibilities of reaching the ear and the soul of others. Sometimes it is not necessary that one should direct one's petition to some particular and definite individual. Everybody knows that a petition sent forth vaguely and generally often touches the heart of this or that hearer, quite irrespective of any personal friendship or any individual responsibility towards the needy suppliant. We ask we know not whom in particular, but we get in response from some one in particular. Men and women out of work insert in the daily papers a statement of their predicament; and their prayer is answered. Somebody hearing of a case of distress announces the circumstances in the Press and vouches for the accuracy of his statement; and the money that is wanted comes. The home in the country which the invalid needed is offered. The journey to a warmer clime is provided. Verily, many have found that a Personal God is round about them, ready to hear and help. Experiences so common as these are known to every one. The only novelty in my argument is that I bring them into relation with the deepest necessities of our lives and open up close at hand an infinite scope for religious trust, faith, and fulfilment.

5. *Prayers that are Overheard*

Sometimes the prayer is directed in no such vague and general manner, but is misdirected. It is addressed to a definite individual, yet one whose heart is hardened or whose eyes are blind or who proves after all incapable of answering our request. And still the prayer is answered. Some chance onlooker overhears and forthwith assumes the rôle of Providence. It must never be forgotten that prayers may be not only heard, but overheard. When not even overheard in the literal sense by one who can answer, they may be reported to somebody else who can.

Nothing could be more naïve in its simplicity than the testimony frequently rendered by evangelical enthusiasts, who boast that in their philanthropic work they have never asked any human being for a penny, and yet the infinite Creator of the universe from on high has heard their prayer to him. Money has poured in from this and that rich man or woman. Such enthusiasts are, without doubt, sincere. But they and the persons who believe their testimony overlook the fact that there are many forms of prayer besides direct begging. People see for themselves a man's sincerity, single-mindedness, and self-sacrifice, and the need in which both he and his work stand. One who has fainted by the wayside need not tell me that he has fainted and requires my help. If I am but half human, I know before he asks, and may answer because he does not ask. So with the self-sacrificing worker among the poor. We see the needs of his mission, and our hearts are forthwith touched to proffer our support. The evangelist who testifies that without natural means the Creator has directly moved the rich to support his mission must prove that some one who has never heard of it or of its merits has sent money. The truth is that dogmas exacting faith in supernatural agencies make those who implicitly accept them blind to what common sense reveals as plainly as the day — the human agencies and the natural connections binding one human spirit with another.

6. *Prayers to Historic Personages*

Petition, however, to one's fellow-mortals is not limited to those actually living. All human agencies who have once constituted a part of the living social organism and whose character and purposes have been preserved to us in books or by tradition are potent factors to-day in the lives of human beings. Literature, in proportion as it is imaginative, poetic, and patriotic in its sentiments, teems with illustrations of direct addresses to human beings long since dead. These addresses consist not only of praise and expressions of gratitude, but of appeals and petitions. If our reasoning thus far has been correct, such petitions do not cease to be prayers simply because they are not addressed to superhuman agents. Upon close analysis we shall, I believe, be forced to confess that they are answered, and not simply subjectively. Take Wordsworth's sonnet, beginning :—

> Milton, thou shouldst be living at this hour:
> England hath need of thee: she is a fen
> Of stagnant waters: altar, sword, and pen,
> Fireside, the heroic wealth of hall and bower,
> Have forfeited their ancient English dower
> Of inward happiness.

The Milton living in history and not simply the Milton already subjectively a part of Wordsworth does, through the supplication, become a more intense, vivid, and potent reality to the petitioner because of his prayer. Milton is one of "the choir invisible," living "in minds made better by their presence," but in other minds as well as that of the petitioner. But more than this, Milton is living in his poems and his prose and in the historical record of his times. No one focussing attention upon Milton, and reconsidering his works and his life, can fail to derive from them new strength and inspiration. It is impossible to say that one studying the works of Shakespeare is benefited only subjectively. It is impossible to say that any one indebted to Shakespeare's liberating and humanizing spirit can turn the attention fresh upon him and not derive from him new, real, and objective inspiration. So with Milton. In opening our minds to him, he becomes more vividly present to us; and thus he makes us better and quickens us to new heroism and new dignity. It is only by prayer to him that more of him enters into us than mere chance allowed. Surely it is a petty and mechanical logic which would lead us to believe that the 240 years between us and Milton are in any way a barrier to his response to our spiritual appeal to him! Time is no barrier. Pathetic is the foolishness of those who, in order to interpret the inspiration which we may derive, feel forced to presuppose that the spirit of Milton is actually present in the sense in which living men are at hand. It is to be hoped that most of us are poets enough, without any spiritistic theory to encourage us and without any materialistic doctrine to prevent, to cry out to Milton, under pressure of our inward shame and conscious of his character: —

> We are selfish men;
> Oh! raise us up, return to us again,
> And give us manners, virtue, freedom, power!
> Thy soul was like a star, and dwelt apart;
> Thou hadst a voice whose sound was like the sea:
> Pure as the naked heavens, majestic, free;
> So didst thou travel on life's common way
> In cheerful godliness; and yet thy heart
> The lowliest duties on herself did lay.

When the services of the Anglican Church become — and they will so become — the native poetic outgrowth of national history and of national character and of national genius, as well as the outgrowth of the religious services of ancient Jerusalem and of the Roman Catholic Church, this supplication to Milton will find its place in England's public worship. The disciplinary efficacy of the repetition of it would in no wise require, as a presupposition, a belief in any doctrine or dogma as to supernatural powers in general or as to the self-conscious living presence of Milton to-day. To the truly historic imagination the past is verily present, not only as the unconscious energizing principle of our lives, but also in the literature and record of its meaning and its lessons.

In a naturalistic view of religion all such appeals as this of Wordsworth to Milton would be recognized as essentially and intensely religious; and such recognition would enhance their beauty, dignity, and influence.

7. *Prayers to Jesus*

Not only, however, will treasures of so-called secular literature be seen to be sacred and be appropriated by the Church. The best prayers of the Church itself, which hitherto have been interpreted in a supernaturalistic sense, will not on that account be discarded by humanists.

Generally in our day nobody prays to Jesus Christ, unless he accepts the idea that Jesus Christ has continued since his death to be a living, self-conscious spirit and is still operating upon human society and coöperating with his disciples to the end of its redemption. But the time will come when persons who in no wise entertain this idea will not be in the least ashamed to turn, as much as any spiritistic Christian, to Jesus Christ for help and inspiration, for strength and consolation, just as they will repeat Wordsworth's prayer to Milton. To-day it may seem almost preposterous to think that such a time will come. But how can the discarding of supernaturalism separate us from Jesus the Man, from Jesus the Christ, from him who exemplified in his sayings and in his life the principle of our humanity to a degree far transcending that of any other character preserved to us in literature and tradition? We need Jesus as we need Milton; and the only way to get him is to turn towards him as we would to Milton — to study his life, picture it, visualize it, know by heart his sayings and his influence, and thus focus our attention upon his unique personality.   To do so mentally will be to cry out mentally, "Christ, have mercy upon us; Lord, have mercy upon us!" and what we shall say in our inmost soul that we may utter with the lips.   Thousands who to-day discard the supernatural office assigned to Jesus are ready to testify to the inspiration of his life.   It is inconceivable that a religion which will turn to the examples of all good men should omit that of Jesus.   Nor will any deficiency of historical evidence as to the actuality of the details of his life have a weakening effect upon the power of his personality, any more than the same deficiency would have in the case of any other man.   In the case of all men the valuable element in their lives depends not so much upon the authenticity of every incident as upon the ideal character which the incidents somehow inevitably suggest or inevitably create through our constructive imagination in our own minds.   The true triumph of Christ will be the survival of his power for good over men after they have totally discarded all belief that he was unique in origin or in kind or even that he actually did or said any one of the things which have been assigned to him.   Somebody, something, many persons or many things, did, somehow, suggest to the writers of the New Testament that ideal of manhood which therein is shadowed forth.   Whatever suggested the ideal there depicted is, in the ultimate analysis, the living reality from which the ideal issued.   Though the whole narrative of the Gospels be proved to be mythical, the reality it presents cannot, from the ethical and sociological point of view, be denied.   The myth somehow grew out of living needs and living experiences.   Destructive critics will have difficulty in destroying the ideal suggested by the story of the life of Christ. Nor can they destroy the belief that it emanated from living experience of some kind.   It, moreover, is in no wise dependent upon the authenticity of the narrative. It is its own witness and its own justification. It will, accordingly, grow more and more to be a positive redemptive energy throughout mankind, in proportion as all spiritism falls away from religion. Naturalistic religion will not only rescue the characters of secular literature, but will deliver Jesus out of the hands of those who in their jealous adoration of him have made him a preternatural — and therefore a monstrous — being.

8. *Prayers to Spiritual Tendencies and Ideas*

Even now we have not exhausted the range through which the spirit of prayer may sweep without passing beyond its legitimate confines. Equally justifiable with petition to living human beings and to the great characters of the past is direct address in the second person to the great tendencies and institutions of human society. The very tissues of the living organism of humanity are sensitive and vibrate in response to our supplications. The ideal relations and standards of human fellowship glow with new life and move responsive to the petitioner's importunity. Such abstractions as America, Democracy, the Spirit of Man, Womanhood, the Moral Ideal; such virtues as Purity, Equality, Fraternity — these are no *mere* abstractions. Although abstractions, they are energies, potencies round about us. To turn the mind towards them, to fix the eye of the spirit upon them, is to cause them to pass from vagueness and indefinite passivity into distinct and precise activity. We cannot mention their names without beginning to grow into their likeness. As ideas, as principles formative and directive in human society, they have a real existence independent of any one individual who may or may not revere them. Take Emerson's immortal prayer: "I love the Right; Truth is beautiful within and without forevermore; Virtue, I am thine; save me; use me; thee will I serve, day and night, in great, in small, that I may be not virtuous, but Virtue." Let any man pray this prayer, and he will see that from Virtue as a real power, from the idea and from the living principle of it in human experience, strength will issue to transform him into its image and into identity with it. The result of experiment with this prayer will be the conviction that even petitions to personal agents, supernatural or natural, are efficacious only in so far as they involve, though but implicitly, an appeal to the abstract qualities of ideal manhood. The suppliant will find that William Blake expresses the inmost truth of prayer when he says:

> To Mercy, Pity, Peace and Love
>   All pray in their distress,
> And to these virtues of delight
>   Return their thankfulness.

9. *Prayer not merely Communion*

If such be the intimate and vital relationship between us and the whole of human society past and present, it cannot be said that there only remains to us a sort of idealistic communion with the great and good, and with those groups which have been the inspiration of the great and good. Besides such union and communion, direct petition is also possible. This being the case, those religious innovators who have discarded supernaturalism, and have on that account felt themselves compelled to discard petition, have erred in judgment.

Typical among such innovators was Dr. Congreve. He retained the word "prayer." But unhappily he went out of his way to assert that from Positivistic prayer all idea of direct petition is excluded. Why should he have excluded petition? Surely only because he had failed to analyze carefully the factors which remained within Positivism. The supreme being to which the Positivists pray, Humanity, is verily present wherever any human beings are present, and hears whenever they hear. To each individual in the congregation all the others are an outside living reality which may and does respond to petitions. But over and above this, did Dr. Congreve even understand the prayers he himself formulated? Was he not still so dominated by the supernaturalistic presuppositions to which in youth he had been trained, that by oversight he failed to recognize the most virile and effectual characteristics of Positivistic prayer? Dr. Congreve's error seems also to have fastened itself upon the understanding of another devout and unflagging disciple of Comte. Mr. Malcolm Quin, who has conducted the services in the Church of Humanity at Newcastle-on-Tyne, England, divides the forms used by him under three headings only, Commemoration, Communion, and Dedication. He allows no place for direct petition. This would exclude the asking that justice be done, that health, wealth, leisure, and knowledge be granted to all those from whom these necessities are now wrongfully withheld. No wonder that the poor and women in general have not been attracted in large numbers to the Church of Humanity! It has fallen into commemoration. It has dropped into quietistic piety and receptivity. It has inculcated dedication of one's powers instead of self-assertion and the demand that forthwith those who can deliver shall arise and redeem.

Yet, fortunately, both Dr. Congreve and Mr. Malcolm Quin have builded better than they thought and professed. In spite of their conscious theory, they have not omitted petition from Positivist prayers. I find in their printed religious services, it is true, no asking for material help. But their prayers are far more than mere aspiration of the individual soul, unrelated to the reservoir of spiritual life

round about. There is in the Positivistic prayers very
much of direct petition for spiritual help from an outside
Being; or, to be more precise, from that portion of the
whole being of Humanity which is outside of the petitioner
himself. What, for instance, are these invocations of Humanity in Mr. Quin's ritual but a direct petition, and what
could be more consonant with the real character of Positive polity than such appeals as these : "Humanity, Spirit
of Love, arise in the souls of thy servants"; "Yea, free us
from this darkness, that we may behold thee in the glory
of thy past"; "O power of present guidance, unveil thy
grace to us and be near to us in these depths"; "O life
that wast, O life that reignest now, reveal to us all the
majesty of thy life to be." Surely here is a petition on the
part of the individual worshipper to some power outside
of his own actualized selfhood. Or take Dr. Congreve's
form for the Sacrament of Presentation of Children. There
you will find this petition, clearly directed to all humanity
as well as to the intelligent heart and will of the parents
who dedicate their child : "Great power whom we adore
as the source of all good to men, Humanity, we thy servants,
met for the consecration of a new life to thy service,
humbly and earnestly pray that the child by this sacrament presented and consecrated may be lovingly, faith-
fully, and wisely trained, that under all wholesome influences of affection and submission and reverence she (or
he) may grow up to be in her turn rich in such influences,
taking her part in thy continuous work."

Thus even those who intend to omit petition spontaneously and wisely retain it. The ultimate substance
of prayer is the act of opening the soul towards the moral
universe beyond oneself. It is a drawing back of the cur-
tain to let in the sunlight. Or — to change the metaphor
— the human spirit, too long shut within the prison house
of the senses and bound to the claims of the pettier self,

is cramped and stifled. It was born for liberty and loving sacrifice; and when it fears that it can no longer breathe, it strikes against its prison windows, and, breaking them, lets the life-giving air from beyond rush in.

10. *Prayer not merely Mental*

From what we have said above, the minor question as to whether prayer shall be purely mental or may also be expressed in words is easily settled. Prayer is, of course, in the first place, mental. But it is a grievous blunder to imagine that it has no need to be formulated in words and uttered in speech. No mental activity can become definite, coherent, and systematic and remain so, except it be embodied and repeated in words. Afterwards we may come to say the words in a suppressed whisper or only mentally; but originally and essentially a prayer to be definite must be formulated in language. And it must be actually spoken again and again, or it will waste away into vacancy of soul. A petition that does not or cannot or will not formulate itself in words and let the lips move to shape them and the voice to sound them and the eye to visualize them on the written or printed page, becomes soon a mere torpor of the mind or a meaningless movement of blind unrest or a trick of pretending to pray. Perfected prayer is always spoken.

11. *Public Prayer*

Moreover, in its fulness a prayer uttered by the private soul alone cannot be adequate to its own fulfilment. One may not say that the prayer in solitude is ineffectual; for indirectly, if not directly, through its effects upon him who prays, it will reach not only the humanity stored up to us in literature and tradition, but the actual living men and women constituting the present-day community.

Nevertheless, it cannot be denied that prayer in its fulness is not only spoken, but is social. It requires for its completeness the presence of two or three uniting together in petition. Ultimately, prayer is the surrender of the individual's private whims to the general will of society; and that general will is most powerfully present and effective when at least a few are visibly together in community of purpose. Again, the very fact that the prayer is entered into by several persons proves that it is already a movement not only of the individual towards the spiritual organism, but of the spiritual organism towards each of its members. It is an insane heresy of religious individualism to regard private prayer as being deeper and intenser than public. According to this heresy, the height of prayer is for the individual to be alone with the Alone — as jealous theists describe it. The truth, however, of our spiritual life is that in order to ascend spiritually we must meet and help one another up. Social prayer is the coming together in order to enter into the unifying spirit of all society. Articulate utterance is manifestly the only means for rational communion, and the words uttered, in order to express the turning of the mind to the redemptive influences within the spiritual organism of society, must consist not only of statements in the third person concerning those influences, but of address. It is not enough that we speak *about* the Being whose help we crave; we must speak *to* it. It is quite true that, when we cease to trust to personal agencies outside of society, we can no longer address *them* either in thought or words; but this is no reason why we should cease speaking to the personal agencies within society. We may henceforward only talk *about* supernatural beings; but surely we are not restricted to talking about our fellow-mortals. We must address them directly.

We dare never forget that moral realities stand to us in a different dynamic relation from the grass and the stars and the sea. No effects upon us or upon these would result from petitions, even of a most righteous man, to them. But no one can deny that prayers to Purity, Serenity, Faith, Humanity, America, Man, Woman, to Milton, to Jesus, do create a new moral heaven and earth for him who thirsts after righteousness.

12. *The Emotional Elevation of Prayer*

It may well be conceded that only when a man's emotions are profoundly stirred and his imagination quickened can he feel the significance and dignity of addressing a petition to such abstract qualities and comprehensive realities as I have been considering. The moral will, although it does go out in supplication to these so-called abstractions and generalizations, never does so when a man is neutral and apathetic. But when in such a state of mind, why should any man trouble to address either natural or supernatural powers? The prayers I have been advocating presuppose exalted states of mind in which principles, ideas, and the main tendencies and goals of human effort are felt to be supreme realities and constitute a living presence. The mood of all prayer, supernaturalistic no less than naturalistic, if it be genuine, is akin to the spirit of poetry, wherein the invisible, the universal, the ideal is felt to be more real than one's own body. It is nothing against the interpretation of prayer which I have given, that it presupposes imagination and a state of profound emotion. The prayer that is prosaic and drags along the ground of literal fact is a contradiction in terms. Let persons who are not deeply moved, and whose spirit is not aflame, speak only in the third person or not at all. The exaltation of prayer which has always characterized it in supernatural religion will be equally required when the redemptive influences to which we turn are wholly within social experience. The emotion must be high; then the speech will correspond. A spoken prayer must give expression to the exalted emotion that inspired it by majesty of style, by sweep of rhythm and greatness of imagery, or else by the closeness and simplicity of its truth.

Some of the Positivist innovators in religion to whom I have before referred attempted to write prayers in an unimaginative mood of cold, logical effort. They supposed that a mere recognition of their right to address Humanity would enable them to produce a prayer. They did not realize that only at the white heat of passion and by creative imagination would come forth a form of petition able to stir moral passion in others. The result of their efforts was sometimes grotesque enough. Yet in humanistic religion a foolish and incapable utterance no more proves the inability of humanism to inspire sublime and stirring expression than would a similarly dull utterance in supernaturalistic religion be a disproof of its possibilities. An analysis of certain prayers which have been offered to the public and are used by English Positivists simply shows that the special writers were not poets; it does not show that Positivism is in itself prosaic, but that Dr. Congreve was not a poet. Let the Positivists wait, if need be, for a Shelley or a Browning or a George Eliot before they begin to offer up prayers to Humanity.

But they need not wait. Already English literature is abundantly rich in Positivistic prayers, as sublime and quickening in melody and passion as anything in the Hebrew prophets or the liturgy of the Church. Let anyone read Swinburne's "Songs before Sunrise." There he will find a whole anthology of prayer suitable for use in the Church of Humanity. Swinburne does not invoke in very name Humanity as a spiritual organism, but he does what would seem less promising. He breathes forth prayers to the Ideal Republic. When "Songs before Sunrise" was written, he was aflame with democratic enthusiasm, and his soul burnt itself in sacrifice at the altar of republicanism. Yet not a line nor a word of his could any one find grotesque. Our conclusion, then, as regards the prayers of naturalism, is that they are in no other position than those of supernaturalism. They presuppose a poet.

13. *Statements of Fact in Prayer*

We have noted that a petition addressed to a Being need not differ in content from a simple statement of fact. Take the General Confession in Morning and Evening Prayer of the English Book of Common Prayer. It is a petition to God; it says, "We have erred and strayed from Thy ways like lost sheep." If we drop the pronoun "Thy" and in its place put words descriptive of what the "Thy" undoubtedly indicates, we shall have destroyed the form of prayer, but the matter of the sentence will remain wholly intact: "We have erred and strayed from the right ways like lost sheep." How little difference, whether we speak to Righteousness or speak about it! We see that the difference between the third and the second person is not a difference in truth or in kind, but only in warmth. The form of prayer marks an intensification of intimacy, but nothing more. We cannot even say that statements about a thing fail to draw it nearer to us. When we declare that we have erred and strayed from the right ways like lost sheep, the right ways become less far off; and they loom higher and grander before our inward vision. They awaken an impulse to start forward and enter into them. Only to speak about Virtue is in fact a supplication. It is an asking without the form of asking; and beyond all doubt such formless prayers are answered.

When speaking of the form of prayer, we found that

it might be addressed to a person or persons within ear-shot or to those living but absent. Or we might ask of the community as a whole, or of persons and tendencies remote in history, or of ideals and abstractions. Now exactly in the same way, although in a lesser degree, to make a statement in the presence and hearing of a person, although with no form of petition, may virtually be a petition. If I come pale and haggard into the presence of some one capable of assisting me and simply declare, "I have had nothing to eat for twenty-four hours and am penniless," the effect is probably quite the same as if I added, "Give me something to eat," or, "Give me something with which to buy food." The efficacy of the statement is of the same kind when the words touch the heart of an absent person whom they indirectly reach. Likewise even the influence of the dead and of abstractions may be secured to our benefit. Almost all the effect of Wordsworth's sonnet addressed to Milton would have been obtained had it been a statement about Milton instead of an appeal to him.

Persons, then, who boast that they have discarded prayer and who regard it as childish or fantastic to address petitions to beings who cannot literally hear, do not escape the charge that their minds virtually go out to meet the great realities of the moral universe, whenever they make sincere and truthful statements about virtues or great historic tendencies. They may say that they have abandoned the form of prayer, but they cannot maintain that they have dropped its substance. Modern indifference and the lack of analysis have led to a widespread discarding of the form of prayer, but we have no reason to think that persons have in any degree ceased talking about virtue or ceased going out to meet it halfway. Nor, in fact, have they, in abandoning prayer to supernatural agencies, fallen off from the poetic habit of using the form of prayer to the dominant factors in moral experience. They have not yet become accustomed to denominate such addresses prayers; but when once the identity, in disposition and efficacy, of petitions to human agents with prayers to super-human beings is seen, the form of petition will not only be used, but will be designated by the religious name for it.

Thus we see that the form of prayer is legitimate whenever the sense of intimacy with the object from which blessing is derived rises beyond the everyday level of emotion. We might say that a statement *about* virtue represents the positive degree of moral emotion, while an address *to* virtue represents the comparative degree. The latter indicates more perturbation of the heart; there is a bursting of the ordinary bounds and channels of feeling; the emotions overflow and rush forth in unwonted abundance and with increased momentum towards the object they seek.

14. *A Mystic Union with God*

There is, however, a superlative degree of moral sentiment. The sense of intimacy with virtue may rise to a level where it transcends even the form of prayer. The plane of feeling where excitement, unrest, and yearning dominate is not the highest. Such a state is often transcended. The soul enters into a realm of spiritual clarity, of calm and radiant fulfilment, where it no longer is aware of any separation between itself and the whole of virtue which it craved. In this state of emotion it becomes as impossible to speak *to* the influences and agencies which redeem as *of* them. The intimacy of the Good in the individual with the Good beyond it has become for the instant identity of being. In such moments of lucidity one neither speaks *of* virtue and the good in the world nor *to* virtue and the good in the world, but lets virtue and the good in the world speak for themselves in and through one's own soul. Thus it was with the ancient Hebrew prophets. They identified God with themselves and spoke in his person. Such, likewise, was the sense of mystic union with God expressed time and again by the Founder of Christianity. He saw himself to be one with the Powers that redeem. The highest state of religious emotion is this, which can only express itself adequately in the first person. And the line of religious development in the future under naturalism will not be marked by a falling short in that emotion which needs the form of prayer, but by a transcending of it.

Not only in Hebrew and Christian literature do we find this higher form in which petition is transcended, but also in the sacred writings of the East. It is likewise to be found in such mystic poets of the West as Emerson and Tennyson. Emerson, without explaining who it is that speaks, uses the first person, where it is quite evident that his own finite personality is not the speaker. In the following verse he uses it as an Eastern seer would : —

> They reckon ill who leave me out;
> When me they fly, I am the wings;
> I am the doubter and the doubt,
> And I the hymn the Brahmin sings.

In "The Higher Pantheism," Tennyson, although he does not use the first person, expresses exquisitely that consciousness of identity with all reality and with the ideal of all good of which we have been speaking : —

Closer is He than breathing, and nearer than hands and feet.

. . . .

And the ear of man cannot hear, and the eye of man cannot see;
But if we could see and hear, this Vision — were it not He?

If in the future the form of prayer is to be less used than it has been in the past, it will not be because we shall fall back in coldness and apathy to the third person,

R

but because we shall more frequently rise, like the great mystics in their rarer moments, to identity with the real and with the good. In its fulness communion with the redemptive powers is such that he who prays is one with that to which he prays.

15. *The Value of Ethical Declarations*

It is, however, an error to imagine that address to God and address by him are the only religious forms of speech. In our recognition of the ecstasies which break out into petition and praise and into utterances as from God himself to man, we must not forget that plain, quiet statements of moral experience and of moral judgment serve the same high ends. Mere assertions of our wants, acknowledgments of our limitations, confessions of our debts and hopes ought to make up the main body of religious utterance. Simple, unimaginative expressions of principles and needs strengthen those principles and meet those needs in ourselves and others. The more sober thinkers of our day have therefore sometimes discarded the form of prayer, only because they were more sensitive and discriminating; they were anxious to avoid the slightest exaggeration. They have disciplined themselves to modest declaration of moral experience. They have preferred to understate in order to escape the vice, to which professional religionists are prone, of overstating the intensity of spiritual desire and hope. They see that religion in the past has often fallen into contempt because of indulgence in the comparative and superlative degrees in speech, when only the positive degree of emotion was felt. It is consonant with the character of true religious feeling to check hysterical talk by restraint of the tongue.

Commendable is the self-control which can feel and will greatly and yet keep temperate in phrase. In nearly all the prayers of the Book of Common Prayer there is an almost imperceptible merging of plain statement, of petition, and of oracular utterance into one another. In the greatest prayers are most frequently to be found plain statements of facts of the moral life. For instance, in the prayer from which we have already quoted the sentence, "We have erred and strayed from Thy ways like lost sheep," there immediately comes the declaration, "We have followed too much the devices and desires of our own hearts." After the clause, "We have offended against Thy holy laws," is the plain statement, "We have left undone those things which we ought to have done, and we have done those things which we ought not to have done; and there is no health in us." Here there is no form of address or petition, but the spirit of prayer is incarnate.

Such merely positive declarations may at any moment mount emotionally and assume the overt form of petition; then, subsiding to a lower level of feeling, they resume the third person. The form is as nothing if the substance be present. To state, "We ask to be forgiven," is not a prayer in form; yet its import is the same as if we had said, "Forgive us!"

In the meetings of some ethical societies are read declarations of principles which make no pretence to imaginativeness. They do not rise above the positive degree of emotion, but — not presuming to — are in taste. They are honest, homely confessions of moral purposes, aspirations, and duties. Yet no one could hear them read and not be aware that they in their degree appeal to the humanity of every listener and set him turning towards all good. They stir in him both a sense of responsibility and a consciousness of his own need. Such a plain, matter-of-fact statement is this : —

We are here to-day to deepen our sense of personal responsibility towards those who may need our ministering care. We dedicate our lives to all with whom we are joined by the ties of duty and by opportunities of service; to our neighbours, to kindred, to the children who are dear to us, to fellow-citizens, to our countrymen and to any one we may help — even to those as yet unborn.

It is a terrible thought that beings, frail, without experience and yet precious, are thrust into a world oftentimes thoughtless, selfish, and cruel. We would offer our lives as a shield to guard the wayward from their own folly and to protect the innocent and ignorant from pernicious customs and the designs of evil persons. We would summon all men and women now living to the high office of benignant Providence, to which their position as fathers and mothers, husbands and wives, as elder brothers and sisters, as neighbours and citizens, and as fellow-mortals calls them. We commend to the fortunate, to the powerful, to those of preëminent ability or in positions of influence, to the governors of our cities and of the nation, all children whose parents are worldly or destitute, illiterate, intemperate, or overworked. To those who might bring relief we cry out: "Have mercy upon these helpless victims, and deliver them out of their untoward conditions; create for them a new environment, both physical and social; preserve their bodies from hunger, pain, and disease; and to their minds bring the truths that reveal the glories of the universe, bestow upon them the beauty that graces life and pour out the love that hallows it."

Above all, we plead that henceforth no human life shall come into existence unless it has been desired, and will be welcomed, cherished, and revered.

Here is a petition to one's fellow-mortals without the form of appeal. It does not pretend to emanate from a mood of unwonted intensity, and so need not attempt to rise above the level of workaday phrase.

As an instance of the natural transition from statements in the third person to direct petitions and then back again, I may cite another confession of moral need, used in the services of some ethical churches: —

To all who might influence us either for good or for evil, we

who are here assembled, being each of us conscious of our own
moral weakness, send forth the time-honoured petition, "Lead
us not into temptation, but deliver us from evil." We cry out
to those about us, appealing to the best that is in them: "Help
us to do through hours of blindness what in moments of insight
we see to be right. Bring home to our unwilling thoughts the
fact that the triumph of righteousness on earth depends in part
on our own effort and our own wisdom. Infuse into us this day
the strength to resist evil and to do good; make us just and kind
in all our dealings. Deepen in us the desire to love, know, and
do the right. Save us from hasty opinions, words, and deeds.
Teach us to consider what we are prone to forget — the cause
of the poor, the unfortunate, the stranger, of the aged, of children, and of dumb animals. Help us to root out from ourselves
race hatred, class prejudice, and religious intolerance, as well as
all other forms of cruelty and malice. Encourage us to make
the common weal our end. Lead us to cherish truth and beauty
and all institutions which make life noble. Lastly and once
more, we ask: Increase our power to live every day of our lives
in the spirit of this appeal."

A statement which never once rises out of the third
person and above the positive degree sometimes reaches
the heart for which it is meant as potently as would a
direct petition. I cite two more ethical declarations which
I have found to be not without the efficacy of prayer: —

The miseries and wrongs which degrade our nation require
no miracle to end them; but only a good heart and willing wit
on the part of the intelligent, the prosperous, the electors, the
legislators, and the magistrates of our land; and, on the part
of the disinherited classes, a burning sense of the wrongs they
suffer. We address ourselves not to beings who are blind, deaf,
remote, or incapable of rendering aid, nor to an invisible deliverer beyond the skies. We importune men — fellow-men,
close at hand — of like nature and in like need with ourselves;
for we know that importunity like ours overcomes both the
heedlessness of the proud and the apathy of the oppressed.

We call upon men and women of all classes, but we especially summon the poor and overworked, to form themselves into a mighty religious movement, for the teaching and doing of the duties of man to man by man. If we who are pledged to social regeneration become an organized multitude, the wrongs of life will be quickly righted, for we ourselves shall have the power to establish justice in the land.

We utter this summons in the glad consciousness that in doing so we are performing a part, necessary though humble, in the great work of human redemption.

Likewise this: —

In the name of duty and humanity; for the sake of the tens of thousands of the suffering poor, for the unemployed, the overworked, the underfed; on behalf of those who have no room to live, and who must die without the sanctities of home; for all who dwell in uncertainty from week to week as to their means of subsistence; for the wives of the needy — especially in time of childbirth; for the children of the poor and of worldly and dissolute parents; in pity for all women whom neglect and want drive into vice; and for the many men and women whom poverty and evil associations tempt into lying, drunkenness, theft, and murder; we call upon all to set aside their vanities, to rise above greed of class and prejudice of birth, and, in the spirit of wisdom and love, with energy and singleness of mind, to look these terrible evils in the face, to trace their causes, and to apply their cure.

The result of our analysis is that the discarding of supernaturalism does not involve the discarding of the form of prayer and does not deprive us of its immeasurable benefits — inward, social, and even material. Accordingly, as regards Christian prayer, the question for religious reformers is not so much one of revising as of reinterpreting. Hereafter when we pray, if we use the old words, we must recall definitely to mind what factors in moral experience are involved. When we remember our own denotation of the terms used, the form in which the thought is cast assumes a fresh and deeper meaning.

CHAPTER XIV

CHRISTIANITY PLUS SCIENCE

1. *New Grounds for Millennial Hope*

CHRISTIANITY, as soon as it has become transfused with the spirit and transformed by the method of modern science, will bring about the Millennium.

This statement is suggested by a sentence of Ferdinand Lassalle to the effect that the millennium will be born from the union of science and social democracy. Lassalle no doubt had in mind the same confluence of historic tendencies as I have; but to me the earthly state of bliss which modern socialists dream of is the same as that which entranced the early Christians. The difference is not in the vision, but in the means for its actualization. If the two dreams are identical, the refusal both of social democracy and of Christianity to recognize that identity must have been an injury to each and to the whole world. In my judgment the socialism of Lassalle and Marx has on this account lacked inwardness, spirituality, and idealism, and has erred in linking itself to a materialistic interpretation of history; while Christianity is still groping ineffectually above the clouds, instead of reconstructing the economic and political life of nations. But if once Christianity be wedded to science, the dynamic of the spirit will forthwith devise, build, and set in operation the mechanism of the coöperative commonwealth.

I here define Christianity by what Christians of all denominations would assent to as its essence — the historic movement emanating from the personality of Jesus Christ and making for the establishment of a reign of personal and social justice and purity throughout the earth. This is Christianity. Its theory and dogma are but devices of the intellect to interpret and justify it to the understanding of man, but its reality is a living tendency in society emanating from the historic Jesus Christ and growing organically in the world. It is to be interpreted by the end it has in view, and no one can deny that its end is the triumph of social justice on earth.

My dictum, then, means that when once this spiritual organism of Christ's Church discards supernaturalistic interests and adopts the method, spirit, and results of science as dictating the means and the policy towards the advancement of social justice on earth, its Kingdom of God will come and come quickly. If the natural and human means be discovered which would establish social justice and personal purity on earth, and if they be applied, it is inconceivable that social justice and personal purity would not come. It is a tautological proposition to which we have reduced the statement; but, being tautological, it is self-evident. The only question remaining is whether it be possible to discover the human and natural means towards the establishment of the Kingdom of Heaven. To many a mind the decision of this question settles forever for the human heart the alternative between despair and life abundant. If we cannot discover and apply the natural and human means to the end of Christ's Kingdom, that Kingdom is worse than a phantom, and it were better for us Christians had we never been born.

2. *The History of the Millennial Hope*

The old-fashioned expectation of a Millennium, being based on a belief in supernatural intervention, was on that account the most unfounded of human delusions;

but, notwithstanding, it was the sanest, sweetest, truest, humanest bent which the moral idealism of man has ever taken. In any case, it began in the third century after Christ to be replaced by a hope of such an existence in a life after death and on another scene than the surface of this planet. But never was there such a fall of man from hope and insight. When the expectation of a second coming of a supernatural founder of the kingdom of righteousness was abandoned and the human heart turned for consolation to the thought of another world, it was the setting in of an agelong night. Since then only for the briefest periods and among small groups has the millennial passion burst forth into flame, but each time it has been quickly stamped out by the powers that be, as if it were the very fire of hell.

Savonarola was a prophet not of a life after death in another world, but of the life on earth in his own time and in Florence itself. But he paid speedily the price for having returned to the millennial hope of Christ and his immediate followers.

Martin Luther after his revolt from Rome was for a time guided by the vision of an earthly Kingdom of God. And he continued to follow this gleam until the peasants, taking fire of hope from him, meant in deadly earnest to end the economic iniquities of the laws of property which had reduced them to abject poverty. Then Luther himself denied Christ and sided with the princes against the peasants. It required, however, the pouring out of the blood of two hundred thousand peasant martyrs to quench the spark in them which he himself had kindled. Before Martin Luther, the millennial hope had lighted up all England for a time. Wiclif and the Lollards were its prophets, but the powers-that-be smothered out the flame. The result was that England during the fifteenth century was intellectually, morally, and as regards joy of the spirit, but a nation of ashes.

Again, the hope of a redeemed earth gained strength enough to flame forth in the moving times of Charles I. The Fifth-Monarchy men under the Protectorate were millennial, but on that account were suppressed as mad. Sir Isaac Newton believed in the Millennium. In the next century Charles Wesley was millennial — that is, despite all his supernaturalism, his hope was for this world, for the poor, for England in his own day.

It was the heat of the millennial passion which in 1789 melted to ruin the ancient *régime* of France. Its fire-flakes were being wafted from across the Channel to English soil, when Burke extinguished them with the floods of his eloquence. It was fanned into flame again, however, in 1849 among the Chartists; and only the Iron Duke could stamp it out by military threat. Yet once more in the eighties in England the millennial hope reappeared — now not so much in the form of heat as of a light diffused throughout all classes of the community. Not only were the poor dockers of London on tiptoe of expectancy of a human time coming for them, not only did the lowest classes of labourers and even of women wage-earners begin to organize their claims for justice, but the towns of England at last received a form of self-government which brought civic idealism from the clouds of dreamland to the solid ground of practical politics. Quickly, however, the forces of reaction set in, so that the last decade of the nineteenth century showed the priests of supernaturalism, the princes of unscrupulous capitalism, and the soldiers of imperial greed more powerfully organized and shameless in England than they had been for seventy years.

America was conceived of millennial faith, and by that same faith she freed the black slaves.

Except for these brief moments, the trend of organized Christianity until the last ten years has been away from a mundane heaven. The authority of teachers and preachers of religion has been used to direct the attention of the masses to a life after death, to find there the consolations for the wrongs suffered here. Even Victor Hugo commended the thought of heaven after death as the only possible palliative to the poor. Within church organizations and from pulpits it was taught to be a heinous heresy to doubt the existence of a life after death. Nor was any other evidence of total depravity required than a lack of interest in that other world. And even to-day scarcely one Christian in a thousand is aware that all this interest is not only unchristian, but antichristian, if we take the personality and thought of Christ as the standard. The New Testament, despite all the supernaturalism of its writers, is from beginning to end millennial; that is, its heaven is one the scene of which is to be earth, the centre of which is the very city from which Christianity emanated, and the time of the beginning of which was their own generation.

The great joy which Christ communicated to the poor who listened to him and whom he touched was the millennial thrill. It was the expectation of the quick coming of justice, love, and the outward health and security which these engender, that excited the first Christians to an ecstasy of self-sacrifice. The Book of Revelation, which is typical and is an authentic document of the sentiments within thirty or forty years after Christ's death of those who had known him personally, is a revelation not at all of another world or of the individual soul after death in its relation to its maker, but of nations here on earth and of a state which was to supersede the organized power of Rome. "And I saw a new heaven and a new earth. . . . And I saw the holy city. . . . And the gates of it shall not be shut at all by day: for there shall be no night there. And they shall bring the glory and honour of the nations into it. And there shall in no wise enter into it any thing that defileth, neither whatsoever worketh abomination or maketh a lie."

To be millennial is to be Christian; whether the forces by which the Millennium is to be ushered in are believed to be human and natural or spiritistic is wholly beside the point. Whether God is to be regarded as a personal agent outside of the spiritual organism of human society, or as the upward gaze, the passionate self-sacrifice in the hearts of men for the establishment of the kingdom, is not of the essence of the message of Christ; all of his language can be interpreted humanistically, and has thus more meaning than if taken literally in the sense of the supernaturalists. The mark of the Christian was his absolute faith in and his restless desire to hasten the coming of the Kingdom, the vision of which had smitten his soul.

We thus see that throughout the Christian era all the periods of millennial enthusiasm have been brief; but they have been the only periods of creative energy, of prophetic originality and of magnificent and ecstatic self-sacrifice.

If we direct our gaze back to Judaism, we discover the same mental phenomenon. The great prophets were millennial in their hope. Indeed, the ordinary Christian, with his spiritual boast of his other-worldliness as the very essence of true religion, looks down upon the Jews not only of ancient times, but even of to-day, because the Jews have preserved as the essence of Judaism the millennial expectation. No oppression, no insult, no contempt, no ostracism could extinguish the divine spark at the heart of the Jew. The only question to-day is whether liberty, social recognition, flattery, titles, riches untold may not kill out what persecution secretly sustained. If so, with the ending of the millennial hope Judaism will cease to be a factor or even a fact in the world. But if the Jew has self-respect enough to withstand the seductions of prosperity, his ancient hope will burst forth anew and organize itself into one mighty flame and again be a light to the whole world, while incidentally disclosing a way to the reëstablishment of the Jews in Palestine.

3. *The False Basis of the Old Hope*

Yet, as I have said, the old-fashioned expectation of a Millennium, being based on a belief in supernatural intervention, was not well founded. Even if it had never been extinguished by hostile powers and interests, it would nevertheless have failed utterly. The old millennial hope bore in itself the germ of its own defeat. Had it been encouraged and favoured, it would have transformed the very kingdom it established into anarchy, riot, violence, and bloodshed. No supernatural redeemer ever did appear on the clouds in glory; nor could he have come; nor would it have been well had he come. There must not be a personal agent outside the spiritual organism of society to establish the Kingdom of God on Earth. If such a deliverer came, it would be our duty to reject him. The very essence of our manhood is at stake. Man must have no kingdom which he himself has not wrought out through experience, by thought, by sovereignty over himself and mastery over nature.

The forces to which believers in the Millennium have trusted in the past for the establishment of a kingdom of righteousness were purely imaginary. Their existence was not verifiable in experience; their control and manipulation were not within human power. On this account, the hope of realizing the vision was an instance of collective insanity. It had no more substance than a sleeper's dream.

4. *A Heaven Material as well as Spiritual*

The new hope of the Millennium is like the old in that it is an expectation of a reign of justice and love throughout the nations of the earth. Both the new and the old differ from the pseudo-Christian hope of a heaven in another world after death, in that they include our material, physical well-being, health, wealth, leisure, and all the manifold richness and beauty of the life of the senses, as well as the perfections of the inward and spiritual nature. It is true that in the New Testament there was an intense and profound inwardness, but always with the full confidence that if the behests of the Spirit were fulfilled, all other blessings should be added. It is true that St. Paul believed, at least at times, in a material resurrection of the bodies of the dead. But this was only to be a momentary catastrophe; and after it the living would go on living; and, so far as one can gather, the whole implication is that human beings would go on propagating after their own kind in the natural way. Furthermore, St. Paul's belief in the immortality of the individual soul never for a moment diverted him away from the earth and the nations of the earth and their future as the goal of all his effort. The millennial hope anticipates, then, a material heaven as well as a heaven reigning within the spirit; and this hope of a material heaven on earth was a part of the original Christianity, as it is of Christianity whenever it reappears as it was in Christ.

5. *The Sanity and Purity of the New Hope*

But while the new millennial hope is infinitely nearer to the old than either is to the counterfeit Christianity which has usurped Christ's organization, the new hope is as sane as the old was insane. Since the advent of science and the awakening of democracy through the blending of Science and Christianity, a man who does not accept the Millennium proves himself at least bad, if not mad. Only prejudice of pride, of greed, of ascendency over others, of class interests, of self-deification, of contempt for the poor and for women can blind a man to the well-nigh infinite resources which the Church of Christ would gain were she to accept the discoveries and inventions of Science and use them and trust to them instead of trusting to miracles, to prayers to invisible spirits, and to the guidance of supernatural agents.

The great material wealth of the modern world has hitherto been associated with pride, greed, selfish ambition, excess, and self-indulgence. But this is wholly because the wealth has accumulated in the hands of a few and at the expense of the many. The wealth, were it co-operatively acquired and justly distributed, would in itself be perfectly right and good and its enjoyment innocent and humane. But, more than this, wealth so produced and distributed would itself favour spirituality, inwardness of life, the love of righteousness, and the readiness to die for it. For then the material wealth and all its blessings would themselves, being just and fair and a result of justice and fairness, illustrate the priority and necessity of the inner spiritual life. It is only wealth unshared that is unholy. But even then it requires little discrimination to see that the selfishness and not the wealth is really the polluted and the polluting thing. We must remember that even the Kingdom of Heaven can only be unlocked by a key of gold. But when the whole community, when the Church herself, holds the key and is ready to open the Kingdom even to the least of these, gold itself will become the symbol of righteousness.

There is no more anti-social teaching than that which glorifies poverty and the renunciation of the physical means of health, strength, comfort, and leisure. It is a self-deception of the rich which makes them imagine that the poor are as happy as those who have security of necessities and a fair share of comforts and opportunities, of education, travel, art, and every other blessing which wealth can give to those who know how to use it aright. Let the poor resent with their whole souls' indignation the teaching of resignation to a poverty which compels them to give nine-tenths of all their attention to the means of a livelihood, while allowing them no leisure to live. When the Church discards her supernaturalism and adopts natural means for the redemption of the world from sin and misery, she will adopt an ideal not of poverty, but of wealth.

There is a powerful argument for a naturalistic millennial hope in the fact that a seemingly slight change in outward conditions or in the social atmosphere of a community may produce well-nigh infinite differences in inward happiness and moral character. In this respect human nature is analogous to vegetable life. Think what a very slight increase of temperature in April over the average warmth of March is necessary in order to produce all the difference in the plant world between an appearance of death and a manifestation of life. Let there be an average increase of warmth of from ten to fifteen degrees, and every seed and branch will burst forth into the splendour of bloom. Precisely parallel is it with mankind. Hitherto for the great masses of the people it has always been winter. Whoever has lived among the working-classes knows that so slight a change for the better as an increase of a few dollars a week in wages throughout all trades makes all the difference to the home life, to the children, in education, in self-respect, in respectability, that April showers and April sunshine make to plant life as compared with March winds and the shorter daylight of winter. A decrease of working hours from fourteen to ten is a change like that from February to June. Suppose the Church transferred all her interest in a life after death to the life before death, from a society of unembodied spirits to the society of us spirits who are dependent for self-realization upon the health and strength of our bodies. Suppose the first object in the Church's policy of human redemption were to shorten the hours of work of all wage earners to the possible minimum, and to raise all wages to the possible maximum. Would it not be "kingdom come" not only in freedom from disease, but in innocence of life, in sympathy, love, and the pursuit of truth and beauty for their own sake?

There is no shadow of ground for doubting that natural means can be discovered for curing the chief maladies of life, in the same way — to take a special instance — that scientific men have discovered the causes and devised a prevention of the blight of the grape-vines of France. Possibly the very method and the causes of the social evils will be found to be analogous. Parasites pierced the roots of the French vines; roots with a slightly thicker bark were introduced; the result was that the parasites could no longer feed upon the vines; and the parasites died. Which things are an allegory.

6. *Children born Unbiassed*

Another argument for a new millennial enthusiasm lies in a fact which for a supernaturalistic scheme had no significance. The fact to which I refer is that the individual men and women of the world at any given time are absolutely removed from it after a period seldom longer than fourscore years, and that the places of the old are taken by new individuals, who come into the

s

world completely ignorant of its traditions, its intrigues, its wrongs and sufferings, and practically innocent. The new-born babe may, it is true, come with predispositions which may tempt it to active injustice and unsocial self-indulgence. But, as we have just been pointing out, the very same nature which certain circumstances would incite to injustice and self-indulgence will, if another set of circumstances act as stimuli, be quickened along lines of humane consideration for others and heroic self-control. One cannot, therefore, argue from any degree of obliquity and weakness which human nature has exhibited under past circumstances of life, that human nature would exhibit the same characteristics if differently played upon from the moment of birth. Those who are discouraged from millennial hope on the basis that human nature is corrupt are, therefore, foolish and thoughtless. The question is whether the corruption of human nature must under any circumstances whatever manifest itself. Would the men who now for the most part yield to excess in drinking intoxicants show this same weakness if for a whole generation the hours of all work were shortened, wages increased, every human being compelled to earn his own living by his labour, and no financial profit allowed to any individual or company, or even to the State itself, from the manufacture and sale of intoxicating drinks? Is drunkenness a sign of the depravity of human nature or a proof of defect in the social and economic environment?

Or take another type of moral irregularities. Suppose men had not ascendency over women by being the exclusive breadwinners, but that women had equal opportunities and were equally incited with men to earn a living and to pursue a career, and that both men and women were made by their teachers fully aware of the social and physiological significance of sex life. Would the horrors that now exist continue? Imagine, then, that all the children in the nation, from the moment they were born, came under the influence of an environment radically changed — as it would be possible even now to change it within a decade, if only the Christian Church were converted to a belief in purely human and natural means of redemption. Then it would seize upon all the means at hand, instead of continuing its colossally time-absorbing and emotion-draining system of intercession with super-human agencies.

I have said that children are born without traditional prejudices; but what does this mean for a humanistic scheme of redemption? It means that children learn from others class distinctions, pride of birth, contempt for women and for persons of other colour and of other nationalities. No child has any such prejudices until these are inculcated by others. Every child is absolutely and thoroughly democratic. No boy naturally and until told counts himself superior to womankind. Free a child from the corrupting contact with these ideas, illustrate in his presence principles of liberty, equality, and fraternity, and there would be nothing in his nature or experience that would ever throw itself against such principles.

7. *Science, Wealth, and Religion*

A scientific religion would be something new. There never has been a religion hitherto which was naturalistic. Yet it would be only relatively, not absolutely, new. It would not be without historic roots. It would be new only as Christianity itself was new, which had been growing in the heart of Judaism for four centuries. It would be new only in the sense in which the religion of the Reformation was new. It would be a child of history and the legitimate heir of all the ages. Its novelty would consist in its arising out of the confluence of streams of tendency which hitherto had been flowing in separate channels. Its novelty would further consist in its arising out of the awakening self-consciousness of a class which hitherto had not had the education or the intelligence or even the leisure to think for itself and to act as a class. Science, so long as its discoveries and inventions were monopolized in the interests of the leisured and rich, did not become a religion; for those classes had already transformed historic institutions into an instrument of their own supremacy and had interpreted Christian principles in a light favourable to their own interests. It is this illicit union of inventive science with class interest that has begotten the monster of modern competitive industry. Once remove Science from private capitalism and join it to Christ and the historic tendency which emanated from him, and there will be a religion new in resources, social philosophy, and cosmic theory, but not new in the direction of hope or in ethical standards.

If I mistake not the lesson of our times, it would be as foolish now not to expect the quick coming of the kingdom of righteousness as in Christ's day it was idle to look for it. The application of science in every direction shortens not only space, but time. By scientific inventions, things can often be done in a day which used to take a year, and in a year which would have taken ages. Thousands of things which never could have been done at all because they could not be done rapidly are now attainable, and are attained. The shortening of time is one of the most important of all conditions in bringing achievements within human reach. Nor is it possible to find any ground for the belief that scientific methods applied to moral and spiritual culture would not be proportionately more rapid than the pre-scientific methods of the old religious discipline.

8. *How Long?*

I am well aware that many scout the idea of the speedy setting aside of institutions which have lasted for thousands of years and the quick liberating and educating of classes of society which have remained in ignorant serfdom from the beginning. That most brilliant defender of government by the privileged few, Mr. Walter Bagehot, somewhere ridicules the notion prevalent among reformers that "in a little while — perhaps ten years or so — all human beings might without extraordinary appliances be brought to the same level." And he adds that of late our perceptions have been sharpened as to the gradual and slow nature of progress. We realize, he says, the tedium of history, and the painfulness of results. Only a few, he points out, have advanced and participated in modern civilization.

We have [he says] in a great community like England crowds of people scarcely more civilized than the majority of two thousand years ago. . . . Those who doubt should go into their own kitchens. Let an accomplished man try what seems to him most obvious . . . in intellectual matters upon the housemaid and the footman, and he will find . . . his audience think him mad. . . . Great communities are like great mountains — they have in them the primary, secondary, and tertiary strata of progress; the characteristics of the lower regions resemble the life of old times rather than the present life of the higher regions. And a philosophy which does not . . . continually emphasize the palpable differences . . . will be a theory essentially misleading, because it will lead men to expect what does not exist, and not to anticipate what they will find.

Here is the opinion of that upper world in which Mr. Bagehot evidently lived and moved and had his being — so far as it has any opinion at all. It is the judgment of the elevated classes of society when they attempt to gaze down from the giddy heights of the drawing-room to the servants' hall in the basement. It is also the philosophy of many upper-class economists, calculators, and sophists.

Now the differences between the habits and conditions of the dwellers in our lower regions and those in the higher strata of society are not exaggerated by Mr. Bagehot. The only point of dispute relates to the time which it might take to raise the masses into that mental and social self-fulfilment characteristic of the upper classes. I maintain that under favouring circumstances, with such appliances only as are already within the reach of practical economics and politics, ten years would be time enough to abolish laws and customs which have lasted two thousand years, and to establish on a firm foundation other systems of production and distribution of wealth and education and opportunity which would remain secure as long as they did not deserve to be superseded by systems socially more efficient. History has shown repeatedly and in many countries the power of man by conscious foresight and energy to do in ten years what unconscious, unplanned natural evolution would require two thousand years to achieve. As regards the appliances at hand which could work such changes, they are extraordinary, not in the sense that they are not thoroughly understood and accessible, but in the sense that hitherto they have been monopolized by the few in their own interests. Multitudes of blessings which now are exclusively within reach only of thousands could, almost with no perceptible increase of cost, be dispensed to millions. We live in an age of duplicators, mimeographs, linotype machines, and rotary presses. These are analogous to many devices for the dissemination, with enormous decrease of cost, of countless opportunities.

Mr. Bagehot forgets that the millions of individuals who to-day live under an oppressive system two thousand years old, came themselves, as I emphasized above, fresh into the world only twenty or fifty years ago; and so recently as at their birth they were altogether human in shape, human in promise, and human in their ability to respond sensitively to whatever environment might close in upon them. When once it had closed in they were soon fixed — doomed. So it is that an accomplished man need only descend to his kitchen and try intellectual matters upon the housemaid and the footman to find that great communities heap great mountains on human beings the instant they are born. Furthermore, even the mountainous weight superimposed upon them does not quite crush out the life. It has been intelligent and rational self-abnegation which has made the poor submissive; they have seen as plainly as day that it was altogether an impossibility for them as individuals to rise. But we are now witnessing the growth of a realizing sense among the poor that what they cannot accomplish as individuals they may by combination. The working classes in more countries than one know that if they combine they can in a decade pulverize structures as old as the Pyramids, and bigger.

The truth is, Mr. Bagehot's view as to the stability of upper-class distinctions and as to the long, long time it will take to render human the lower strata of society is altogether superficial, pedantic, and mechanical. Human beings, at the bottom even of Mr. Bagehot's England, are not as yet by any means exhausted centres of spiritual and social power. They still think, aspire, renounce, suffer, and wait. In the highest things it is quite possible that the housemaid and the footman are nearer the insight of the Founder of the Kingdom of Heaven than is the accomplished man who thinks it will take them countless ages to reach to the moral and intellectual standard of the higher regions of present-day society. Upper-class men lack sympathetic imagination, or they would see that their theories are unscientific as well as inhuman. They now fail to detect so patent a fact as that which Lowell depicted.

Thrones and altars are built on the bodies and souls of living men. We hear bitter cries under the very foundation-stones; we mark great fissures that rend the walls and open wider as the living foundations heave and sigh. Surely in ten years it will be possible for Christianity plus Science to lift the maid and the footman a little higher than the drawing-room of to-day? Whatever height one man has reached to-day, although it has taken ten thousand years for the achievement, may easily be accessible in ten years to every man and woman in the nation. Discoveries known only to the finder one day may be the possession of the whole intellectual world the next, and of every schoolboy the following year. One invention, the secret of one man to-day, may revolutionize the practice of ten thousand years in one year, and does so.

When considered from the point of view of psychology, the permanence of the differences of education, taste, and capacity in the various social strata is seen to depend almost wholly upon the unconsciousness of the masses to-day as to their own power and opportunity. Until a century ago, the masses of no nation could read or write. Now that they can and do both read and write, and that literature in their interests is being systematically circulated among them, it would seem no difficult feat, should a few set about the task, to wake them up fully to their responsibilities and privileges. There is no reason for not hoping for what at first thought seems the most unlikely of all occurrences — the conversion of the priests and preachers of Christianity to the spirit, method, and results of Science and to her mastery over nature as the legitimate and rightful means in hastening the coming of the Kingdom of Heaven.

If Mr. Bagehot intends to imply that the inborn brain power of members of the lower classes of society is as far behind that of the upper classes as was the brain power of all men two thousand years ago, the answer is that the brain capacity of people of the same race two thousand years ago was, for all we know, in no wise inferior to brain-power to-day. There has been no evolution of the stock of the upper classes as distinct from the stock of the lower classes, and there has been no evolution of the stock of the race in two thousand years, or apparently in ten thousand. So it is fairer to Mr. Bagehot to assume, as he does not say, that the inferiority he attributes to the working-classes is not at all that of congenital capacity, but of arrested development due to adverse environment.

9. *The Religion of Eugenics*

This question of native power and capacity leads us to another aspect in which Christianity plus Science will be able to do mightier works than ever did Christianity plus Supernaturalism. The whole knowledge of our day, especially that of plant and animal life, leads to the belief that we can not only transform man's environment so that it shall be favourable to whatever powers the individual has, but that we may develop the stock of the race itself. Man's artificial selection and control of the stock from which plants and animals spring, and his gradually increasing knowledge of the laws, both qualitative and quantitative, which heredity reveals, together with our new sense of the necessity of improving the human stock, point to the prevention of the practice of bringing undesirable human beings into the world. Persons not fit to propagate the species will either voluntarily abstain from doing so, or will be forced by public opinion to abstain. On the other hand, when once the situation is laid bare to the imaginations of men, those who could transmit qualities desired of the nation will have large families by personal preference, or will be moved by public opinion to render such service to the nation. If not in our day, there is reason to believe that in the course of a century of such investigation and reflection as have taken place during the last decade a knowledge will be attained which will guide us in these matters. Already we know that families distinguished for sobriety, intelligence, integrity, and sympathy transmit such qualities to offspring, and that persons descended on both sides from what is recognized as excellent stock are more capable than others of serving the nation well.

Imagine now that all the priests and preachers of America, adding Science to Christianity, should transform it into a Religion of Eugenics, and — never once dogmatizing beyond the tentative results and theories of observers — should preach the duties of motherhood and fatherhood as the foremost responsibility of woman and man. What a revolution, what a new strengthening of the foundations of the nation! Knowledge of heredity inevitably would direct the choice of human beings in the selection of mates. Those who know most of the psychology of sex know that there is no instinct in human nature more susceptible to domination by ideational forces than that which attracts the sexes. Thus the successors of Christ in the organization for the founding of the Kingdom of Heaven, besides the new mastery of environment, will have also the new mastery of man over his own offspring. Even the numbers of the population of any nation are in the control of the religious teachers and educators; the quantity as well as the quality of human beings will henceforth be under the Providence of the nation, the State, the Church of Christ.

CHAPTER XV

1. *Church Services to express the Democratic Faith*

NOBODY seems to deny the failure of the Christian churches to attract to themselves the masses of the people. The outstanding fact to-day of gloomiest import is not so much the breaking up of the Christian community into mutually antagonistic sects as the division of the nation into those who have some sort of religion and those who have none — at least none that is articulate and organized.

All America is divided into two classes — those who have only their labour and self-respect to live by, and those who, owning land and capital, control the labour of others. The interests and sentiments of these two distinct sections of the community are not only different, but mutually repellent. The class war is on; and agitators are inciting to class hatred. Now the churches have hitherto appealed to the self-respect and self-satisfaction of those who possess, or expect to possess, land and capital. In other words, the churches have appealed to the class that support them financially; and they who pay the piper of religion call the tune. That tune is discordant to the ear of the intelligent proletariat. Those, accordingly, who have only their labour and their self-respect to live by are outside the churches. They have no organization, no recognized preachers of religion who appeal to their self-consciousness and their craving for self-realization.

The inability of the churches to attract the working people has seemed of late deeply to alarm and set musing the professional leaders of religion. But these seem wholly incapable of detecting that peculiarity in themselves and in their equipment which is the cause of their inability to draw the masses. They are conscious of no obliquity in their own hearts; they want to do good to the wage-earning classes. In our day they not only desire to save souls, but to rescue the masses from poverty. One notes how often they enjoin thrift upon the very poor. They have not realized that however pure their hearts, their intellectual outlook is wholly inadequate and has become the cause of the churches' shame.

The whole tradition of preachers for centuries has taught them to care very much for purity of heart and almost not at all for intellectual grip of present facts. It is this one-sided tradition which has led them on a false scent in seeking out the causes of the religious apathy of the masses.

When the spirit of social democracy enters into the heart of the preacher and the method of modern science becomes his habit of mind, his eyes will be opened. He will see the inadequacy of the faith he has been preaching, and he will begin not only to present that view of life and the universe which modern science and critical philosophy have begun to take, but he will turn back also to that kind of economic teaching which first rang forth from the lips of John Ball in England in the fourteenth century: —

Good people, things will never go well in England so long as goods be not in common, and so long as there be villeins and gentlemen. By what right are they whom we call lords greater folk than we? On what grounds have they deserved it? Why do they hold us in serfage? If we all come of the same father and mother, of Adam and Eve, how can they say or prove that they are better than we, if it be not that they make us gain for them by our toil what they spend in their pride? They are clothed in velvet, and warm in their furs and their ermines, while we are covered with rags. They have wine and spices and fair bread; and we oat-cake and straw, and water to drink. They have leisure and fine houses; we have pain and labour, the rain and the wind in the fields. While it is of us and of our toil that these men hold their state.

The ruling classes of his day thought John Ball mad; and the rich parishioners of our time will either leave the churches or dismiss the preachers of social democracy.

In another chapter I point out that the preaching of the twentieth century is often ahead of the teaching embodied in our traditional forms and ceremonies. I there have in mind not social democracy, but only the methods, spirit, and results of critical philosophy. It is equally true, however, from the point of view of democracy. Our present-day preaching is deplorable enough, but our old-fashioned rituals are abject. Our prayers, extemporaneous or written, as well as our hymns, anthems, and litanies, give the lie direct to the democratic faith, namely, that salvation, spiritual as well as physical, can come only by the intelligent enterprise of the whole people. Our hymns, anthems, and prayers, it is true, need not be wholly rewritten; but only because they can be freshly interpreted. Even then they will prove an inadequate expression of the new sources of human hope; original forms by the living poets of democracy must supplement them. Only a democratic ritual sung by a whole people can bring about the long-delayed fulfilment of that prophecy in the Magnificat: "He hath scattered the proud in the imagination of their hearts. He hath put down the mighty from their seat: and hath exalted the humble and meek. He hath filled the hungry with good things: and the rich He hath sent empty away."

2. Sir Henry Maine's Error about Democracy

Many critical writers of the nineteenth century protested against the association of popular enthusiasms and millennial visions with the word "democracy." They seemed to think they could dampen the ardour of democrats by pointing out that democracy is, after all, but a form of government. And how, they asked, can any one grow enthusiastic and poetic over such a thing as a mere form of government? To them, differences of government were only differences of machinery and routine. This was the attitude taken by Sir Henry Maine, in his book on "Popular Government," where he devotes a whole chapter to the attempt to eradicate enthusiasm from the breasts of democrats. How can any sane man, he argues, wax enthusiastic over a mere form of government? Those who do so, he declares, must be ignorant of what they are talking about and need to be enlightened. He instances Mr. Edward Carpenter, although he concedes that Carpenter's little volume entitled "Towards Democracy" does not lack poetic force. He says: "The smallest conception of what democracy really is makes his rhapsodies about it astonishing. . . . If the author had ever heard of the dictum of John Austin or M. Scherer that 'Democracy is a form of government,' his poetic vein might have been drowned, but his mind would have been invigorated by the healthful douche of cold water." But surely Sir Henry Maine misconceives the situation. He can point to no single word or line to prove that Mr. Edward Carpenter was not fully aware that democracy is never anything but a form of government. Indeed, this is the very thought which created in Mr. Carpenter's poetic mind its ruddy glow of enthusiasm. And how could it be otherwise? How does it diminish the significance of democracy when we see that it is only a form of government? Suppose the effects of that one form upon mankind at large are stupendously beneficent? Let any one read the poems of Whitman, Lowell, Swinburne, Carpenter, and Markham, and at the same time repeat mentally that the thing these poets find so inspiring is only a form of government; he will see that the dignity and meaning of the democratic chants, instead of being diminished, are enhanced. Indeed, the wonder of it all is the greater, that a merely mechanical device of politics should be fraught with well-nigh infinite weal to mankind.

The truth is that Sir Henry Maine was overlooking the effects of the democratic form of government upon those human energies which combine to create it, and those other human energies which through it are liberated and made effective. He abstracted it from the appetites and passions, habits and fears, ideals and systems of philosophy which beget it and which it in turn begets. He regarded it simply from the point of view of social statics. He thought of it out of relation to human causes and human effects. But the real meaning even of a trick of politics can never be seen or appreciated until it is understood in relation to the purposes and imagination which conceived it and to the ends which it serves.

3. *The Dynamics of Democracy*

Poets have never praised wine on account of its chemical composition, but they have very often sung in honour of it because of its cheering effects upon the mind and body of those who drink it. Likewise they praise sunlight, not for its inherent nature as vibrations, but because of its immediate glory to the human eye and its beneficence to all living creatures. Accordingly, if one must disparage democracy because it is merely a form of government, one must likewise argue that there is nothing glorious, for instance, in a mere prism because it is only a shape of glass. Yet into that prism the light from the sun pours white, but rushes forth drenched in all the hues of the rainbow. And on this account there are some of us whose hearts leap up when we behold the prismatic splendours, and who are not ashamed to transfer the delight that we have in them to the mechanism which produces them. We maintain that it is folly to abstract the prism from the light which it refracts. Indeed, to us it is a prism by virtue of the effects it produces; its meaning and value do not exist for us otherwise.

The truth is, a merely statical study of popular government is superficiality itself. The student must move on to consider the dynamics of the institutions he is examining. Then he will be rewarded with real insight into causes and effects. And if he be capable of awe, admiration, disinterested terror, and humane sympathy, he will find himself thrilled by the mighty meanings of that which at first was merely a form of government. For in the end he will discover that democracy is a gateway opening into the City of the Light. Or, if he have no faith in the people, it will inspire him with alarm, as it did Edmund Burke, when he sounded the note of terror against the French Revolution.

That which stimulates historians, statesmen, and poets to outbursts either of terror or admiration when they regard democracy, is the unprecedented magnitude of the capacities of popular government for evil or for good. What a people, when fully awake and determined, may do through a democratic form of government is beyond all measure greater than what any king or nobility or middle class may achieve, while the masses of the people lie apathetic and passive. Nero were innocence and harmlessness itself compared to a whole nation of men and women, able to express their will through their form of government, in moments of national vanity or lust for revenge. Something like this Edmund Burke foresaw in France and feared for England. On the other hand, imagine a whole nation, each one of its members inspired with an ideal of human service and efficiency; imagine each man and woman contributing genius, skill, self-control and provident pity, and expressing character through a form of government happily devised to this end.

4. *The Inside of the Democratic Cup*

The dynamic point of view alone opens up to us the essential secret of popular government. It furnishes us the only approach to the inside of social institutions. The study of social dynamics is an investigation in human motives and outward stimuli to those motives. The forces that make and unmake institutions are men's hopes, ambitions, appetites, fears, fancies, doctrines, and faiths. It is true that these psychic forces themselves are reacted upon and modified by different institutions, but inasmuch as institutions, economic and political, do react upon men's hearts and minds and wills, they must never be regarded as merely mechanical. They are so many irritants to thinking, feeling, and willing. They must be viewed as psychic factors in the moral universe of man, and not as inert and outside facts. In studying the relation of popular government to organized religion, of social democracy to church discipline, it is especially worthy of note that this dynamic point of view — the study of motives as the cause of institutions and the study of institutions as stimuli to desires — is the one which each person always assumes when observing and estimating himself. He sees and feels himself to be a creative agent. Although he sees himself to be a creature as well as a creator, he is conscious of himself as not having been fully created as yet. He is waiting a chance to be created and is conscious within himself of adequate power. He may be fully aware that his character at any given moment is a balance of impulses in equilibrium, but to him that balance is not a finality. Even from within himself he may disturb it. He is, more-

T

over, never interested in himself as an accomplished fact, but always as a potentiality. He knows himself to be capable of responding to forces that have not yet had a chance to operate upon him. He is "moving about in worlds not realized"; and when he judges himself he includes in his selfhood what he aspires to be equally with what he has been. He takes to himself credit for what he might have done but was prevented by accident from achieving. For he knows his own secrets; and while others may mistake his actual record for a revelation of himself, he counts it rather as a concealment of what he really is. He knows well enough what other circumstances might have brought to light and life. It is as if gunpowder were conscious beforehand of what the accidental discoverer found out only after a spark touched it. Now this inward point of view in investigation and criticism is the only scientific one when the subject for consideration is oneself, another man, a nation or any institution within a nation, even a form of government. The dynamic study of social phenomena also furnishes the only standard for judging of the moral worth and the political significance both of individuals and institutions. Nor can any one doubt that the exercise of sympathetic imagination, which sees every human being as a point of creative energy, which views every one from the inside and recognizes him as a creature sensitive to stimuli from without, is the motive and original attitude of the Christian religion. There is, therefore, an identity of nature between Christianity and democracy; they both unlock the hidden and secret springs of spiritual energy within every individual breast. If this be so, however, there is a tragic irony in the tradition of the churches, which have held out longer than any other human institutions against the spirit of democracy. Religion to this day has been less touched by that spirit than any other human interest.

5. *The Religious Individualism of Professed Socialists*

But the churches must become social-democratic; or the people will see to it that they are "cast as rubbish to the void when God hath made the pile complete." The religious organizations must act on the presupposition that their whole end and essence is to develop the nation into a spiritual organism; that is, one in which every moral agent is at the same time both means and end to all the others, no one in any particular being used merely as a tool by others or by the whole, and no one becoming exclusively an end, but always serving in turn. Such a nation would be the Kingdom of Heaven — on earth.

The professed Socialists have always been blind to the identity of religion and nationality. They believe that religion is purely a private affair. But one is justified in asking them whether they know anything about the real nature of religion, or have ever carefully studied the sociological function of the churches. Have they worked out a philosophy of religion by noting its social causes and effects, do they believe in religion at all, in the way in which they believe in their economic remedies and political theories? It must never be forgotten, moreover, when the authority of present-day Socialists is cited, that their Socialism itself is still so permeated with its very opposite — philosophic Anarchy — that it is not yet half itself. Before one pays full respect to the authority of any man who calls himself a Socialist, one must give ear to detect whether it be the Socialist or the Anarchist in him that is speaking. Social reformers, furthermore, have hitherto so exclusively concentrated attention upon economic and material wealth that they have fallen into the error of imagining that physical possessions constitute the whole domain for the application of the principle of nationalization. This again proves that many so-called Socialists are half Anarchists. They relegate to Anarchy one whole half of human life, and that the better half — the higher life. A thorough social philosophy would believe in the nationalization not only of man's labour, but of man's love.

6. *Isolation fatal to Churches*

If I be right in contending that the churches of a country are to be judged as centres for the moral education of the nation, they have committed an almost fatal blunder in holding aloof from politics and economic reform. They have each shut themselves off from regenerating touch with the present-day life of the world outside their own organizations. Each denomination began with a protest against traditions which it believed to be evil; yet they are all to-day devoting the whole of their energy to the upholding of some peculiar tenet which the critical world at large regards as obsolete. Accordingly, each denomination has ceased to be a running stream of the waters of life, and has become a stagnant pool of ancient beliefs. Originally, every sect sprang from the democratic spirit; but they have all in turn, for the sake of self-preservation, guarded their doctrine jealously from the modifying influences of new thought and experience. Not a single Protestant denomination fell back, as it ought to have done, upon the authority of living reason and the progressive conscience of the nation when it threw off the authority of priestly Councils. In place of the priests it set up the Bible. It did not look for redemption, as it would if it had originated in an age like ours, to the quickening and illuminating power of the living social will. Every denomination also continued to trust to an outside and miracle-working Deity. Nothing could have been more anti-democratic and unmodern. The religious ideas of all the churches are an inheritance from times against which the modern spirit has revolted. That the churches still cling to their old traditions can only be explained by the fact that when they abandoned the ideal destiny of the nation as their own goal, they cut themselves off from the source of spiritual insight. Whatever institution severs itself from the currents of national life is foredoomed, unless perchance in the throes of some great social upheaval it again allies itself with the aims and visions of the common life.

Nothing but the isolation of each denomination from all others and from economic and political interests can explain the appalling fact that no religious sect has ever received any new revelation after the initial impulse which organized it. The only eternal revealer is the reason of a whole nation, the living conscience of an entire people. To that source of light and life no church, except at its inception, has ever appealed. No wonder, then, that the religious organizations of the nation are not in the vanguard of science and reform. No wonder that they bring no message to our day. Their religion is out of touch with modern thought in the sense that its fundamental principle is antagonistic to the motive, method, and results of modern research.

7. *Not Toleration, but Coöperation in Religion*

The various religious bodies, in accepting toleration instead of coöperation among themselves and with the world at large, have rejected the democratic principle of religion for all and by all. Yet in spiritual as in civil life, the application of this principle is the only possible method of arriving at the moral unification of a people. It is also the only way of attaining eternal and universal truth. Every denomination has thus far closed its heart in pride against the redemptive power of social democracy. It has failed wholly to see that contact with the surging and conflicting thoughts and efforts in the whole nation is necessary if it is

to keep quite sane and broadly human in its religious beliefs.
It has failed to realize that every devout person must put
himself into receptive yet alert relation with the entire
genius of the times, in order to be able by reaction to contribute his own wisdom and experience to the nation's
spiritual fund. As with each individual, so with every
religious society. As compared with the general life and
thought of the world to-day, the churches have become
morbid and dogmatic, priggish, self-satisfied, and almost
unconscious of the defects which their isolation has bred in
them.

From the point of view of social democracy, sectarianism
— the splitting off of sect from sect, and of all sects from
the nation as an organic unit of spiritual life—is a great sin.
Nor has that sin been without its inevitable punishment.
Witness the moral evils which have settled down upon
John Wesley's once vital and quickening movement because
it cut itself off, or was content to be cut off, from contact
with the historic Church. Wesley's movement during his
life was the most ethical and vital since Luther's, yet until
quite recently it went on splitting up and splitting up again
within itself, and becoming more and more aloof from the
main currents of life. And each new group of Methodists
grew proud of its own aloofness.

The glorious movement of the Society of Friends reveals
the same tragic decay from within because it also has not
remained in organized unity with the whole nation's life. At
first the Quaker movement was not only quickened by the
spirit of democratic and national unrest; it was also clearly
conscious that the democratic spirit was the Holy Ghost.
The Society of Friends, however, as an organization and as
an upholder of the simple life, has until quite recently been
dying out. As a quickener of the nation's fundamental
thoughts it is still practically dead. But concerning none
of the denominations do I speak as a prophet of evil; I

believe in the resurrection of nations, I believe in the resurrection of religious bodies; and I also believe in the resurrection of parties. There is no inherent necessity that any organized group of spiritual or social life shall ever die. It may revive after continuing to exist for generations in a state of suspended animation. But let me return to the melancholy history of one other religious denomination which began with glorious promise.

Witness the devitalization of Unitarianism. It was the only religious organization to champion human reason; yet it has scarcely been able in the last decades to preserve its earlier hold in the community. Some Unitarians themselves incline to believe that its work has already been accomplished. They think that it has sufficiently permeated with its thought all the other religious denominations to justify it in retiring from aggressive propaganda. But one must ask: Why has the Unitarian body absorbed no new light, no added strength, no fresh enthusiasm? Were there no further revelations ahead in the direction of its first philosophic discoveries? Were there no improvements possible in its methods? Could it not have become the conqueror of new worlds of principle and fact, of policy and discipline? I cannot otherwise explain the lamentable decline of Unitarianism than on the ground that it is always a fatal error to accept isolation and toleration instead of demanding full recognition and complete organic inclusion in the total religious organization of a nation.

Indeed, as one reads the history of all the denominations, from their thrilling origin to their pitiable resignation, one feels that to be content with isolation is worse than an error. It is a sign of spiritual pride. It is a proof that it has turned in some degree from social humility to self-worship. And nothing blinds the judgment like self-centred pride. It has been, therefore, not only an error, it has been a sin of the churches that they were willing to be in the nation but not of the nation. The deadening effect of this sin in the case of all the denominations has set rapidly in; in a few brief generations the strength had gone out of each of them.

8. *Debate to be an Item in Public Worship*

Social democracy in religion, as distinct from religious toleration, would subject the moral idealism of each church to incessant debate by the laity. Social democracy always means correction and reform through debate. If it entered into the churches, it would instantly begin to set up a process of reorganization. It would mean in religion what it would mean in industry — ownership and control by the living community. The ownership would be that of the powers in man and nature which make for righteousness. Social democracy in religion means the ownership and control of the instruments of disciplining character, of fostering virtue, of opening the eyes of the spirit, of training the moral judgment by bringing the attention of every man and woman and child to bear upon the great issues of life. Social democracy in religion means that the nation itself shall lead the way to spiritual salvation, to moral health, long life, and innocent gladness. Social democracy in religion means a church of the whole people, by the whole people, for the whole people — women and men alike.

When we begin to compare the principles, methods, and outlook of social democracy in religion with the forms of anti-democratic government and teaching which have prevailed among all religious bodies, we are especially struck by one peculiarity which makes the prevalent governments and doctrines of the churches harder to reform and remove than are similar customs and prejudices in any other department of life. If, for instance, we consider the existing systems of land tenure, we find that while the form of ownership is that of the few for the few at the expense of the many, nevertheless the few for whom the land is monopolized are always at least the living, and never the dead of a past generation. The monopoly is preserved in the interest of the present landlords and of their children. But if we turn to the systems of religion, we note the absolute dictation of a few persons of a past generation. The churches are to-day preserving methods that spiritually were of help in the time of Edward VI or Oliver Cromwell or Charles II or George III. All of them are upholding practices made by a few of a former generation for a generation long since dead. The Methodist churches of our day, a century and more after the death of Wesley, are still governed by his thought, and for a kind of people under a kind of conditions which no longer exist anywhere. Social democracy in religion would mean the spiritual life throughout the whole nation organized and reinterpreted year by year by all the men and women who are interested in the ideal aims of humanity, in the interest of the citizens of all future time.

Let it be clearly observed that a recognition of the claims of social democracy within the sphere of religion does not involve a committal to any specific creeds or rites. The responsibility to determine rites and doctrines must rest with the people of any given time or place. Consistent with this liberty perpetually to recast statements and adopt new principles is the whole argument of this book. I have not been pleading that my own individual convictions and tastes deserve to be adopted. I have had no more in mind than that my peculiar beliefs should be allowed a place side by side with hundreds of others in an organized coöperation of all religious bodies in the service of the nation. I have advocated religious inclusion and coöperation. I cannot see why the champions of a hundred rival creeds and forms should not work together in a national church in the same way in which men of conflicting political and economic theories work together on municipal and national councils. And there is no reason why majorities in religion should not respect minorities as majorities do in politics.

I believe that as a result of centuries of coöperative effort complete uniformity may be brought about. But variety of conviction and practice would be far better than any forcible suppression of any one's individuality. There need never be any danger that the teachings and disciplines of the past will ever again trammel the spiritual evolution of the nation. It would seem that we are on the threshold of an epoch in which religious controversy will dominate as never before. We are entering upon an era not unlike that preceding the Civil War in England in the sixteenth century. But then the leaders attempted to suppress free discussion; now the religious organizations themselves will probably invite and stimulate the fullest and freest expression of the most original opinions. For many within the churches see that honest doubt is the only way to positive faith. Inside authority, as Whitman says, must take precedence of outside authority. Private judgment will be encouraged because it is the only way for the individual to arrive at universal reason. Only if a man thinks freely can he think fully; and to think fully is to drop all eccentricity or whim or private bias. At first, if there be many minds, there will be many opinions, but after a time a consensus of opinion is inevitable if the minds be sane.

We have, I believe, already entered upon an era in which many religious leaders are ready to act upon the principle formulated by Milton, when he says: "Where there is much desire to learn, there, of necessity, will be much arguing, much writing, many opinions; for opinion in good men is but knowledge in the making." We are all coming to see with Martineau that, "A religion forbidden to improve, instead of growing upwards into statelier propor-

tions, breaks into lateral deformities as the only vent for
its vitality." Or, to return to Milton : "Truth is compared
in Scripture to a streaming fountain. If her waters flow
not in a perpetual progression, they sicken into a muddy
pool of conformity and tradition. . . . He who thinks we
are to pitch our tents here, and have attained the utmost
prospect of reformation that the mortal glass wherein we
contemplate can show us, till we come to beatific vision :
that man by this very opinion declares that he is yet
far short of the truth. . . . The light which we have
gained was given us not to be ever staring on, but by it
to discover onward things, more remote from our knowledge."

9. *The Social Psychology of Religion*

All the churches of Protestantism in their rebellion against
Rome have rejected the organic and social conception of the
church and have adopted an atomistic and individualistic
psychology of religion. They regard themselves as aggre-
gates or federations of voluntary human atoms which
come together. They count themselves as nothing more
than the arithmetical sum of their separate members.
They are instances of Rousseau's social contract ; they are
private enterprise concerns as much as any business company, into which people enter on a bargain of gain and
mutual benefit. No Protestant, historic in temper, respects
his church more than himself, or certainly not more than
he does all the members. An organic philosophy of religion tends on the other hand, so to speak, to a deification
of the church. It is the Bride of Christ. Its unifying and
quickening spirit is Christ, living and working in the world
to-day. According to the social psychology of our times, a
church is an organic unit of spiritual life, and the individual
man or woman is but a constituent part. According to
this new view, it is not so much the individual who gives

its moral power to the church as the church that quickens the individual. The general is prior to the particular in the order of a spiritual philosophy of society.

There can be no doubt that the real source of moral enthusiasm is always the general will of a group of persons in devotion to an ideal. If the Holy Ghost be interpreted as the organizing spirit of the church, the unifying will of its members, then some sort of a deification of the church would seem justifiable. The group in its unity is felt to be the indwelling Christ, the living God.

10. *A Religion teaching Self-respect*

Having set forth the vital significance of social democracy as it bears upon the church problem of our day, let me now indicate one of the chief characteristics of social-democratic religion as contrasted with what is offered to the poor in the sermons of the traditional churches. No religion can be compatible with the spirit of social democracy which does not teach self-respect as the primary religious virtue. Sacrilege has been committed against the highest in humanity by those teachers of religion who have traced to a superhuman and supernatural source everything in man that was beautiful, pure, and holy, giving man no credit for it, while they have assigned to human nature whatever was base or mean. In order to glorify their transcendent Deity, they have attempted to strip man of every vestige of self-respect, declaring that whatever emanated from his own heart was to be counted but as filthy rags. Their method of conversion was first to awaken self-loathing and self-abasement and a sense of dependence for any spiritual strength upon a power which was neither man nor nature, but which held man both soul and body in its almighty grip. So far as I am aware, no single religious denomination that has acknowledged the divinity of Jesus Christ has rejected this teaching; even George Fox the Quaker, when questioned by Oliver Cromwell, asserted that the inner light was not man's light. When Cromwell assented to the existence of the inner light, but insisted that it was natural to man, George Fox protested that it was supernatural. Thus every recognized Christian denomination has given the lie to man's higher nature, to the very essence of his selfhood, to the witness of his own conscious spirit. No wonder that the people, accepting the priest's low valuation of themselves, have fallen under the power of spiritual dictators and their allies, the princes. How deep is the infamy of the priest's wrong against human nature, we can see when we realize that even after well-nigh two centuries of growing democracy in all other spheres of human interest, religion is only now beginning to see the spiritual significance of democracy. Only now is the doctrine of God's immanence in the social conscience beginning to be preached. Only now is it realized that God is identical with the saving powers in our social humanity and with the regenerating energy of our higher selfhood.

At last we see that the perfect is the fulfilment of what is prefigured in the constitution of man, despite his wickedness and error. We see that evil is an abnormality, and contrary to the fundamental trend of the human will. It is true that evil is a part of the universe, and that therefore the universe itself, being both good and evil, may be said to be neither good nor bad. We see also that human beings are never wholly good nor wholly bad. But the good is organic, structural, and constitutional, while the bad is recognized as a foreign growth. We further find that man, in his conscious purpose and in proportion as his intelligence is awake and his experience wide, is distinctly on the side of his own constitution and against the evil that preys on him. This is true not only of individual human beings, but also of the general purpose of social life. The will of the community, when awake, always sides with the good, and sets itself to extirpate the bad. It is grossly untrue and cruel, therefore, to assign only the evil to human nature and to attribute all goodness to the inflowing of superhuman grace. This is as false as it would be to say that insanity only is natural, and that sanity is supernatural in its origin. But we know perfectly well that in proportion as a man is not sane he is not a man. Insanity is natural in him; but it is not constitutional, structural, or organic; it is something external, which obliterates the human. What could be more unpardonable than that the guides of the people should attempt to persuade men that lunacy was the inevitable condition of every mortal, except for some superhuman power, which by its own grace — that is, irrespective of man's right and desert — should communicate understanding and wisdom? Yet it is just such an unforgivable wrong, and a worse one, which traditional religion has perpetrated. What could have been more detrimental to man's spiritual insight than first to persuade him that he was blind? Indeed, there can be no doubt that the teaching has produced blindness. The idea thrown out has taken demoniacal possession and worked out its detailed effects; and then the induced blindness has seemed to substantiate and fortify the lie that induced it. I will not say that all those who have taught that goodness comes from a transcendent source of grace have been conscious deceivers; but one is justified in asserting that this doctrine arose among people in the ruling classes of society who had tasted of power and found it sweet, and were tempted to secure their privilege and prestige by teaching a philosophy favourable to their own ascendency. This doctrine sprang up as the Christian faith began to take possession of the ruling classes of the Roman Empire.

Social democracy is at last beginning to interpret itself

spiritually and ethically; it sees the majesty of its own motives. This revelation could not have come about were it not that now for more than a hundred years, in the actual struggle of class with class, the higher nature of man has been asserting and organizing itself into a mighty power for social redemption. Filled with a new sense of justice, the people have risen up and thrown off tyrants; the mountains are being brought low, and the valleys are being raised. Out of these experiences and social trends, to account for them and give them place in the philosophy of life, has sprung up the doctrine of the immanence of God, of his identity with the truly human. What zest, what clearing of the eye and steadying of the gaze, what new elasticity of tread and consecration of the human body, what a sublime sense of personal responsibility and of the dignity of every human life, become the heritage of the common people, with the throwing off of the old dogma, and the taking to heart of the new philosophy of religion! After a generation has been reared on the doctrine that one's deeper self is God, there will be no drunkards, no prostitutes nor suicides, none driven to despair and madness by the meaninglessness of life. After a generation has been bred to the teaching of the religion of self-respect, there will be no outcast class, no army of the unemployed, no children born of self-indulgence. The old-fashioned teaching was a direct disparagement to righteous conduct, to moral originality, and to enthusiasm. To teach men that it was impossible to do right except as a superhuman power came into them and communicated its energy was equivalent to discouraging them from exercising the power they possessed and turning to their neighbours for support.

We now see that the grace which was attributed to some being outside of organized society really issued from the stored-up virtue of the social life about them, and the creative energy latent within them. But not to see this, not to have realized that men do good as naturally as they open their eyes, was to discourage them and to coerce them into intellectual conformity and economic submission.

When the churches become democratic, they will bring about such a revival of religion as the world has not known since the founding of Christianity. And this religion will in turn enlighten and strengthen democracy in economic and political life. The cause of social justice has only needed the backing of organized religion in order to sweep away the entrenched iniquity of ages. For that iniquity, although the support it received was disguised, has hitherto been upheld and sustained by the churches. When social democracy enters the domain of religious life, it will seize the churches, and will convert them from defences of private monopoly in land and capital into strongholds of economic equality.

PART III

CHRISTIANITY TO BE EXPRESSED IN SCIENTIFIC LANGUAGE AND DEMO-CRATIC SYMBOL

PART III

CHAPTER XVI

THE NEED OF A NEW MANUAL OF NATIONAL WORSHIP

1. *For the Storage and Transmission of National Idealism*

My proposition is that all the various religious denominations should so transform their respective services as to make them instruments of modern hope and modern thought and modern faith. What we need is a manual of religious worship that will serve for the social storage and transmission of modern ethical humanism.

It may seem to some preposterous that a mere manual of new church services could have any such effects as I anticipate. But it can appear so only to those who have overlooked the importance of other similar devices in religion and of machinery in other spheres of human enterprise. We are apt to forget that preaching is a mechanical device; yet the invention of it secured the spread of Christianity throughout the Western world. We are liable to forget that the keeping of one day in seven sacred to the moral interests of a nation is a mechanical device of a very evident order; yet it was the means of preserving Judaism for many centuries even after the Jewish nation had lost its independence. It must be remembered that social meetings at stated intervals for the worship of a nation's God are nothing but a tool shaped and used for certain ends. Yet that tool has been the means of accomplishing those ends. It should further be remembered that these purely mechanical, natural devices of human ingenuity are the means by which supernatural religions have been perpetuated. Their efficiency is beyond all question. Who, therefore, can doubt that these same means, if used consciously to the end of national ethical idealism, would prove equally efficacious?

Now, one of the many mechanical instruments for the promulgation of religious ideas is this which I have been advocating — a manual of services fitted to a nation's present needs — but it is an instrument which has been almost forgotten. Nobody could fail to see that any new religious movement must naturally resort to preaching as a method of propaganda; and, in fact, such a method is adopted. Nor do many persons question the rightness and appropriateness of using one day of rest in seven as the most opportune time for the oral spread of new ideas. But a manual of religious rites and ceremonies has been wholly discarded by those who have rejected supernaturalism. They seem to have imagined that such a thing is in its very nature fit only to be an instrument for the propagation of spiritism. They refuse to use it because it is associated too unpleasantly in their minds with the beliefs which they have outgrown. The result is a predicament of the gravest nature.

How can the new moral idealism be spread and become a mighty national asset; how can it change from an exclusive philosophy of the few into an energizing religion of the whole nation, if it allows the enemies of science and democracy to hold a monopoly of the chief mechanical means of communicating from one man to another religious principles, sentiments, and inward meanings? Formulæ, rites, and ceremonies used by a social group constitute that chief mechanical means.

If any one wishes to know why humanitarian freethought has scarcely made any progress in two thousand years as an organizing, nation-building force, let him not imagine that it is because it is inherently negative, disruptive, or destructive. Let him be well assured that it is because freethinkers have in the past never realized the supreme importance of concreting their humanistic idealism into a cult; while on the other hand the champions of super-naturalistic religion have fully appreciated the necessity for such devices. In the past, rationalistic idealism has always been individualistic and non-æsthetic. It has always undervalued the debt which original minds owe to the common mind about them. It has always de-preciated the artistic, poetic, and symbolic way of com-municating ideas. It has always overestimated the independent resources of the individual — especially of his reasoning powers. We have no evidence of the failure of a rationalistic idealism which was at the same time social in spirit and symbolical in its methods of presentation. Accordingly, we are justified in thinking that psychological socialism and ritualistic methods of propaganda would prove as powerful in the spread of ethical realism as they have been in the perpetuation of supernaturalism. We have, therefore, reason to believe that whoever prepares a book of common humanistic devotion, adequate for a scientific and democratic age, will do for the spread of humanistic religion such a service as Marconi or Edison or Lister or Pasteur has done for trade, commerce, and medical and sanitary art. Until the new idealism possesses its own manual of religious ritual, it cannot communicate effectively its deeper thought and purpose. The moment, however, it has invented such a means of communication, it would seem inevitable that a rapid moral and intellectual advancement of man must at last take place, equal in speed and in beneficence to the material advancement which followed during the last century in the wake of scientific inventions. Only the instrument for the storage and transmission of the new idealism has been lacking.

2. *Services as compared with Sermons*

If my contention for the unique value of a humanistic book of religious services be opposed on the ground that simple informal preaching of naturalistic moral idealism would be far more effective and more congenial to enlightened men, a complete answer is ready at hand. Preaching presupposes preachers. But the great lack is an instrument to educate the majority of preachers. A small minority could prepare a manual, which the less gifted could adopt. Preaching presupposes also a wealthy and powerful organization to support and direct these preachers. But with a millionth part of the wealth required to do this, a suitable manual of ethical services could be printed and placed on sale in every town throughout the English-speaking world. Then, without any elaborate organization or great expense, any group of sympathizers anywhere could organize themselves and hold regular meetings where the services could be practised. A meeting using the hymns, canticles, selections from literature, and statements of principle contained in such a manual could create within itself an atmosphere of moral faith and enthusiasm which would quicken into new life every one who participated in it. If such a manual also contained marriage and funeral services, it would make it possible immediately to conduct wedding and burial rites.

Nothing has more astonished me than the actual experience of this one great difference between the preaching of a sermon and the celebration of a ceremony. I have often regretted as a preacher my inability to be in a hundred places at once. This inability limited each sermon to its one utterance or to a wearisomely slow repetition week after week. But having twenty years ago elaborated and conducted an ethical marriage ceremony, I was immediately invited to lend copies of it to various persons throughout England, and they reported to me that all who were present where it was used by them were gratified that at last a marriage rite consonant with their own convictions and not too defective in form had come into existence.

In the same way, by means of a manual of services, it might be possible for one organization inspired by humanistic moral idealism to spread its ideas a thousandfold more rapidly than it could otherwise do.

3. *Christian Science an Instance*

Many persons have been astonished and possibly even terrified by the rapid development of Christian Science during the last decade. This teaching is already in evidence in England, as well as America, even in brick and stone — which, whatever else it means, proves that many persons of wealth believe that Christian Science has come to stay. The rich, however lavish in expenditure upon pleasures, seldom give to good causes which they believe are only transient crazes. So astonishing has been the organized growth of Christian Science that many have sought to explain its spread as one more evidence of man's innate love of mystery. Many have even been tempted to find in it a proof that unregenerate human nature craves for the supernatural. I myself knew no other cause to which the phenomenon could be traced until, drawn by curiosity rather than by any intention of discovering its causes, I attended a Sunday evening meeting of a Christian Science Church. I entered the auditorium of this Temple, with its chaste and simple style of architecture. I had known nothing whatever of the order of a Christian Science meeting.

Imagine, then, the revelation it was to me, who for years had been drifting, by some inevitable train of logic and experience, into a realization of the necessity for rites and ceremonies to supplement preaching, to find that here there was no preaching at all. Reliance was placed exclusively upon a set and prescribed ritual.

Some great organizing genius had been preparing practical means for the transmission in the most effective way of the Christian Science gospel. Into my hand was placed a leaflet containing references to a hymn-book, to Mrs. Eddy's "Science and Health," and to the Bible, arranged for use for every Sunday in the then current quarter of the year. Thus it had been made possible for any little group of Christian Scientists immediately to conduct a religious service of an hour in length. No great organization was required. I have since been told by members of the Christian Science Church that generally the religious services of any new group are at first conducted in the drawing-room of a private house. Such has been the ingenuity and foresight of the organizers of this movement. Its statesmen have proved themselves worthy to be leaders of the Order of Jesuits, so subtle and instinct with common sense has been their judgment in constructing out of materials almost hopeless, as I should have thought, a ritual full of variety and interest and yet centring in one dominant idea. As I went away from the meeting, blessed by its elevated influence despite my rejection of every tenet of its metaphysics, I found myself mightily reënforced also in the conviction that the ritual is the thing. National idealism needs what its disciples have all along till now been too dull to think of giving it. I said to myself: "This sectarian doctrine of the Christian Scientists, which takes a truth of limited range (the power of ideas to beget health, happiness, and character) and extends it into a universal law, has been embodied in a liturgy which is rapidly winning converts. How much more rapidly would a religion of national idealism spread if it had but found its poet-statesman, its prophet-priest, shrewd and wise enough to have constructed its ritual, not omitting from it either man or woman or rhythm or song or social silence or the voices of the congregation speaking in unison or the powerful reënforcements from the literatures of the world ! How rapid from state to state and city to city would be the growth of the social-democratic church of America the moment an adequate manual of national idealism was at the disposal of every little group of men and women to which social service was the essence of true religion."

4. *Preaching alone Inadequate*

The inadequacy of preaching alone as an instrument of propaganda, at least at the beginning of a new religious movement, arises from the fact that inevitably there are never more than a few preachers who grasp the real character of any new message. The result is, if it spreads rapidly and forms groups of disciples, the new movement is sure to break loose from its original moorings and to drift. Almost imperceptibly it suffers an unintended mental change. Nothing could prevent this alteration unless the spoken word of the preacher was somehow kept close to the central thought of the movement by written and more or less authoritative statements, which were recognized by the whole group as containing its essential meaning. As such statements are often to be consulted, they should embody the message in condensed and vivid form, in a style suitable for reading again and again, and should prove inexhaustible of meaning after many ponderings. So, while it may be granted that a manual of religious services alone could scarcely draw disciples in the first instance, but would require also the ini-

tial impulse either of some spoken word or of some book
not prepared as a manual of services, it is equally true
that such spoken word or such a book alone would be inadequate.   Indeed, even the preachers themselves of a
new movement, however intimate their relation to its
founder and their study of its authoritative scriptures,
would need the manual of services to keep them to their
moorings.   At least, only the greatest moral and intellectual geniuses will not drift unconsciously to other than their
original foundations.   The minds of ordinary men are by
nature no more fixed than floating islands.

A manual of humanistic devotion could also be used on
occasions where no original discourse was to be delivered,
as at family devotions and at morning and evening chapel
in schools and colleges.   But it would be equally adapted
to meetings where the central feature was a sermon.

It must furthermore not be forgotten that, whatever the
differences between services and sermons, the sermon
itself, in proportion as it is really great, powerful, and of
lasting value, partakes of the nature of a service.   The
two great differences between it and the other parts of the
service are that it is the one item not fixed and determined
beforehand, and also the one which does not lay any claim
to being cast into a form of enduring value.

However important preaching may be, the set forms
may at least be held to be more independent of it than it
of them.   For they will always present the fundamental
ideas and the deeper trend of the faith embodied in them,
and will do so in literary form; while one never could
be secure of the same effects from the preaching itself.
The preacher's theme is left to his own selection; it may
be wide of the main issue, and will inevitably be dependent
on the mental gifts of the particular man and on his
momentary fitness.   It is at any rate clear that from the
start a manual of services must supplement preaching.

It would be the primary instrument for insuring permanence and consistency of propaganda. It alone could sustain and educate the nucleus of a new group of disciples and could steadily knit fresh recruits into an abiding and vital unity.

A further reason why the use of a manual of services has not been appreciated by men of ethical and scientific faith as compared with preaching is that the set services familiar to us — those of the Anglican and Roman Churches — happen in our day to be far less ethical and rational, far more occult and doctrinal, than a good deal of present-day preaching. The preaching even in orthodox churches, being in great part dependent upon the judgment of the preacher, has been more expressive of the needs of the hour than have the church services. It is behind the times, but not, like the Episcopal Prayer Book, three hundred years behind. It has somewhat reflected the trend of the age, which is increasingly ethical and naturalistic. We are therefore liable to fall into the error of imagining that somehow preaching is necessarily more ethical and progressive than a set service. But this conclusion presupposes on the one hand that the set Anglican and Roman forms are the only type possible. On the other hand, it implies that preaching is necessarily ethical. This is the point of view held by a recent writer, who has cited the low moral stage of the Church in Spain to-day, and attributes it to the fact that there the Church has neglected preaching and had recourse almost exclusively to ceremonial. But had the ritual to which it had recourse embodied the ideas of social democracy and naturalistic humanism, it would have lifted not only the religion, but the whole life of Spain out of the mire. On the other hand, what proof is there that Spanish priests, had they opened their mouths to preach in place of conducting formal services, would have inculcated the virtues of self-respect, intellectual honesty,

democratic equality, and reverence for the moral personality
of women? What reason is there to suppose that they
would have presented the moral character instead of the
supernatural functions of Jesus Christ? It will be readily
granted that in the historic Christian churches the
preaching is to-day for the most part more ethical and
scientific than the services. It is the service that now
retards sincerity and freedom of intellectual and moral
faith. These old forms are concretions of the supernaturalism and the metaphysical doctrines of remote ages,
together with ancient ethical sentiments and human aspirations. But it is inconceivable that any preaching could
be more ethical and more in accord with the spirit of science
and of democracy than formal services would be if expressly
written or selected to embody the spirit of science and democracy.

The fact that the Anglican and Roman services are not
up to the ethical and intellectual standard of our day and
fall morally and scientifically far below the preaching of
the most powerful living representatives of those churches,
is one of the reasons which make it especially worth
while to prepare a new manual of services. Bewildering
is the contrast between the springs of conduct which
preachers touch and the weaknesses and emotions upon
which the sacrifice of the Mass plays. The spiritistic occultism, the supernaturalism, of this mysterious ceremony
of the Real Presence often has no more relation to the fundamental presuppositions of the sermon than the thoughts
of a Caliban to the character of a Miranda. It is not the
sensuous splendour of the form of the Mass that strikes one
as barbaric, but its idea of a supernatural blood-atonement.

In the Anglican Church there is often a similar preposterous incongruity between sermon and service. Fifty
minutes to an hour are devoted to a prostrate crying out to
a supernatural agency — at least, so the worshippers them-

selves interpret the ritual — to save us; then one may hear for twenty-five minutes a most searching sermon teaching us to save one another, and thereby incidentally save ourselves.

Let it be conceded, then, that the preaching of our day is comparatively not unethical or unscientific; it is the forms that are chiefly at fault. This stricture applies as fully to the Evangelical churches as to the Roman and Episcopal communions, and as much to Quaker and Unitarian as to Presbyterian and Methodist practices. My impression as to the attitude of mind of Unitarian preachers towards the services which they are required or expected to conduct is that half of the preachers, except for their saving sense of humour and expectation of speedy revision, would be agonized in conscience by the compromise with supernaturalism to which the traditional forms compel them to submit.

If we consider the special case of the Anglican Church, we notice that only the Romanizing party have had the insight to see that living ideas must penetrate not only the sermon, but also the ritual. Accordingly they have done their utmost — even (in England) beyond the limits of legality — to embody their convictions in ceremonial form. In this they have proved themselves to be statesmen, psychologists, and historians, as well as religious enthusiasts. They know the practical power of symbolism in conveying an idea into the heart and will of the people. Superficial and blind by contrast is the attitude of the Broad Church and the Evangelical parties, who know no better means of checking the Romanizing tendency than by proving it illegal and preaching legality as the highest clerical duty. If they but knew it, the only efficient way by which the Romanizing movement could be counteracted would be to legalize forms of service which should embody principles of democracy, science, and national idealism. Along these

lines preaching is already permissible and is to be heard
from many pulpits. But when once formal services con-
gruous with such preaching are equally allowed, old-fashioned theologians will have something bigger and stronger
to fear than Rome. They will have the modern nation
herself to cope with — a nation awake as a living church.
Towards this end a manual of modernist services is more
urgently needed than a new outburst of pulpit eloquence.

Those who have not long reflected upon the problem
here under discussion may think that somehow formal
services are in the nature of the case further behind the
times than preaching. But this again is a mistake.
Indeed, it is the survival of the old forms which accounts
for the fact that the preaching is not far more advanced
than it is. Only the most daring and original preachers
think beyond the forms. But at first, and for generations
afterwards, these forms did not cramp. It is not of the
essence of a formal service that it should have been perpetuated unchanged for centuries. It is, as I point out elsewhere,
perfectly possible that there should be an organized body
of the best intellects and most spiritually minded souls
in the churches continuously at work upon the revision
of services. And it would be possible that at stated intervals, a decade apart or less, the results of their labours should
be submitted to the lawful authorities, and that those new
forms which commended themselves should be sanctioned,
and permission granted for their use side by side with old
forms. There is nothing inherent in the nature of church
services to occasion the retention of any obsolete ideas or
rites. Just as the criminal laws and civil statutes of the
nation not only require but may receive constant revision,
so with church laws and statutes. Nowadays, under a
democratic *régime*, it is inexcusable for any but embittered
Anarchists to interpret all legislation as the tyrannical
empire of past ages over the living present. Sane persons

see that it is our own fault if we have not cast off the dictation of the dead and have not formulated the social conscience of our own day. In similar manner, before long, all except blind haters of social discipline of every kind will enthusiastically help to revivify the churches by revising and reinterpreting their rites and forms.

5. *Ethics and Ceremonial*

Until quite recent years nearly all persons who had discarded the old forms, on account of the error in them, were prone to be chary of all common devotion. They cried out, "The world needs no kind of an ecclesiastical religion with priests and prayers and holy books. It needs a religion of justice. In the new religion nothing will count but clear thoughts and honest deeds." They did not realize that if this attitude were adopted, religion in the old sense would cease to be. Politics, economics, art; science, and spontaneous morality would take its place. But here, again, we detect the vitiating blunder of the old individualism to which I have already referred. As if a man by himself alone — nay, rather in defiance of organized attempts at spiritual discipline — could attain to clear thoughts and honest deeds!

Now, the older prophets, despite their trust in personal agencies outside of human society, were well aware that only by the systematic concentration of a nation's attention upon righteousness could a people ever reach honesty and the clear vision. The whole apparatus of Judaism and Christianity was instituted and perpetuated for the attainment of justice, by creating in the minds of the people a love of justice. The old worship, with its priests and prayers and holy books, was in ultimate aim a religion of justice. Its end was right. Its means unhappily were pre-scientific, but they were, however falsely interpreted,

natural and human. If by "ecclesiastical religion" is
meant a looking to supernatural persons for help, let us
away with it. If prayer be but a petition to superhuman
agencies, we have had enough of it. If books cannot be
holy unless they teach submission to invisible and incorporeal beings, then without doubt the world needs no
such things. But unassuming teachers and preachers of
human ideals, confessedly fallible but well disciplined in
the method and spirit of scientific test and search, are
needed by the world more than ever. And a systematic
turning for help to human and natural sources of redemption is indispensable. So, too, holy books are required, if
holiness means, as it always has meant, not pandering to
selfishness, vanity, or lust, but on the contrary ministering
to the spirit of self-sacrifice for great human ends.

Among nineteenth-century prophets no one was more
alive than Emerson to the fact that religion is turning
away from the subtleties of scholasticism to morals, and
that this change is altogether an advance. He was supremely the apostle of clear thoughts and honest deeds.
But his mother-wit prevented him from falling into the
error of thinking that these could be attained without
the natural means of regular religious practices in common.
The passage in his essay on "Worship" in which he pro-
phesies that "there will be a new church, founded on moral
science," is often quoted in witness of his prophetic instinct.
But the special evidence of genius in this passage is not
his saying that an ethical church will come, but his recognition
that it will of necessity begin, as he characteristically puts
it, "at first cold and naked, a babe in a manger again, the
algebra and mathematics of ethical law"; at first "without shawms or psaltery or sackbut." Emerson, although
he recognized the necessity of it, saw no virtue or permanence in this initial state of nakedness. The new church, he
went on to add, "will have heaven and earth for its beams

and rafters, science for symbol and illustration." He accordingly foretold that it would "fast enough gather beauty, music, picture, poetry." Still more directly in his essay on "The Sovereignty of Ethics" does he give his sanction to a church that will educate and discipline men into clear thoughts and honest deeds; but with greater emphasis also does he insist upon the necessity of rites and ceremonies.

"It accuses us," he says, "that pure ethics is not now formulated and concreted into a cultus, a fraternity, with assemblings and holydays, with song and book, with brick and stone. Why have not those," he asks, "who believe in it and love it, left all for it, and dedicated themselves to write out its scientific scriptures, to become its vulgate for millions?"

But even Emerson, as can be seen in these passages, suffered perhaps under the limitations of his age. He speaks of a new church, as if a new organization was to be founded and as if the old churches would not transform themselves. Now, it must be granted that the old did not base themselves upon moral *science*, because science had not yet come. But science having now arrived, the notion is inconceivable that the old churches should continue resting on a foundation of trust in supernatural sources of redemption. Surely the old churches will refound themselves, and this time on a scientific basis — on science humane and therefore moral. But in so doing, the churches will discard only so much of their accumulated beauty, music, picture, and poetry as is positively an affront to the truth which we modern men behold. It is a fact that *pure* ethics has not yet concreted itself; but impure ethics — ethics transfused with a certain amount of trust in supernatural agencies — has long since done so. The organizations which have achieved this work, there is every reason to hope, will themselves, thanks to the prevalence of the scientific spirit, now drive out super-

x

naturalism — which after all was never the real treasure of the Church. They will remove the dross for the sake of their own pure gold. At least in America the churches are still alive; their members have, moreover, been permeated with the new hopes and ideals. The churches surely then will know how to continue to keep alive and to grow into the Church of Men to Come.

Sir John Seeley saw as perfectly as Emerson that religion is moving steadily away from scholastic subtleties to the science of ethics; and that a church with assemblings and holydays, with song and book, with brick and stone, is an indispensable accessory to national character. But, unlike that of Emerson, Seeley's historic sense was disciplined and strengthened by systematic scholarship. He therefore would hear nothing of a new church organization, but only of the old churches renewed. All that Emerson deplored in the teaching and practices of the dominant religious institutions Seeley equally lamented. But the defects of the churches are not their essence. The organization has lived in spite of defects, at least in spite of their perpetuation. Those who love the old institutions most, and who are most ready to sacrifice all for them, shall be brought to distinguish what is vital in them from what is extraneous and may prove fatal.

6. *The Revision of Church Services*

During the last half century religious controversy has raged around the Bible. During the next half century the storm-centre will be a new manual of church services.

In the sixteenth century there began in Christendom the evolution of two new ideas, the idea of science and the idea of democracy. These ideas have now developed into full self-consciousness and definite outline. A point of view has come into existence from which the Bible itself is being

interpreted differently. We now understand the Bible
not to mean what those imagined it to mean who reconstructed its substance in the formularies of the Protestant
churches. It is therefore possible for us to-day to embody
in new or in revised national manuals of religious rites and
ceremonies the teaching and spirit of the Bible as we now
interpret it. Such manuals would preserve to us the religious treasure of the past; but they would also communicate to the people the new method and spirit of science,
and the new outlook, strength, and self-reliance of social
democracy.

7. *Science unifies Men*

At the outset, one cannot but lament the conflict that
has prevailed between believers in science and the upholders
of religion. Hitherto the whole tendency of the scientific
method and spirit, so far as it has touched the religious consciousness at all, has been centrifugal and disintegrating.
It has divided and isolated men. It has driven them from
churches, but has not drawn them to any new centre of
spiritual life. Science has become wedded to commer-
cialism on one side, and on another is running into theo-
sophic freak. For four centuries the right of private judgment has tended to this splitting up of churches, until
now among the foremost of the scientific world every individual man has become a church unto himself. What is
needed is a scientific instrument of religious cohesion.
That such an instrument can be found is the more likely
because, despite all appearances to the contrary, science
both by its method and spirit ultimately tends to unity.
What is science, but the dropping out as unverified of what
cannot be demonstrated to every rational being to be
true? And what has taken place in the domain of each
special science, except a unification of thought and an agreement and consolidation of men? The whole evolution of

science is from a variety of opinions to a common judgment. Every year, every month, disputed points are
settled and intellectual harmony is established. It is only
in reference to religion, the one domain of human interest
which has not yet come under the scientific spirit and
method, that scientific men still differ one with another,
although they all agree in rejecting the intellectual tradition of past ages as it is manifested in the churches. If
once the rites and ceremonies of public worship could be
so transformed as no longer to violate the fundamental
methods and spirit of science, is it quixotic to hope, as I
do, that the whole nation would soon be drawn into one
religious fellowship? Would not the most powerful engine
for bringing about such a revolution in public worship be a
manual — democratic and scientific — of church services?

Science, I have said, has thus far been centrifugal in
tendency; but in the fulness of time it will be centripetal.
It has destroyed religious traditions; but all the applications of its methods to chemistry, to physics, to botany
and biology show its truest work to be constructive and
synthetic. The old-fashioned notion still widely prevails
that if people are allowed to think for themselves in religion, each will go his own and therefore a different way.
But if people really think for themselves, they will learn to
think according to the method and spirit of science; and
the result will be that in each going his own way they will
all go the same way.

The cleavage which now exists between science and religion, moreover, is not identical with that between church
members and those who on intellectual grounds have been
compelled to withdraw from church membership. Intimate acquaintance with present-day religious thought and
scientific education exposes to view the fact that thousands
of preachers and members of churches have been as much
touched by the spirit of science as those persons have who

have broken away from religious organization or who were born and have been reared in circles wholly out of sympathy with religious traditions. Scientific minds within the churches, however, have until now remained quiet and passive. In church conferences and services they do not demand any expression of the new ideas which they have adopted. They carry on no active propaganda of science in the domain of religion. The result is that at present within the churches old-fashioned notions seem to bear completer sway than is actually the case. They still dominate the set forms and phrases; but, notwithstanding, the new notions are alive and strong in pulpit and pew. A crisis at any moment may precipitate them into definite expression. Any day these modern men within the churches may speak out the new faith that is in them. They have remained within and kept quiet, because in the interest of religion and the nation they were waiting for the right opportunity. They have seen that there is a time to keep silent and they have respected its claim; but only because they have been sure that their time to speak would come. These men of science have remained within because they shrank back in bewilderment and alarm from the moral isolation which severance would entail. They have had a deep sense of the ethical benefits of spiritual fellowship. They have believed, and not wrongly, that spiritual isolation tends to engender, even when it does not always produce, laxity of life. In terror at the isolation which seemed to await them if they were to follow truth whithersoever it might lead, they have apparently drawn back the deeper into the twilight of the old faith. They have clung to what had so long stood fast rather than yield themselves up to a stream which seemed but to flow into a sea of negation. It appeared to them that if they should be forced to decide on the instant, they must make a choice between truth and righteousness; and they have not been ashamed temporarily to prefer concrete righteousness to abstract truth, abiding the time when these would cease to be in practical antagonism.

8. *Outside the Churches*

Of the two classes of persons — those who break with all religious association on account of new ideas and those who, although adopting them, remain quietly within the churches — it is quite possible that the latter class have chosen the wiser course and have manifested the deeper ethical insight. They have seen that science, while it has meant knowledge, accurate, systematic, and verified, has not yet meant wisdom; and they have preferred wisdom unscientific to science unwise. But were science now to become wise and stoop to the service of those very ends to which religion has always ministered, these seemingly more timid natures within the churches would forthwith declare themselves disciples of science. But only a scientific transformation of the rites and language of the churches will demonstrate to the devout and to the masses that science has at last been allowed or compelled to enter into the service of moral idealism. For the sake of the churches the leaders of scientific thought and of critical philosophy must become the reorganizers of religious forms. The psychologists and sociologists of religion must not only furnish a restatement of the creeds, but embody the new view of the universe and of man in rites and ceremonies. The first result would be a return of the intellectuals and of the masses of the nation into the churches.

9. *The Warring Sects*

Comparatively happy would the religious state of America be to-day if the only breaches in her life were those between the scientific and the unscientific. But equally great and deplorable are the chasms which separate and divide among themselves sects and groups within sects which have been wholly untouched by the doctrine of evolution and the philosophical criticism of our day. We need some instrument of cohesive power to bring together Evangelicals and High Churchmen, Unitarians, Baptists, Calvinists, and Methodists, who are separated not by science against dogma, but by dogma against dogma. The same reasons, however, which make me believe that modernist forms of public worship would heal the breach between science and Christianity compel me to hope that they would exercise a similar influence amidst the warring sects.

There have been many attempts to effect a union among the Christian bodies by means of a compromise. It has been thought that all the sects will unite if only they can be induced to drop points of difference and cling to points of conscious agreement. But every such attempt has proved futile. It has led to a colourless and impotent undenominationalism, which perhaps produces an armed truce, but settles no differences and assuages no antagonisms. Undenominationalism is an abstraction which will only pass muster as a religion in the interregnum between two great national ideals. So long as all the theological sects believe in supernaturalism, for each sect not to dare to point to the special supernatural agencies it believes in nor to its own particular means of conciliating its invisible deities, for fear of awakening sectarian bitterness, is to cry halt just when the nation needs to march on. No! Nothing but a new instrument which will render vivid, concrete, and beautiful the new synthesis of social democracy, science, and Christianity can unify Christians among themselves. The new bond will, therefore, be an idea which is as yet wholly outside the consciousness of the majority of orthodox Christians and is directly in antagonism to the supernaturalism of the churches. It is true that the new idea has not yet begun to win the extremely orthodox believers in Christianity, nor has it begun to transform and vivify even the centres of religious radicalism. But it must be remembered that the new synthesis has never yet been concreted into a cultus. Such a concretion is exactly what I am pleading for when I urge a revision of religious rites and ceremonies.

Lest the force of my argument be lost by not appreciating how such a revision is to be achieved, it must be borne in mind how other reforms have been brought to ultimate triumph. Judging from analogous cases, I have given it as my opinion that various individual persons must first, as I am doing in this volume, offer tentative suggestions as to revision. These should be applied and made the basis of new forms. At the same time, since rites and ceremonies can only be tested by being actually practised, religious meetings of those sympathizing with such attempts should be held, in which the new forms were used as the order of service. By trials of this kind, in proportion as the services fulfilled their object, other assemblies would adopt them.

Such experiments have now been made for more than twenty years at the Ethical Church in London, England. The results were published and thus made accessible to the public in the summer of 1913 in two large quarto volumes entitled "Social Worship," issued by George Allen in London and the Macmillan Company in New York. Volume I contains the Introductory and Dismissory sentences, the Meditations, the Lessons from universal literature, the Invitations to Church Membership and the Special Services for the religious Dedication of Children, the Receiving of New Members, for Marriage, and for Burial. Volume II contains the words and music of the Canticles, Hymns, and Responsive Services and the words (with bibliography) of the Anthems. All these items have been selected as expressive of the living conscience of the modern world. Some of them refer exclusively to England, but others are derived from American literature; the great majority, however, are expressive of the universal spirit and vision of our day in every nation of the world. These two volumes of " Social Worship," being in the main but a collected anthology from the greatest writers of modern times and the masters of thought and expression in all ages in so far as they represent the point of view of humanistic idealism, science, and democracy, must be an approximately adequate embodiment in literature of the Soul of America. They are offered to the public, however, only as a tentative and first contribution. They have sprung from the same effort and the same sense of need which have produced Professor Rauschenbusch's volume of prayers entitled "God and the People," and Professor Patten's "Social Hymns" and the collection, under the same name, which appeared in *The Survey* of January 3, 1914.

10. *The East*

I have said that the outcome of our task might prove a benefit even beyond the borders of Christendom. We are to-day face to face with new religious problems arising from the contact, now for the first time, of China and Japan on equal terms with the civilization of the West. China and Japan are already losing their belief in invisible and incorporeal agencies as the source of human weal and woe. Their intellectual classes are discarding the naïve spiritism involved, if not expressly declared, in the old cults, and are reinterpreting their ancestor-worship in terms of social idealism and of the historic unity and solidarity of their countries.

Some merriment was awakened a few years ago throughout the Western nations by a report that Japan, not many years before, had sent representatives to the West in search of a religion which would be to the benefit of Japan and suitable to adopt as the State religion. If the Japanese did take such a step, it furnishes only one more proof of their consummate statesmanship and originality. There is not a nation of the Western world but as a nation is alarmed at the decay of the old Western faiths and puzzled and bewildered how to keep up the moral idealism of the people, now that the old dogmas and forms have lost their hold of the popular imagination. Further, when the relation of religion to national idealism is fully comprehended, it will be seen that there is nothing grotesque in an attempt to find a religion for a nation. Such an attempt means an effort to bring into definite outline and shape, and to organize systematically, what had hitherto been the inarticulate and undirected idealism of the nation. When it is thus realized that, after all, a religion at its best and fullest is nothing else than the nation's idealism organized into a system of moral education, it will be seen that not once but always should a nation be on the lookout for improvements in its religious methods and principles.

That Japan found no religious system of the West suitable for her needs is again a proof of her penetration and discrimination. Is it, however, foolish to believe that if in America since her War of Independence all religious bodies had been revising, readapting, and perfecting their religious institutions and teachings, so as to bring them every decade abreast of America's own need, Japan would have found in the United States such a manual of religious worship, ceremonial and dogma as with very slight readaptation would have ministered to her newly awakened consciousness? Japan found for herself in the West a science of chemistry and chemical laboratories; she found methods of manufacture and agriculture; she adopted systems of sanitation and medicine. Had our religion of the West

been as up to date as our science, those Japanese representatives who went in search of a religion would not have
returned to the East empty-handed.

Few have realized that Christianity entered upon a new
era the moment Japan conquered her Russian assailants.
That moment, for the first time in fifteen hundred years,
Christianity stood again face to face in intimate relationship of equality with pagan ideas and principles, and in
full consciousness of the fact of that equality. Japan not
only gained a material victory, but won the moral admiration of the world. And now China has done likewise by an
internal revolution towards science and social democracy.
Historians have noted that so long as Christianity in the
early ages was in intimate and reciprocal contact with
heathen culture, she was constantly deriving from it as
many benefits as she gave. They have pointed out that
after she had once conquered the whole range of civilization
and was no longer confronted with conflicting principles
and ideals of religion, she lost those benefits which always
come of comparison and contrast. Without fear of challenge, she could assert and impress upon the minds of her
ignorant subjects the notion that she possessed a monopoly
of divine wisdom. Now again after fifteen hundred years
the people of Christendom will be forced to compete, as
it were, in the open market of the world for the acceptance
of her religious wares.

CHAPTER XVII

THE GROWTH OF LITURGIES

1. *By Effort*

It must be borne in mind that modernist modes of devotional service will never come of themselves. They will not be hit upon by happy accident. And without a mighty struggle on their behalf they will never be introduced either into the historic or into new religious organizations. Even in the latter there will for a long time be a strong party opposing outward forms of any kind. It may be, as Emerson says, that

> The litanies of nations came,
> Like the volcano's tongue of flame,
> Up from the burning core below —
> The canticles of love and woe.

It certainly is true, as he says, that

> Out from the heart of nature rolled
> The burdens of the Bible old.

But false would be the inference that because the litanies come naturally out of human love and woe they therefore come without effort, purpose, and plan. If the volcano's tongue of flame does not issue by design, it is in so far not like the litanies of nations in its energizing force.

The belief prevails that litanies spring out unintended from unconscious impulses. And when persons undertake to-day, by effort and with beneficence prepense, to make or remake litanies suited to the new needs, they are met with the scornful rebuke that religions cannot be manufactured — that they are not made, but grow.

There is no doubt in my own mind that the progress of religion into a democratic and scientific scheme of moral regeneration has been retarded for ages by the notion, never allowed by priests to die, that religious forms and ceremonies cannot be invented and manufactured. This notion, kept alive by conservative interests, and sincerely believed because accepted without question by the multitude, is doomed soon to be exploded. For the fact is writ large on every page of Church history, and in the narrative of all great religions, and needs only to be known: that so long as religions have been alive and growing, the vital force which produced their teachings and practices has been the conscious effort of bold, patriotic statesmen. These saw that ethics, whether pure or impure, — ethics somehow, the best they could have, — must forthwith be concreted into the most attractive, vivid, and inspiring cultus they were able to devise. Churches have always and everywhere manufactured their ritual.

Nevertheless, it is true that the ritual is a natural growth. Human manufactures always grow. Unless one is admitted into the secret of the psychic forces that create them, they bear all the marks of spontaneous, unpremeditated development. Religious statesmen construct them as inevitably (although designedly) as the wood-bird weaves her nest

> Of leaves and feathers from her breast;

or as

> the fish outbuilds her shell,
> Painting with morn each annual cell;

or as

> the sacred pine-tree adds
> To her old leaves new myriads.

It is hazardous to affirm that bird and fish and tree quite spontaneously and unconsciously construct their temples for body and home. The finest and closest observers of animal and plant life are more and more hesitating to believe so. There is no proof of unconsciousness or effort-lessness. Both in the case of plant and animal it is an unfounded assumption to deny even effort. And as regards all beautiful forms of religion, what we do know of them from intimate and universal experience and direct observation is this: that they have come first by the effort of patriots; then they may have continued spontaneously, and probably only at last survived unconsciously. We know further that the unconscious production of beautiful things is no more worthy nor admirable than activity which is all tingling with conscious design. It is also a perversion of judgment, due to conservative self-interest, to cast dis-credit upon laborious effort as compared with spontaneity, whether conscious or unconscious. Only let the results of agonizing enterprise be compared in their beauty and utility with products of effortless impulse, and not pre-judged adversely because they have cost self-control, sacri-fice, and the concentration of intelligent will.

2. *Emerson on Adaptation*

It has not been to the interest of the official priests of churches to acknowledge that forms and ceremonies, litur-gies and the Bible grew by a process of revision. Accord-ingly, they did not see this process, and they honestly fancied that the products of ceremonial art sprang quite otherwise into existence. But any one not biassed knows that the same process is exemplified in the religious forms of every nation. Nowhere is it more fully exemplified than in the origin and development of the English Bible and the Book of Common Prayer. Admirably has Emerson pre-

sented the facts and appreciated them in this passage from
his essay on Shakespeare : —

It is easy to see that what is best written or done by genius
in the world was no one man's work, but came by wide social
labour, when a thousand wrought like one, sharing the same impulse. Our English Bible is a wonderful specimen of the
strength and music of the English language But it was not
made by one man, or at one time ; but centuries and churches
brought it to perfection.   There never was a time when there
was not some translation existing.   The liturgy, admirable for
its energy and pathos, is an anthology of the piety of ages and
nations, a translation of the prayers and forms of the Catholic
Church — these collected, too, in long periods, from the prayers
and meditations of every saint and sacred writer all over the
world.   Grotius makes the like remark in respect to the Lord's
Prayer, that the single clauses of which it is composed were
already in use in the time of Christ, in the Rabbinical forms.
He picked out the grains of gold.

But there is a still more pertinent hint in this same
essay of Emerson's, to encourage and embolden to revision
those who feel that during the last two centuries and a half
the people of Christendom have been denied the right to
breathe the breath of their new life into their church services
and to let that new life reshape, as it must, forms which
are inadequate. "Shakespeare," says Emerson, "in common with his comrades, esteemed the mass of old plays
waste stock, in which any experiment could be freely tried.
Had the prestige which hedges about a modern tragedy
existed, nothing could have been done."   I know the retort
will be made that this was all very well for Shakespeare
and his immortal comrades, but that until a man has
demonstrated that he is the peer of Shakespeare he has
no right to lay his unconsecrated hand upon the sacred
literary heritage of the past. But note that Emerson
insists that even Shakespeare, for all his greatness, could

have done nothing had the prestige which hedges about a modern tragedy prevented his esteeming the mass of old plays waste stock. If Emerson be right, Shakespeare's greatness itself, or at least the world's possession of his greatness, was due to the liberty taken by him of experimenting freely with the literature he found at hand.

Once let the devout world be converted to the dignity and necessity of human effort in the writing of Bibles and in the formulation of religious cults, and in a century religion will make more progress in beauty, reasonableness, and humanity than it has done in two thousand years. The notion that sacred scriptures emanate from supernatural agencies and that rites are enjoined by invisible intelligences has generally paralyzed by suggestion the efforts of religious reformers. These have waited for that to be done by superhuman persons which they ought to have undertaken forthwith. But luckily this erroneous notion is losing hold of intelligent minds.

With the shifting of trust from supernatural to human agencies, we abandon the idea that independently of us the universe has a purpose which we are to serve. But the notion that we therefore abandon all belief in rational cosmic purpose and fall back upon blind evolution is as crude as it is dangerous to the higher interests of humanity. In abandoning superhuman personal agencies we do not fall back upon subhuman and impersonal or even merely human forces. No human will is merely human will; it is also natural, just as all nature is subject to the forms and laws of the human mind. Instead, we replace the idea of extra-human cosmic purpose by that of human cosmic purpose — humanity being the crown of the cosmos. Combined human foresight — the general will of organized society — assumes the rôle of creative providence.

Consistent with this new conception of the Church and of human design as a factor in religious evolution is

it that we should appropriate and adapt the materials
furnished us by the rites and ceremonies of the historic
churches. We who love the old organizations and are true
to their spirit are rightful masters of their letter. As the
wood-bird, bent on building her nest, in lieu of better
materials, makes it of leaves and of feathers from her breast,
so may we use what is familiar, old, and close at hand. It
is all ours, and the homelike beauty of the Church of the
future will be enhanced by the ancient materials wrought
into its new forms.

3. *The Right to adapt Creeds and Hymns*

The right to appropriate and modify materials at hand
to serve new needs has only been exercised in the few
and short periods of creative work in Church organization
— those who effected the changes believing themselves to
be guided by some supernatural agency. By such men
at such times no forms or symbols were counted too holy
to be touched. There is little doubt that out of the Creed
of Irenæus (A.D. 170) was built up the Apostles' Creed,
through the deliberate attempts of many. This in turn
was worked over into the Nicene Creed, to meet the new
attacks of heretics by rendering explicit various points
of Church doctrine. The Apostles' and the Nicene Creeds
must have been held in execration as an unpardonable
parody by those who on principle opposed all tampering
with authorized documents. The Nicene Creed itself
soon becoming inadequate as an instrument of Church
defence, the Athanasian Creed was constructed out of two
existing formulæ as to the nature of God and of Christ.

In the case of these creeds, there was no deviation in
the new statements from the old meanings — only a bringing out of what was implicit and understood, or the addition of new materials to buttress the old. Yet the right

Y

to appropriate and modify has not been confined to cases where the old idea was preserved. The early Christians put quite different meanings into the words "Messiah" and "the Kingdom of Heaven," as into the use of one day of rest in seven and into the Passover Supper. They did not stop short of appropriating anything that would serve their cause.

It is not only creeds that have been reshaped and bent to serve new needs; the same has been done with prayers and hymns. It is sometimes supposed that these latter, being lyric and emotional, have spontaneously sprung into existence, and, being living organisms rather than mechanical structures, cannot be modified without laceration. But such a distinction of creeds, as compared with prayers and hymns, is wholly without foundation in fact. The most subtle and metaphysical of all the creeds, the Athanasian, is itself a superb psalm, and as such is used by the Church. It is a living organism, but we must remember that in matters spiritual the life-force is often conscious effort and intelligent design. As to hymns, whoever is intimately acquainted with the evolution of anthologies is perfectly aware that the lyrics undergo modification the moment the intellectual soil and environing atmosphere have changed. What is more to the point, the most sweetly lyrical of all Christian hymns, those of John and Charles Wesley, found their origin in a systematic intellectual scheme. The Wesleys wished to embody their peculiar theological doctrines in a form which should become familiar to the masses. The hymn was the one possible popular vehicle. Accordingly, the whole of the Methodist scheme of salvation was poured into melodious rhyme. As regards the spontaneous perfection, and therefore inviolability, of prayers, it must not be forgotten that a number of those in the Book of Common Prayer are compilations.

Church literature cannot and must not be the product of individual and isolated minds. It still must be, as it always has been, the work of a continuous group of organizers and worshippers thinking and feeling together like one mind and embodying their common sentiment in fitting formulæ. One person preëminent in logical clearness throws out the new idea ; another soul gifted with song breathes into it the breath of life. By use the substance becomes strengthened and compacted. Church literature has thus the characteristics of folk-lore.

A redeeming circumstance in such appropriation, as compared with the seizing of material wealth, is that the old still survives intact under the former ownership, after it has been taken and adapted by innovators. The Jewish use and meaning of the words "Messiah" and "the Kingdom of Heaven," as of the institutions of the Sabbath and the Passover, were not extinguished, but were compelled to compete henceforth with what the Jews would have called parodies.

There was a similar seizure by the early Christians of pagan materials — festivals and phrases, as well as temples.

At the Reformation, likewise, when the Church of England was organizing herself as an independent body, she took every form and phrase she wanted, modifying language and rite by omissions and additions and by the introduction of fresh ideas and meanings, according to the living sentiments of the hour. "In the Mass," says an historian of the Book of Common Prayer, "the order and contents of the Sarum service were adhered to, but stress was laid upon the communion of the people, by the incorporation of the 'Order of Communion,' and the Canon was practically rewritten, expressions being omitted which would be thought to countenance the doctrine of a repetition of the sacrifice of the Cross, and the then preva-

lent form of the doctrine of Transubstantiation. . . .
The direct invocation of saints and expressions connected
with the mediæval doctrine of the state of the departed
also disappeared."

Only in these great creative periods of national religious
life have existing materials been intentionally transfused
with new meanings and reshaped. In periods of timid
conformity thinkers have seen what needed doing, but
have not dared, or have not cared, to do it. At most,
some one has prophesied that another would come, who,
being bolder, would do, instead of announcing, what ought
to be done.

4. *An Anglican's Plea for Revision*

All persons likely to be interested in the revision of
church services might for our purpose be conveniently
divided into two classes, as the obstacles to revision be-
setting each of these are quite different: preachers and
literary laymen.

Such is the peculiar position of the body of ministers in
any denomination that it cannot well conceive any one's
beginning the work of readapting services to the future
needs of the nation until the authorities of any denomination
have moved in the matter and authorized and appointed
a committee of men to undertake the task.

There can be no doubt that thousands of ministers
deplore their bondage to tradition. But those who thus
regret their bondage can do nothing more specific than express their regret; and this they are continually, but ineffectually, doing. Typical of these expressions by the
Anglican clergy are the letters which appeared some time
since in the London *Spectator*. One contains the following
passage: —

How different would have been the history of the Christian
Church in England if the compilers of the nation's Book of

Common Prayer had definitely fixed some date, such as the first year of every century, for its revision! They made no secret of the fact that their work would periodically need to be brought up to date. Were they not themselves revising venerated liturgies, handed down to them, in order that they might be better adapted to the knowledge and the needs of the people of England in their own day? Would not the arguments which they used in their Preface to convince gainsayers be equally applicable to future generations? They both knew and foreknew the hold of customary forms and phrases over men's minds. They had seen and must have foreseen the danger "lest one good custom should corrupt the world." . . . Who can doubt that as godly a body of men of piety and learning will be found for the task to-day as at any period of the Church's history? Even Church doctrine, which is spoken of sometimes as if it were a petrified tradition, means neither more nor less than the teaching of the living Church of the day, as expressed in authorized formularies by the help of the living Spirit. Such formularies must be kept in constant refreshing touch with the heart and mind of the nation if the national Church is to be worthy of its name, and not decline and fall into a mere denomination among denominations. The sense in which the compilers of our Prayer Book meant Church doctrine to be "distinctive" — a much abused word, surely — was chiefly, if I mistake not, in its simple, broad, and therefore comprehensive character. It was their ambition that all Christian people should be able to use the services supplied with comfort and profit, whether their family tradition and personal leaning inclined them to Rome or to Geneva.

How pathetically handicapped must be the man who would attribute the inactivity of the Church of England since 1662 in this work of revision to the mere negative fact that the compilers omitted to fix a definite date, such as the first year of every century, for revision! That omission surely can be no cause for the apathy and stolid conservatism of the Church. And what good would a fixed date, once in a century, for revision be if during the

ten decades preceding there had not been the liberty given
to each of the bishops, if not to the rector of every church,
to compose and use, besides the authorized forms, others,
according to his own genius and the seeming requirements
of those to whom he ministered? A revision that could
not be tested by actual experience in common worship,
although it were the work of a great poetic prophet, might
fail absolutely. Forms for actual use in church, like plays
for actual performance upon the stage, presuppose on the
part of those who devise them intimate acquaintance with
the stage management and the actual performance, so to
speak, of the ritual. I will not say but that it would be
better than the present inactivity if after every hundred
years there should be five of hurried effort to improve
the rites of the Church. But the very spirit which would
promote such periodical revisions would be sure to sanction
continuous tentative work by recognized authorities in the
Church.

If such privileges were conferred upon the bishops of the
Church of England, what a stimulus would be brought
to bear upon all the literary geniuses born to England!
As the Catholic Church called into requisition the creative
powers of architects, painters, and musicians, so all denominations should at last summon to their service the
greatest lyric and dramatic poets. Suppose Shakespeare
had been called as were Raphael and Michel Angelo.
And if only Milton, or George Eliot, or Browning had been
summoned to this task! But to return to the painful facts.
Nobody in the Church of England for more than two centuries has tried to construct any kind of a religious ritual.

5. *Lord Morley's Plea*

Even the belief in an inevitable upward evolution of
human institutions cannot justify the notion that religious

forms would adapt themselves without effort to the new demands of science. Without a struggle for existence between the old and the new, in the persons of the champions of each, how could the new gain a permanent foothold? But before there can be a struggle for existence, that which is to struggle must exist. And how could a new creed or litany or hymn or order of religious service enter into competition with the old, unless first some one had thought it out and written it down and published it and defied public opinion to the extent of using it at religious meetings of those who believed it better and truer than the old?

Fully illustrative of this attitude of waiting for some other to do what needs now to be done in liturgy is the following passage from Lord Morley's volume entitled "On Compromise" (which, let me say, has not been without its influence as one of the causes of this book) : —

The tendency of modern free-thought [said John Morley, writing in 1877] is more and more visibly towards the extraction of the first and more permanent elements of the old faith, to make the purified material of the new. When Dr. Congreve met the famous epigram about Comte's system being Catholicism minus Christianity, by the reply that it is Catholicism plus Science, he gave an ingenious expression to the direction which is almost certainly taken by all who attempt, in however informal a manner, to construct for themselves some working system of faith, in place of the faith which science and criticism have sapped. In what ultimate form, acceptable to great multitudes of men, these attempts will at last issue, no one can now tell. For we, like the Hebrews of old, shall all have to live and die in faith, " not having received the promises, but having seen them afar off, and being persuaded of them, and embracing them, and confessing that we are strangers and pilgrims on the earth." Meanwhile, after the first great glow and passion of the just and necessary revolt of reason against superstition have slowly lost the exciting splendour of the dawn, and become diffused in the colourless space of a rather bleak noonday, the

mind gradually collects again some of the ideas of the old
religion of the West, and willingly, or even joyfully, suffers itself
to be once more breathed upon by something of its spirit.
Christianity was the last great religious synthesis. It is the
one nearest to us. Nothing is more natural than that those
who cannot rest content with intellectual analysis, while awaiting the advent of the St. Paul of the humanitarian faith of the
future, should gather up provisionally such fragmentary illustrations of this new faith as are to be found in the records of the
old. Whatever form may be ultimately imposed on our vague
religious aspirations by some prophet to come, who shall unite
sublime depth of feeling and lofty purity of life with strong
intellectual grasp and the gift of a noble eloquence, we may at
least be sure of this, that it will stand as closely related to Christianity as Christianity stood closely related to the old Judaic
dispensation.

By following the hint contained in Dr. Congreve's
formula for Positivism, the religion advocated in this
book might be described as Christianity plus Science plus
Social Democracy. The task of one who would compile
church services in harmony with such a formula would,
if he had but the destructive and constructive imagination,
be simple enough: to strike out of existing forms everything that offends against social democracy and against
science, and to add all that is necessary in order to instruct
and inspire the public mind with the spirit and method,
the ideal and goal, of knowledge devoted to social service.
But we dare not wait for the genius who is equal to the
imaginative destruction and construction that are needed.
We must prepare for his coming. The discoveries and
inventions of the greatest minds always have foundation
in the thousands of minor contributions, half-successes
and experiments that failed, but taught avoidance of the
same mistake. It is not only "natural," it is necessary,
that we should gather up the illustrations of the new faith
to be found in the old. In so doing, we are not simply

beating time while awaiting the advent of the St. Paul of the humanitarian faith of the future; we are actually securing his coming and preventing its indefinite postponement.

One would have thought that since Lord Morley published " On Compromise " countless experiments along the line of concreting Dr. Congreve's formula would have been made; and that now we should have the results to profit by. But nothing has been done, except what Dr. Congreve himself did; and the general tone seems more timid than ever.

It is probable also that Dr. Congreve's attempt at adapting old forms to the new idea of faith in Humanity has injured rather than advanced his cause. He started from the wrong motive. He confesses his object in adaptation to be to make his own expression in its form continuous with the religious worship of the Christian churches. But this is a vitiating aim. The one object should have been to make his own expression adequate to its own idea, and not to borrow simply because it is desirable to preserve an outward semblance of similarity. If there is to be borrowing, it must be wholly because the thing appropriated is in itself the best possible material. If outward similarity, without being sought for, happens to be preserved, well and good. But the slightest suspicion that the similarity is only outward and not due to inward identity is fatal.

6. *Ancient Forms were New Once!*

The general attitude towards the making of liturgies, even on the part of persons most in sympathy with humanistic religion, is well exemplified by one distinguished writer of our immediate present, who has published this curious betrayal of halting between two opinions: "A ritual," he says, "cannot be invented; antiquity appears to be of the essence of its power — though, to be sure, rituals must have had a beginning! — and, as experiment shows, it is difficult to take seriously any new attempt in this direction." If rituals had a beginning, to the starters of them they must have been most powerful. There was no antiquity hallowing the custom of those who in memory of Christ first broke bread and drank wine. And yet how thrilling, how overpowering, must have been this new experiment in ideal communion! Antiquity is not of the essence of ritual. On the contrary, old rituals keep themselves alive and quicken us in spite of their antiquity. And it is only because we lack courage and creative originality of faith that we halt. Religion is monopolized to-day by vested interests, which spread it abroad against us if we attempt to bring up the form to the living faith. We are tasteless innovators, it is reported — vulgar nonconformists.

"Though, to be sure, rituals must have had a beginning," yet undoubtedly experiment shows that it is difficult to take seriously any new attempt in this direction. Nobody that was anybody took seriously — at least, not for several centuries — that breaking of bread in memory of Jesus. Evidently it began in a circle so removed from the refinement and power of the worshippers of antiquity as never to have heard that the experiment was ludicrous. Beneficent crudity! Yet let us again forget the periods of timid conformity; let us again drink of the spirit of prophecy; let us save what is worth saving in Christianity and the churches, by keeping everything that is consistent with science and true to the vision of social democracy and discarding the rest.

As I am devoted to the purpose and spirit of the Hebrew prophets and Christian Apostles, and convinced that a transference of religious faith from superhuman to human agencies does not touch the essential message of the Bible and the Church, I have dared to think of myself in publishing this plea for revision as in a line of Church-reforming successors to Cranmer, the arch-appropriator and adapter of ancient forms to new meanings. I would fain hasten that Reformation of the Reformation which Milton prophesied.

I have said that if I do not believe in waiting for the St. Paul of the humanitarian faith, it is because I believe that we must prepare the work or he will never come. And I am not without hope that this volume may lead to experiments in revision and to original forms. The chief glory of each output of such successive efforts will be that it helps to bring forth that which will deserve to supersede it. I anticipate that men of the highest ability — poets lyric and dramatic, patriot-musicians like Wagner, statesmen who are also orators and prophets, men of more than Renaissance versatility — will some day create a form of public worship which for music, eloquence, and action, for closeness to experience, depth of meaning, scope of vision, elevation of sentiment, and reach of purpose will transcend any art that the world as yet has known.

The preparation must consist in creating a demand for church services which only great literary and religious geniuses can produce. We are apt to overlook the fact that men of original and constructive mind in any age bring forth works of art after whatever kind the public opinion of that age effectively demands. The Elizabethan era required simply the patching up of the Roman Catholic liturgies in the spirit of cautious compromise. No wonder, then, that the poets, like Spenser and Shakespeare, and the thinkers and masters of prose, like Richard Hooker and Francis Bacon, did not bestow their gifts upon the Church's forms. The hasty and shrewd adaptations and revisions of Cranmer were enough for the English nation in her new

self-consciousness as a Church. But is it inconceivable
that Shakespeare and the rest of his kind would have re-
sponded to her call, had she but called?

7. *The Poets Called*

Let the present-day situation in all its realism be kept
clearly in mind. By an effective demand is meant not
merely one that honours the poet with wreaths of bay,
but one that secures him a better livelihood than he can
win by turning his genius to any other application of his
art. Men of genius rightly are drawn to that domain
where they can find most honour, most recognition, the
greatest leisure, the fullest trust, the completest command
of all the materials needed and the widest scope for the
realization of ideas and the manifestation of their creative
power. Constructive artists do not defy and stem the
main currents of their age. On the contrary, they are
most sensitive to the drift. What they think and feel and
do is an index of the newest life and impulse of the times.
And the test of the times is the effective demand which
they make upon the artist.

Those, therefore, who have not the poet's nor musician's
nor dramatist's gift may at least help to create an active
public opinion. It is a lamentable characteristic of our
age that the new faith seems to lack understanding of the
means towards the realization of its great end. In striking
contrast to its impracticality is the efficient grip of conservative religionists upon means for bolstering up obsolete
doctrines and symbols. Illustrative of the whole question
here under consideration was the remark of a famous
designer of stained-glass windows: he was a man scientifically trained and imaginative, in sympathy with all the
newer ideals of the people; yet the best years of his life
were spent in designing and painting for church windows

illustrations of the cosmogony of the first chapters of Genesis, of the conceptions of angels found in Ezekiel, and of the New Testament miracles — in no one of which he believed. When asked how he could lavish beauty upon and thus perpetuate ideas which he counted false and pernicious, he replied, "The patrons of my art give me orders for these things, whereas the believers in the new ideals send me no orders."

To put it bluntly, we must go straight to the poets of all sorts and tell them what we want. We should begin with the great writers of our day. Many of them are eminently capable of bodying forth in sublime forms the national idealism of our day. We who demand need not even give a hint of what it is we want as regards actual structure; that is the poet's function to discover.

The best writers of our time are all gone astray on lines infinitely less congenial to their genius than a new liturgy would be. They could express the aspiration and buoyant confidence of the rising social democracy, of woman, and of childhood. I will speak only of British writers, who well might serve even America. Take the case of that profoundly passionate prophet of the new life, Mr. Israel Zangwill. His little book of poems, entitled "Blind Children," exhibits such strength and closeness of phrase as would suit a litany. The passion of his poetry is of the ethical order. Tell him that Christendom, which is still using in its liturgy the poetic utterances of his spiritual and natural ancestors, wants the religious genius of Judaism brought up to date. We need a Temple service which shall be as native to us as was theirs to the ancient Jews.

Consider for a moment the pathetic waste of Mr. Rudyard Kipling's bold imagination and virile tongue. To what end has he written? To delight us and our children, and to back British territory-grabbers. Or import Mr. William Watson, prophet and poet of the higher patriotism. Not one in a thousand of his contemporaries is familiar with the majestic rhythm of his lines. Besides Mr. William Watson, democratic America should call to herself Mr. Edward Carpenter, in order that labour might cease to be only a groan and not a voice — that the churches might again articulate the people's need and guide their hope.

And what might we not do with Mr. Shaw? Why not retain him, the humanist, as sensitive as St. Francis himself to the sufferings of the poor and of dumb brutes, as chivalrous as any knight of the Round Table, as candid as truth itself, and yet possessing the supreme grace of humour and that practical skill of stage-craft which is indispensable to the deviser of rituals? Why should his great gift of dramatic presentation not be utilized by the churches, as the principles of moral pedagogy require, for the storming of the senses of the people in the interests of the Soul of the nation?

And as England fails to do so, why should not America summon the musical genius of Sir Edward Elgar? To think that England's one really great and internationally renowned inventor of harmonies should have been setting to music that ghastly offspring of scholasticism, born five hundred years after due time, Cardinal Newman's " Dream of Gerontius " ! Sir Edward Elgar should have been retained by England to transform into convincing melody the dream of England's women, her children, and her poor.

8. *The Humanists in Religion*

What is needed within the churches is an ethical-democratic party, which shall look to the interests of the new idealism. Indeed, such a party has already sprung up in every denomination and is making steady advance. It is taking up the point of view of the Humanists of the sixteenth century. It is continuing the work of Sir Thomas More and Erasmus, who sided neither with Luther nor with the conservative party of Rome, but on the principle of Catholicism plus what was the Science of their day would have transformed the Roman organization and rites. The modernists are humanists of the twentieth century. The specific work of this party must consist in constructing religious services adequate to the science and the spiritual needs of the present day, in experimenting in the actual conducting of such services in religious assemblings, and thus educating the public and winning converts to their party. Thus would be ushered in an era when all the different tendencies of faith would be equally recognized. Side by side, rival forms could be practised and each group of worshippers could choose those commended of its own judgment. There would be no need to suppress any innocent forms which satisfied peculiarities and even eccentricities of temperament and intellect. Such would be the ideal method of religious evolution; and such, there is reason to hope, will be the actual process, now that America for half a century has been disciplined to the idea of experiment and of deference to the spiritual individuality of others.

It is wholly inconsistent with the policy of the humanist party to wish to introduce uniformity by compromise or by terrorizing either a minority or a majority. Humanism as a religious policy can adopt no other method than tentative adaptation; there will be no need to clamour or wrangle or resort to the subterfuges of a cunning opportunism.

CHAPTER XVIII

PREJUDICES AGAINST RELIGIOUS FORMS

1. *Familiar Acquaintance Needed*

As this volume is, in one aspect, an invitation to the public to give impartial consideration to the claims of church services which would be new in their object and inward meaning and partly new in outward shape, it may not be superfluous to indicate what the conditions are which enable a person to judge competently of any religious form.

If a person has been accustomed to the elaborate ceremonies of the High Church and has derived his spiritual strength through them, he will be astonished, upon his attending a Quaker meeting for the first time, that human beings, apparently of like susceptibilities with his own, could sit speechless and motionless with others for ten, fifteen, or thirty minutes together. But upon reflection it becomes perfectly evident that no one attending a Quaker meeting for the first time can be a competent judge. Its effects upon him are exceptional, and are the opposite of those produced upon the minds of Quakers themselves or of persons who have in some period of their life grown familiar with the meaning of its massive silences and its unpremeditated outbursts of speech. Here are two opposite effects produced by the same form. That upon those habituated to it is peace, love, clearer insight, new power of self-control and of self-sacrifice: that upon the stranger is a feeling almost of repulsion. The silence to the stranger is empty, the motionlessness stupefying. The speeches and prayers bear none of that majestic poetry and manifest none of that mental vision which he has been wont to consider as the distinctive mark of utterances inspired by the Most High. Of these opposite effects, it is clear that the one which should be accounted the standard is that made upon the mind of the person who is familiar with the form.

The first rule, then, to which the judge of a new liturgy must submit is that he make himself intimately familiar with it and suspend judgment until he has done so. I set forth this rule of criticism not only in order that my readers shall discount the prejudices which they might feel towards forms of the kind which I propose; my chief motive for calling attention to this first canon of criticism is that persons who are wholly in sympathy with the fundamental ideas of what I call ethical religion should prepare themselves to become appreciative and constructive critics of Roman Catholic rites, of the High Church liturgy, of the forms of service prevalent in all the Protestant churches, and even of the ritual of the Greek Church. The St. Paul-that-is-to-be of the humanitarian faith must know all things that work effectively upon all men and be willing to introduce every invention that shall foster spiritual energy. To prepare oneself for scientific and democratic revision, one must study even priestly and occult rituals sympathetically, psychologically, and sociologically. Whatever power for good or evil such forms have had, it was due to elements within them which were purely natural in their operation. But these elements cannot be judged justly if they still awaken a feeling of revulsion due to strangeness. One who has studied them long enough to be rid of the sense of novelty will also find that he will have outgrown that well-nigh universal prejudice which shrinks from reintroducing in new connections any music or ceremonial act or object that has been associated with supernaturalistic ideas. A man may test his unfitness to judge of religious

z

services by the degree to which he shrinks from forms the
ideas of which he has discarded.   It is an error to transfer
the dislike for a principle to the outward form through
which that principle has been able to propagate itself.
For that same form may be the best means also for the
transmission of the opposite idea.   The shrinking from the
unfamiliar prevents our widening our acquaintanceship
with religious expressions and recognizing the possibilities
of utilizing those expressions for the communication of our
own living faith.   I am not sure but that it is more important for a man to gain an expert knowledge of the ceremonies of other religions than to become an authority in
regard to his own.   If ever a ceremony arises so beautiful
and full of meaning as to commend itself to the judgment
of the nation as a whole, it will spring out of the labours and
insight of men who count all the forms of all the religions
of the world as new material to be used and transformed
to the needs of the nation.

2. *The Effect on the Believer*

The second rule for judging any religious service is that
no one should attempt to do so by its effects upon himself,
unless he believes in the truth of the idea which it embodies.
A form incorporating a thought which we believe to be
false seems like mummery unless for the time being we
force ourselves to forget our own convictions.   It must be
remembered, however, that what is objectionable is not
the form, as such, but the idea, false to us, which we see
exercising over others what we believe to be a deplorable
influence.   The attack, therefore, in such a case, should
never be upon the form.   By sweeping that away one would
not dry up the evil at its source.   Those Protestants err
who assail the forms instead of the substance of the Roman
Catholic Church and deplore any approximation to them

on the part of the Episcopal communion. If the ideas which animate Episcopal forms are the same as those which have found concrete embodiment in the Roman ritual, the attack should be directed against the ideas, not against the ceremonies.

In short, nothing in a ritual which to us is absurd, because the idea which it embodies is absurd, should be counted as an objection to the ritual itself. A ritual is a means towards an end. The end is that a certain idea, which is in the mind of some persons, should be communicated powerfully to the minds of other persons. But no evil inherent in the idea should be blamed against the medium which has been able to convey it. We must not complain of the ceremony of the Mass in the Roman Catholic Church if it succeeds in creating in the minds of the worshippers an overpowering sense of the immediate presence of the living spirit of Jesus Christ in the consecrated elements; for that is the very idea which the Mass was meant to convey. If we suppress the Mass, we must remember that we are overthrowing only the means by which the idea was communicated, and not the idea itself, which may still live in the minds of the Catholic priesthood.

Instead of attacking a symbol of an idea we hate, we ought, on the contrary, to feel towards it as the Government of one nation might towards some new device for military or naval defence which another nation had discovered and failed to keep secret. In spiritual warfare it is justifiable to rejoice when one is able to steal an enemy's gunpowder. Every symbol of every doctrine I abhor shall teach me how to convey the doctrine I love. In judging of my spiritual enemy's symbol, therefore, I must not be biassed by the fact that for me it is mere mummery, or worse.

3. *The Value of the Thing Symbolized*

A third canon which should be borne in mind is that no symbol should be judged by its effect upon us, even though we be familiar with it and though we count its teaching to be true, provided the truth it conveys is in our opinion of very little worth in the relative scale of human values. No form which conveys a truth to us insignificant can impress us. It leaves a sense of insipidity; and yet the form, both bodily act and words, may be quite perfect as symbols. A philosophic agnostic or rationalist, if he finds himself more intensely bored by the forms of the Episcopal Church than by the services of other Protestant bodies, ought to remember that this effect upon him is due to the greater efficiency of the more finely finished forms. They more powerfully convey to his mind the doctrines which he hates than do the less literary and classic rites. We must put ourselves by force of sympathetic imagination in the position of the devout and enthusiastic worshipper. When we have done this, we are able to detect just how much of the effect of the religion we are studying is to be traced to the idea itself and how much to the ceremonies in which it is embodied. We then are also able to detect what elements in these are capable of complete detachment from the special ideas which they serve and can be appropriated by a religion which wholly discards trust in superhuman agencies as the source of moral inspiration.

4. *Minor Cautions*

Another rule which will aid towards an impartial judgment of any religious rite is to bear in mind that it is not essential to any ritual that it should be repeated every day or twice every Sunday, or even once a week or once a month. Unhappily, the churches of our day which depend most

upon liturgy iterate and reiterate the same forms *ad nau-
seam*. Many, even, who devoutly believe the ideas conveyed, find the reiteration intolerable. This satiety from
too frequent hearing and seeing of the same forms accounts
for a very large part of the prevalent dislike of ritual; and
yet that dislike is purely accidental. If the Episcopal
Church should adopt quite different forms for morning
and evening service for every day in the year, varying the
order and presenting different aspects of its great teachings, it might be able to draw all Protestantism into one
fold, and help persons who have outgrown supernaturalism
to see the possibilities of using ritual in the interests of
national idealism.

In lieu of any such introduction of infinite and delightful variety into the services of the Episcopal Church, it
would be well if those intelligently interested in the religious life of the nation would remember that the monotony
attributed to ritual to-day is wholly extraneous to its essential nature, and that the ritual of the future may reflect
the exhaustless fulness of life itself, and thus meet that
intellectual need which psychologists call the law of variety.

Another caution may here be in place. A religious
ritual may leave us apathetic, not because of any defect
in itself as art or because of any falsehood or insignifi-
cance in its idea, but because it goes counter to some
self-interest which we are unwilling to sacrifice to the interests of humanity at large. Our judgment may tell us
that the idea conveyed is true and good and that the means
by which it is conveyed are beautiful; and yet we may
on this account be alarmed. Were the idea, by means of
the symbol, to penetrate into our inmost self, we should be
compelled to let go some treasure which we clutch. Let
us imagine a person quite prepared in all other ways to
appreciate the lines from George Eliot's "Spanish Gypsy,"
which I would suggest as an appropriate utterance for the

opening of a confirmation rite when the churches have become humanistic :

> Ours is a faith
> Taught by no priest, but by our beating hearts:
> Faith to each other; the fidelity
> Of men whose pulses leap with kindred fire,
> Who in the flash of eyes, the clasp of hands,
> Nay, in the silent bodily presence, feel
> The mystic stirrings of a common life
> Which makes the many one.

The truth and beauty of these words may be felt to be un-
impeachable; but on that account they may be hateful to
a person who, despite his better nature, loathes "the great
unwashed." Liberty, equality, and fraternity are all very
well in the abstract and as a watchword of a political party;
but fraternity in a church's rite of admission to membership, committing every one to social recognition of the
crowd who make up the congregation, might be exacting
too great a sacrifice of many a refined, exclusive soul.

Another prejudice inevitably confronts one who asks
the public to sanction democratic and modernist innovations in church services. A critic hearing a new ritual
imperfectly rendered should discount the imperfections of
the rendering and not attribute to the special form offences
attributable to defects of execution. An exquisite poem
or magnificent prose utterance may be so stammeringly
spoken as to make it impossible for the listener to realize
the beauty or the moral dignity of the composition or the
possibility of its being impressively rendered. A certain
degree of skill must be evinced before even a fair jury would
be able to pronounce a just judgment. What is true of
mere elocution is to a greater degree the case in regard to
instrumental and vocal music. The general public never
discriminates between bad music and a bad rendering of
good music; but a critic of unfamiliar forms of public

worship can train himself to detect when the rendering is the cause of offence.

The old-established forms possess an enormous advantage over new and democratic symbols. They command the best music, the finest architecture, and all other accessories. The further one goes from the churches where the aristocratic and wealthy worship, the more one finds not only ideas which would offend their preconceptions, but also forms and renderings of forms which would outrage their standards. The classes most cultivated æsthetically have nevertheless not had enough intellectual training to be self-critical; they attribute to the new forms and ideas offence due merely to crudities of execution, which may be owing to the poverty of believers in the new ideas.

Still another caution must be given for the guidance of the critic of new religious forms and proposed revisions of old. Ritual, like the drama, can only be judged when it is witnessed in actual execution. The items of the rite and the directions for production when merely read in a book will not disclose their possibilities even to an expert. It is a commonplace of experience that until a drama is actually performed nobody can tell how it will "take." The dramatist himself does not know. Actors and stage-managers are proverbially liable to erroneous judgment. They reject pieces which prove afterwards the greatest successes, and expend vast sums of money on the performance of plays which fail utterly.

There is no occasion for us to enter into the essential differences of a literary composition when read in a book and when recited in a church. But the difference is astonishingly great. A religious rite in the pages of a book is to its actual celebration very much as a corpse to a living body. A sentence or a ritualistic sign takes on new and unexpected vitality the moment it is uttered or enacted before a public assembly convened for that purpose.

CHAPTER XIX

THE PSYCHOLOGY OF PUBLIC WORSHIP

IT would not be difficult to prove, both historically and analytically, that where there is no ceremonial there is no religion.

1. *Historical*

The historical proof lies in the fact, disclosed by thorough research, that every nation or race known to us as holding religious ideas possesses some form, however rudimentary, of ceremonial. In the main, with the complexity of the ideas, the rites develop; although there may be counteracting tendencies which prevent the same pace in each. It is generally thought that as a religion grows more spiritual it loses in ceremonial complexity, and that the inwardness of one's ideas of God naturally militates against outward forms; but even this is found not to be the case if we take a psychological and, so to speak, physiological, and not merely a spectacular, view of ceremony. The case of the Society of Friends is one in point. Superficially and outwardly it would seem that persons who sit motionless in a meeting for an hour together, and dress with severe simplicity, are anti-ritualists, and disprove once for all the dictum that where there is no ceremonial there is no religion. But first let us remember that symbolical dress is the most striking element in the furniture of even spectacular ritual. Further, in proportion as Quakers have discarded their peculiar garb, they have generally discarded their peculiar tenets. But, quite apart from the question of dress, for a number of persons to sit silently together is the most dramatic and eloquent ceremonial ever invented. Physiologically, also, there is no action involving more self-control, more domination of every nerve and muscle, than motionlessness.   Think of the tongue, with its proneness to move when the mind is bursting with ideas to be communicated.   Think of the eye that so easily wanders; of the ear solicited by every stray sound.   Consider, again, the tremendous physiological self-consciousness developed by the silent presence of others, unless one is dominated by an overpowering idealism.   We need only to peep beneath the surface of things to see that here is action — and action that requires not only an almost hypnotic control of a whole assembly by a single thought, but also action which produces upon every onlooker a most powerful impression of the reality of the thing signified.

Again, to some persons the fact that religion is a function of ceremonial, and *vice versa*, is obscured by the æsthetic meagreness of many ceremonials of which the underlying religious conviction is highly intellectual and inward. There is a tendency to imagine that rites which are not æsthetic are not ceremonial, and that an absence of the fine arts proves an absence of ritual. This, however, is utterly a mistake. The sacrament of the Lord's Supper has not in and of itself any æsthetic element; or, if it has, it is only what is borrowed from the general social grace and manners of the persons who communicate. It is quite possible that many among the humble folk who entered the Christian movement at the start, because it was a burial and sick-benefit society, partook of the Lord's Supper in a manner not more graceful and charming outwardly than they ate any other meal. Likewise it is difficult to see very striking æsthetic elements or any elaboration of the various fine arts in the rite of immersion. If there were anything beautiful in the ceremony, it could only be something quite accidental — as that the Church official performing it happened to be graceful in the movements of his body and well developed in physique. Even then, however, it is hard to imagine that men with their clothes dripping with water would conform to our notions of beauty in drapery. Likewise the dripping face and streaming hair must be such as at least no ordinary person would count æsthetically attractive compared with the face when dry.

What is true of the Lord's Supper and baptism from an æsthetic point of view holds equally of the details of all the essential features of the Catholic ceremonial. The making of the sign of the Cross has nothing in itself of the beautiful; nor has the elevation of the host; nor have the forms of the marriage rite and of burial. It is altogether a mistake, then, to identify ritual even in its most elaborate forms with the fine arts, and then to argue from an absence of the latter that the former is not present. Even if we confine ourselves to the elaborate services of the Roman Catholic Church on Sundays and the great festival days, of the splendour of which one hears much, we must admit that the ritual proper, except in colour, is not splendid. There is nothing especially beautiful in a man's kneeling many times, in the bowings of others before him, in his muttering of the words of a book, in his turnings about, and in the changes made in dress.

Probably the right relation between the fine arts and ritual is that suggested by a passage in Mr. Dearmer's "Parson's Handbook," where he says that many persons are kept away from the Anglican Church on account of its bad music, and for this reason he pleads that the music shall be good. This suggestion is sound, both religiously and psychologically. In a community accustomed to music of a high class you must either have none at all in your public worship or a kind which will not give offence. If robes are to be worn, they must harmonize in colour, shape, and quality of fabric with the community's feelings of the appropriateness of all these to the occasion. We thus discover the whole principle of the relation of the fine arts to ritual. If the ceremony is to be in a building, that building must meet the requirements of the people architecturally. But whether the costumes and the building are really æsthetic or not is wholly beside the mark. The one question is, Do they keep any one away on account of their ugliness?

Perhaps the proposition that where there is no ceremonial there is no religion should be taken as true not of an individual human being, but of a nation; and not of a nation at any one instant, but throughout its history. It is possible that after generations of ritual, religion without the visible signs might continue to live. It is certainly possible that in a community where various religious rites are regularly practised by various groups of worshippers, many individual persons who never participate in these rites may be most devoutly religious. In such a case, however, it may be questioned whether such persons do not constantly have the fundamental problems and sentiments of religion thrust upon their attention by the very ceremonials which they themselves abstain from witnessing and perhaps regard with loathing. The credit, therefore, for the religion even of those who have no ritual must in such cases be assigned to ritual.

After these explanations, it is probable that no one will contend against the general proposition that in a nation where there is no ceremonial there can be no religion.

2. *Analytical*

Philosophically, the case stands thus: Religious ceremony is in its very nature sacramental, if we take the Prayer Book's definition of a sacrament as an outward and visible sign of an inward and spiritual grace. A ceremony which did not signify an inward and spiritual grace, and which was not thought, at least by the devotees themselves of the cult, to be necessary to the conveyance of the grace, would never have been adopted. A man might possibly, on philosophical and ethical grounds, reject every sacrament as unnecessary and even pernicious. Still he could not deny that those who did practise a religious rite believed in the necessity for it, and therefore, under the domination of this belief, positively needed it.

But why is a sign necessary? Or rather, what is the nature of the inward and spiritual grace which requires a vehicle? If, again, we take the point of view not of the individual alone, but of the community or the nation, we shall easily be convinced that every spiritual grace is dependent upon an outward sign. If such a grace is something that is communicated from the heart and will of one person to the heart and will of another, through their conscious intelligence, it becomes almost self-evident to anybody who knows human life, that there could be no communication of it without a sign as a symbol of the thought of the one understood by both. The whole of language is nothing but a system of signs, and at bottom every communication of an idea from one person to another, if that idea be true or be felt by both to be true, partakes of the nature of a sacrament. What is the conveying of an inspiring thought from one to another by an outward and visible sign but an instance of the very thing which the Church of England declares to be a sacrament? One may readily concede that the word sacrament does not apply unless the grace communicated is some religious principle or virtue. But then one cannot deny that religious ceremonial is only a specific variety of a whole genus of rituals, which, in proportion as the matters with which they deal are sacred, are sacraments. Any word which is the exclusive sign of a special meaning is essential to the conveyance of that meaning to another. Words, however, constitute only one system of signs. Gestures make up another, dress another, styles of architecture another.

We cannot understand the philosophy of ceremonial in religion unless we understand its use, and the necessity for it, in other domains of human interest. There is very much in human life which is ritualistic, yet which we fail to recognize as such. Every act, in so far as it is an arbitrary sign of something in the mind of him who performs it, by which he is able to communicate that mental something to the mind of another, is an act of ritual. Persons, therefore, who disapprove of religious ceremony on the ground that ritual altogether is an absurdity and without foundation in practical necessity, must be ready to sweep it away from its other domains as well. Let a man strip from human manners all that is not an immediate necessity of direct satisfaction, and he will begin to realize that, whether the similar statement be true of religion or not, it is literally a fact that where there is no ceremonial, there are no manners. If there were no acts agreed upon arbitrarily by the community and performed as signs of deference, of respect, of cordiality, of trust, of affection, of acquaintanceship, of being strangers, to what a state of barren crudity and isolation should we be reduced!

In another volume I remind my readers that some sort of a sign of entrance into a church, a physical act understood to indicate the mental act, must be submitted to, else it is inconceivable that a church could ever acquire new voluntary members. Of course a church might count itself synonymous with the nation, and say that every person born on the soil of the nation was a member. But then it becomes quite clear that the necessity of a sign has not been done away with. The sign ceases to be a voluntary act, but the fact of being born within the

geographical area of the nation becomes itself the symbol;
and, as it is an event not within the arbitrary will of the
individual, such a church thereby ceases to receive voluntary
members.   Here, accordingly, the necessity for arbitrary
signs is confirmed instead of being disproved.

In business life ritual is as important and prominent as
it is in religion.   Constantly the commercial community
must by common consent seize upon some one act or circumstance which is to serve no longer in its ordinary and
natural capacity alone, but as an arbitrary sign which, once
chosen, possesses almost a magical power.   What a difference between the spoken word of an agreement and the
signature to a written document!   The difference is not
in the natural inferiority of the word or in a lack of honour
on the part of the man who feels at liberty to break his
word.   The difference between the spoken word and the
signature is that the community has never stamped the
spoken word as the legal sign committing the speaker.   If
once the word spoken in the presence of others were to be
made the sign, one would find that the sense of inviolability
now attaching to the signature would be transferred to the
verbal symbol.   In escaping from religion, one has not
escaped from ritual.   One has only escaped from the word;
and quite possibly it is *that* in religion, and not the thing,
which gives offence to many.

Ritual as a social phenomenon is extremely complex.
For instance, I have been speaking of acts chosen arbitrarily as signs of some inward and spiritual grace.   Now
if a totally new set of acts that had no meaning otherwise
were chosen, the case of ritual would be comparatively
simple.   But nearly always an act serves in a double capacity, both as an arbitrary sign and as an actual direct
benefit to oneself or another.   For instance, to drink a
glass of wine may be a direct service or disservice to oneself.   This would be quite enough to insure the practice

or condemnation of it. Yet it is just such an act as drinking a glass of wine which is seized upon and made to do duty in another capacity. If you drink in the company of others, it may be taken as a symbol of friendship, of fellowship. To refuse to perform the act in this way may be the grossest insult. To perform it with certain persons may be the occasion of losing caste with others, and may act as a signal for a social boycott.

It requires considerable alertness and acuteness in watching one's conduct throughout a single day to discover how many acts, which one does as if they were of direct expediency, serve also in the capacity of symbols. Unlike the lifting of the hat, the shaking of hands, the formal greetings with friends, which are purely symbolical acts, nearly everything we do is just as much serviceable as it is ritualistic. The ritual nature of these acts which have another import is one which we are prone to forget entirely in the ordinary course of life.

3. *The Symbolism of Dress*

Take, for instance, the kind of clothes we wear. How few of us fully realize that the distinction between the conventional dress of men and women is a matter of ritual. It would be almost impossible to detect at a distance whether most human beings of the age of forty were men or women if they were dressed alike, if the men were shaved, and the manner of wearing the hair were the same. Because of this possible confusion it is that the law makes it a criminal offence for men to wear women's clothes or women men's. It is here, however, wholly a question of ritual. The woman's dress, besides serving as a convenience and a decency, serves as a sign to announce that she is a woman. So of a man's dress. This difference, however, is no more striking than that in the costume of different classes of society.

We are so accustomed to wear clothes which immediately declare the class we belong to, that we do not
realize the effects that would come were we suddenly to
don the style of dress of people of another station. Only
when we imaginatively picture the consequences do we
realize the deep psychological hold which the signs have
upon the mind of the community and upon our own habits.
No people who are not working-men dress like them; which
means, not that the dress of the day-labourer is inconvenient
or not beautiful or is necessarily untidy, but simply that
any man above the working-class would almost as lief die
as be identified by the community with those who are disinherited from all the greatest privileges of humanity. He
might also shrink from the suspicion of insanity which would
be hurled at him if people, knowing him to be rich, saw him
in the garb of a day-labourer. It is equally true that the
moment people of the working-class, by any accident of
fortune, become rich, they instantly assume the dress of the
classes of society above the working-class; not primarily
because that dress is æsthetically or hygienically preferable,
but because it stands as a symbol for social position and the
command of power and opportunity.

When certain classes of persons wear distinctive uniform, it becomes more immediately evident that their
clothes are not only for convenience and decency, but that
the peculiar colour or shape or ornamentation is a sign of
their social position or function. Yet it seems so natural
that the postman, the soldier, the sailor, and the professional nurse should wear uniforms that we easily forget
that it is only by making the dress arbitrarily a sign of
something with which it has no inherent connection that
we are able instantly to recognize in the distance the postman, the soldier, sailor, and nurse as such. What a mar-
vellously efficient system of communicating a knowledge
of such invisible yet powerful realities as social function

and position through the eye! How terribly cruel was
the use made of the ritual of dress in the case of the Jews
in the Ghetto! How horrible it is in the present custom
of a prison garb and a poorhouse uniform! But all these
cases prove at least the universal secular recognition of
outward and visible signs for organic social functions and
relations. It is then a little strange that persons who
accept, for instance, as altogether suitable the costume for
the nurse or the uniform for the postman should speak
with contempt of a distinctive garb for priests. Logically
and practically the transference of one's contempt from
the priest to the dress he wears is altogether unjustifiable.
For his office would be just as contemptible, if it were contemptible, whether he dressed in uniform or not. But the
tremendous efficiency of ritual is proved by this almost
instinctive transference of horror for the inward reality to
the outward and visible sign. The only justification for
wishing to remove the priestly garb without abolishing the
priesthood is that you would be removing one powerful
means by which the priesthood announces its existence to
the community. Nothing is more striking upon the first
visit of a stranger to Rome than the enormous number of
priests who throng the streets. The impression is created
of the ever-present power of the Church. Strip from the
clothes of the priest the signs of his office and this reminder
of the existence of the Church would vanish instantly. In
Berlin the officers of the army, thanks to the military use
of ritual, are in similar domination over the mind of a
stranger. One never can escape the sense of the haunt-
ing, alert presence of the military power.

So true is it that the unseen functions and relationships
of human society are dependent upon systems of arbitrary
signs that one may well say that with the abolition of all
the signs would ensue an annihilation of the functions. If
not only the distinctiveness of his garb, but every other

2 A

arbitrary signal of office of the priest were removed, he would no longer be a priest, in that he could not possibly be recognized; and, not being recognized, he would not be allowed to perform the very rudiments of the priestly function.

As a part, then, of a general policy for abolishing the social function of any class it would be justifiable to attempt to forbid their ritualistic dress. But if one's hatred of the thing signified is to extend to some of the signs by which it is signified, it ought to extend to them all. If the object be not to abolish the function of a certain class, but only to repress it, to deprive it of part of its power and restrict it within narrower limits, then to strip it of some of its symbols while allowing it the use of others is justifiable both logically and practically. Undoubtedly one sees in the relative amount of symbolism in the dress of Roman Catholic priests, Anglican clergymen, and non-episcopal preachers an expression of the different degrees of ascendency of the officials in these three religious communities.

An individualistic philosophy of religion, politics, and economics is the only point of view from which the ritual of dress can be opposed. And historically it has been opposed by anarchistic and anti-socialistic theorists. It will be found that in proportion as a man's social function and position are counted to be of less significance than his all-round individuality as a human being and than his own private liberty, in that proportion symbolic dress has been abolished. Individualistic religious liberty has been the source of the hatred of the social function of the priest and preacher and of the churches, and is thus the origin of the hatred of the official's dress. It is equally the origin of the abolition of uniform generally. The officer of the English army is not in uniform except when on duty. He is a civilian among civilians in his everyday life in England.

Uniform prevails there to-day only to mark the disgrace of poverty or crime, or to serve commercially and as a defence for property or to announce sex. The postman has a uniform because the function of transmitting written communications is considered so important in business that the postman's individuality is as nothing compared with his official responsibility in delivering letters. Likewise the policeman is dressed symbolically. The individuality of the policeman is as nothing compared to his defence of property. A policeman is ten times a man, and therefore we dress him as a superman. But what a commentary upon our modern society that the social function of the policeman is counted thus infinitely more valuable than that of the school-teacher! The authority of the school-teacher would be enhanced and the work made easy were he or she, at least in school hours, to wear a teacher's dress. And this will surely come as we again recognize the intellectual and moral functions of the State.

Carlyle's humorous philosophy of clothes was but a chapter in the philosophy of outward and visible signs of inward and spiritual graces. Carlyle perhaps exaggerated the significance of clothes. We should not be reduced even outwardly to a level if all symbolic dress were discarded. Other arbitrary signs would be chosen which would indicate differences of sentiment, prejudice, spiritual power, origin, ancestry, and what not. Indeed, Carlyle himself takes clothes but as a type of all forms of symbolism.

We have seen that there is nothing peculiar to religion as distinct from manners or commerce which makes it dependent upon ritual, and have found that as an actual fact manners and commerce are just as ritualistic as religion. One may say of commerce, as of the other two: where there is no ritual, there is no trade. Where there is no outward and visible sign of the inward and spiritual grace of exchange of ownership of commodities, there is no exchange. Accordingly, when the Founder of Christianity insisted upon immersion as a sign for admission to the Church and upon a common meal as an evidence of loyalty among members, when he declared that baptism was essential to salvation, he was doing nothing different from that which the business man does; nor were his reasons different.

4. *Not Supernaturalistic*

When we bear in mind that it is no peculiarity of religion which makes ceremonial a necessity for it, we see how false is the generally prevalent notion that the supernaturalism of religion is what makes the resort to signs and rites indispensable. It may well be granted that if the spiritual grace to be communicated is the favour of some personal agent beyond man and nature who requires formal homage, then the making of the signs that please him would become the *sine qua non* of gaining his favour. But here again we note that the sign is necessary not because the agent communicated with is supernatural, but simply because he is another personal agent, and that a system of signs must always be set up if one of two persons is to communicate a knowledge of his inward disposition to the other.

This statement opens up to us a second phase of the nature of ritual, suggested in the Prayer-Book definition by the words "inward and spiritual."

5. *The Ethical Meaning of Ritual*

The spiritual grace is never merely a general idea unrelated to the persons who communicate or receive it. There is never simply a sign of a general or a particular fact, such as a scientific formula might be, or an account of some event which took place in ancient Athens unrelated

to the persons by whom and to whom to-day the sign is
made.   Always his own will and his own heart are committed by the person making a ritualistic sign and are
received and accepted by those to whom it is made.   Par-
ticipation in an act of ritual is a personal commitment or
pledge, and therefore is an event in the moral and social
history of the participants.   The woman who assumes the
rôle of bride in the marriage ceremony is actually thereby
becoming the wife of the man who stands by her side.
She is not simply symbolically illustrating in fantastic manner some general principle of monogamy.   She is staking
almost all her chances for happiness in life upon the act
she is performing.   The marriage ceremony is infinitely
removed in its nature from a show or a symbolical repre-
sentation of some real event which took place elsewhere.
A great event is always taking place in the life of the persons who are participating in any religious ritual.   In a funeral rite, that which is conspicuous for the mourners is
the immediate reality of their bereavement.   They have
lost a relative, a friend.   The mourning garments are
symbols of an actual state of heart and will.   The deference shown to the dead might be shown in some other
manner, but that other manner must needs be symbolical.
A man going through the ceremony of taking holy orders
is actually committing himself to a profession.   To take
part in the ceremony of becoming an Episcopalian clergyman while being at heart a Roman Catholic or an Atheist,
is to commit a deed of unutterable perfidy.   The girl who
goes through the ceremony of taking the veil as a nun
is setting her life's destiny on the act.   If she does it in-
sincerely, she is wrecking both her character and her happiness.   If she is forced into doing it, those instigating
the coercion are committing a heinous crime.   The little
child baptized may never afterwards wholly escape from
the moral and social effects of the fact that his parents and

the priest committed him to the Roman Catholic or some other communion.

In the light of this terrible realism, one wonders how the expressions "mere ceremony," "mere ritual," have come so generally into use. Who has ever seen such a thing as a mere ceremony or a mere ritual? For if there were such a thing as the word "mere" implies, how could the act be fraught with far-reaching and unescapable consequences? There are persons who speak lightly of the marriage ceremony, as if it were a mere form and as if it could make no difference in the duties and responsibilities and the affection of the woman towards the man, whether she went through the marriage ceremony or not. Yet no woman ever defied this "mere ceremony," who forgot her defiance to the end of her days. There is no such thing as a mere ceremony of ritual; for the moment it ceases to be an indispensable sign in the eyes of the community, it is not the sign at all.

6. *The Difference between Ritual and Acting*

Thus we see how absolutely mistaken is the judgment of those who associate elaborate church services with stage performances and theatrical displays. There are three fundamental distinctions which place a world-wide difference between ritual and drama. In drama the actor only pretends to be the person he represents. In ritual he actually is the person. A man who was not a priest, were he to personate a priest in the performance of the Mass, would expose himself to being stoned to death by the outraged members of the Catholic communion. And he would deserve severe punishment. On the other hand, what could more outrage our sense of human dignity than that an actual cardinal of the Church of Rome should personate a cardinal on the stage in a play of Shakespeare's? How is it that we have this terrific sense of the incompatibility of ritual and drama, if there be anything essentially akin in the two? It violates every principle of dramatic art to attempt to attract the public by any kind of realism whereby the original persons should, so to speak, play their own parts. Even when contemporary events are depicted, in proportion as the drama respects itself, it preserves its method by which one person pretends to be another. In Miss Elizabeth Robins' recent play, entitled "Votes for Women," it might have been easy to draw larger crowds, and secure a longer run of the play, if the original women conspicuous as "suffragettes" had themselves taken the chief parts in the performance. But they knew, and the writer of the play and its stage producer knew, that the play would have lost its entire force as a political pamphlet, if notoriety and success had been bought at this price. It is true that on the vaudeville stage persons conspicuous in real life sometimes exhibit themselves for money to the gaping crowds, but scarcely ever is there such lack of taste shown as that they should assume a part analogous to their own in real life. So there is no question here either of art or of ritual.

The second of the three chief distinctions between ritual and drama is closely akin to the first. All the events on the stage must be a mere pretence. One can imagine that the "suffragettes" might have acted in "Votes for Women," and drawn the crowd, and yet the actual incidents in the play might have been purely fictitious. So a totally distinct characteristic of stage plays is that what happens is understood not actually to be occurring. As a fact, nobody is dying, no one is stealing, no one's heart is breaking.

In church ritual no deed done is at all a stage performance; it is the original. Not only are those who officiate actually, legally the persons holding the office which they seem to hold, but they are positively doing the things they seem to do.

The third point of difference between ritual and the drama is that in the former all the materials used are exactly what they pretend to be. If it is not so, an offence is committed against the fundamental principle of ritual. It is permissible that an actor on the stage personating a monk and imitating the celebration of the Mass should wear a wig to produce the appearance of a tonsure. But we would resent it if in a church service a real priest, celebrating Mass, were to appear in such a headgear. We require that his head shall not only seem to be but shall be shaven.

This principle of realism applies to all the objects seen, beginning with the church itself. On a stage, for the purposes of a play, a cathedral may consist of a wooden frame and painted canvas to imitate stone and arches. But the cathedral itself, where a ritual is performed, is actually built of stone shaped into arches. Any sort of made-up structure may serve for a pretended pulpit in a play; but the pulpit in a church must be what it appears. Even the details of the dress must be made of the genuine stuffs and substances which they look to be. The embroideries, the gems, the gold are real embroideries, gems, and gold. Any mere tinsel is out of place; whereas on the stage, for the actors to wear crowns really made of gold would be to distract instead of concentrating the attention upon the true art and nature of the performance. In a play on the stage, if a meal is represented, it is preferable, as art, that the bread and wine should not be real, and the people only seem to eat and drink. But it were a scandal in church to introduce substitutes in this manner. In Wagner's " Parsifal " there is a scene of the Communion of the Lord's Supper where the Holy Grail glows with a wine-like light of what seems the actual blood of Christ. It is far more impressive as dramatic art, although we know the effect is due to a mechanical trick, than anything in any actual celebration of communion. But such a device in a real communion service would be blasphemy.

Not only devout worshippers, but every other honest man would be horrified to hear that any celebrant of any religious service had in the least particular introduced any merely dramatic effect. It is important to bring home vividly this aspect of the realism of ritual. To do so, let me ask the reader to contrast a burial service upon the stage with a real burial service in a church. It is not only that in the latter the mourners are the real persons and the ceremony an actual deed of homage to the departed; but his dead body is verily in the coffin. If one hears or knows that in the coffin on the stage there is nothing of the sort — it is empty or filled with stones — no offence is given. To introduce a real corpse on the stage would be — such a thing could not be. But suppose the whisper went through the congregation at a burial service that the coffin was empty, how could one explain the moral resentment which would be felt, except on the principle that ritual is never a mere formality? On the stage, without offence, we often see a woman carrying in her arms what purports to be an infant child, while we know that there is nothing of the sort there. But it is hard to conceive the consternation that would ensue, were the priest in church to discover that he was baptizing not a live baby, but a rag doll. Yet why, if ritual is even remotely akin to theatrical performance?

Perhaps, if we turn from religious to political ritual, we shall more keenly realize the unjust prejudice against ritual which inclines to dub it theatrical. Suppose Parliament is to be opened by the King and Queen of England. It is unthinkable that any substitutes should be found to perform their parts. It is inconceivable that the ceremony should take place when there was not actually to be an opening of Parliament. It would be shocking to our sense of the dignity of the kingdom that the crowns worn should be gilt paper and the jewels paste. A pantomime at Drury Lane is as far removed from the spectacle of an actual royal ceremony as is fiction from reality and fancy from fact. An American who may have seen hundreds of pretence kings and queens in theatres longs to see the real King and Queen of England, for there is a whole world of difference between the theatrical and the ceremonial. Yet the King and Queen are by ritual king and queen. They are outward and visible signs of an inward and spiritual social function and relation.

7. *Ritual and Real Life*

I have said enough to prove that acts of ritual are deeds in real life. But how, then, do they differ from other deeds which are not ritual? In the first place simply in this, that they are symbolical, and by means of arbitrary agreement effect mighty moral and social changes in the relations of individuals to the surrounding community. In ritual outside of religion, the difference between ordinary acts of life and ceremony is not so strikingly conspicuous, and the two blend in such a manner that we scarcely are aware when we pass from the one to the other. But religious ritual differs from the rest of life, ritualistic or not, by so much as religion differs from other spheres of human interest and activity. Now it is to be remembered that religion, as we have seen, deals with what are believed to be the supreme concerns of life. It is a turning of the attention to the ultimate source of life's highest blessings, in order to gain them. The dignity of religious ritual differs, then, from the dignity of political, commercial, or merely drawing-room ceremony by the superiority of the relations of which religion treats. Here, of course, I assume that the persons participating believe in the worth of religion. But in cases where they do not, the same principle is illustrated. Their bitter hatred of religious forms and ceremonies cannot be because form and ceremony in itself is pernicious or is an empty nothing, but because they count the religion to be hostile to human interests. They dread the ends the religion has in view, and therefore they hate these potent means by which the ends are achieved. In the same way, those persons who do not hate but have a patronizing contempt for religious ritual simply transfer their contempt for religion to its forms. Such adverse critics, however, if they were logical and practical, would be compelled to concede that the vanity or the positive evil of religious ceremonial casts no discredit whatever upon ritual in general.

8. *Social Democratic Ritual*

I have given this elaborate analysis because, as it seems to me, ninety-nine persons out of a hundred who hold my fundamental views in regard to the principles of ethics, religion, and politics incline to disbelieve in ritual altogether. Having turned from the forms and ceremonies of supernatural religion, they are filled with horror at the very suggestion that the new ideas of naturalism, social democracy, and national idealism must concrete themselves "into a cultus, a fraternity, with assemblings and holydays, with song and book, with brick and stone." They fail to see that in order to counteract the influence of Rome it is necessary to set up a ritual of Reason. They are not ashamed to declare a distaste for any and every sort of religious ceremonial. But in assuming such an attitude, if my analysis be correct, they are doing nothing less than refusing to naturalism, democracy, and national idealism a system of signs by which the deepest personal responsibilities of social life might be announced and established among the many. They are unwittingly robbing humanism of indispensable organs, and reducing it to the most beggarly and inarticulate means of actualizing its ideal throughout the community.

Fortunately, these opponents of outward and visible signs of an inward and spiritual grace are not so ruthlessly logical as to abandon all use of human speech. They would permit persons who have discarded supernaturalism to reason and argue, and, if possible, be eloquent in public speeches, pamphlets, and books. But nobody must wear a garment which shall stand to the community as a sign that he who wears it is one who repudiates supernaturalism, miracles, presumptions of an aristocratic priesthood, and the like. Yet let us suppose that in New York or San Francisco alone there were five hundred men and women devoting their lives to the spread of democratic and naturalistic religion. Think what an easy means of propaganda it would be that these persons, wherever they went, should wear a dress as distinctive as that of the Salvation Army workers, with the words printed on their caps and bonnets, "Democracy in Religion," "The Religion of Social Justice"! Such signs would challenge more attention than could be gained by a hundred times as much labour and cost in any other one direction. Suppose, too, that a person — the chosen speaker and preacher, let us say, of a democratic ethical church — should wear, when preaching, a robe selected and sanctioned by the society as the distinctive garb for its official preacher. Is it wrong to think that instantly at a meeting where the speaker wore such a symbolic dress, the impression made upon every attendant as to the earnestness and strength of conviction of the members of ethical societies would be a thousand times stronger than if the man merely appeared in his everyday clothes? It must not be forgotten that even those everyday clothes are a symbol. If he is a working-man, his dress will betray it. If he is well-to-do, immediately,

without his saying a word and without his wishing it, his
dress shows his social position and suggests the size of his
tailor's bill. These matters, taken at their least, are dis-
tractions. A social-democratic preacher should appear not
as a man of this or that birth or ancestry or family connection or means of livelihood, but simply as a teacher —
as one enough respected to have been selected as a preacher
of social duties and an inspirer of moral enthusiasms.

The prejudice against so subordinate a sign in religious
ritual as dress naturally extends its censure to the adoption
of any conspicuous signs to indicate the great events of
life from the point of view of social idealism. It would
seem to me that the greatest service which any little group
of ethical idealists could render in our times would be to
concentrate themselves upon the elaboration of a ritual
which would adequately express their new thought.

In the past, religious ceremonies, being anti-democratic,
unscientific, and occult, have strangled liberty and intellectual honesty. They have overpowered the imagination
of the people, and allured them into willing subjection to
human and superhuman masters. But the worst of all
their effects has been this unthinking and bitter hatred
and distrust aroused in naturalists and democrats for any
and every form of religious ritual. Until this distrust is
removed, science and social democracy can never throw
off princely and priestly domination and the superstitious
authority of invisible agencies. Until a ritualistic religion
be constructed on the basis of science and democracy,
science and democracy will be almost exclusively confined
to the domain of material wealth and politics. They will
be occupied with the machinery instead of the dynamics
of social justice. They will fail in the supreme art of
generating the enthusiasm and guiding the loyalty of the
masses of the people.

9. *Ritual and the Fine Arts*

I have attempted, as far as possible, to dissociate ritual from the fine arts, and have implied that the fine arts shall be introduced into it only in order that no æsthetic deficiency may offend the community and thus alienate minds highly cultivated in taste. But this problem of the relation of the fine arts to ritual is extremely complex, and therefore one aspect after another must be dealt with.

In the first place, it is essential that a church service shall be conducted, as far as possible, by persons whose speech and bearing conform to the educational standards of the nation.

As for singing and instrumental music in church services, they must never be primarily for æsthetic delight. The compositions must be restricted to that class which produce emotions akin to those produced by the ideals of social righteousness and by the responsibilities of social duty. Certain tone-compositions do undoubtedly arouse an enthusiasm or a dignified calm allied to ethical moods. The Roman Catholic Church has rightly recognized of late the necessity of banishing from the Church services forms of music which are not strictly subordinate to the ends which religion serves. It is conceivable that churches might give such beautiful secular music that many would attend for the æsthetic treat; but they would thereby defeat their own end. Church music, however perfect, must be so subordinate to and so permeated with the church's dominating idea that it will inevitably direct attention to her principles and create an emotional state receptive and favourable to them. It should be so winning in its plea for that which is higher than itself that the ungodly will keep away in fear of being converted.

Literary art in public worship must always be the highest which the nation can procure, because true literary perfection, meaning simplicity, directness, and dignity of speech, is always the most powerful means of reaching the ear and soul of the less educated. But it must never be forgotten that in a community where taste for it is not highly developed, mere literary style is by no means essential to the communication of ideas and principles of character. In childhood most persons learn the rules by which they live for the rest of their life from mothers and fathers who speak ungrammatically and whose utterances never pretend to assume the form of connected discourse. It is the veriest pedantry that would identify the power of preaching with eloquence or oratory as we know these in the art of Edmund Burke or of the famous speakers of classic antiquity. Almost incoherently a man may blunder out the message of Christianity, and yet its essence will not be lost nor fall of its work.

Architecture as an element in ritual may be of the most primitive kind and yet powerfully effective. As the service is inside the building, the effect is almost entirely due to the interior. As the right proportions and colours of a room are independent of its exterior, isolated church edifices are altogether a costly extravagance, so far as concerns the spiritual atmosphere of the church service. With architecture, even more essential than its actual art-merit is the association of the building in the mind of the worshippers with the special objects and work of religion. Paintings and sculptures may assist mightily, but as symbols rather than as art, provided they give no æsthetic offence.

By universal consent, ritual is more intimately identified, as we have seen, in the mind of the general public, with drama than with any other art. The reason is quite plain. Acting is a pretence of action; ritual is action. And generally it is action comparatively dignified, graceful, and effective. Acting also is symbolic action; unlike ritual, however, it symbolizes not some real change in

social relation and function in the life of the actor himself,
but simply some universal and general truth or principle.
Yet the fact that it is symbolic action brings it into close
line with the action of ritual. Now, the priest, in order
to reach the altar or the pulpit, must walk, and in this he
does the same kind of thing that the actor must do to pass
from one part of the stage to another; yet the priest's
act is no more acting in this case than is the movement
of any human being from one point to another whither
his social duty calls him. The priest must turn and speak
to the audience, and in a manner removed from ordinary
conversation. Again, although he is not acting, what he
does is parallel to the actor's art. The priest, addressing
a whole assembly, naturally and rightly uses gesture more
than would prevail in private conversation; and again
he resembles the actor. He may lift his hands in bene-
diction, he may make the sign of the Cross, he may kneel;
again, action. And to the persons in the congregation
who have never been in his position his actions assume
a distinction not felt in those commonly done by every one.
Inevitably, also, persons going through actions in the
presence of a public assembly are compelled more or less
to conventionalize their motions. They may not study
for effect upon the congregation, and yet instinctively they
will learn the art which the actor on the stage in the same
way learns.

Thus it comes about that, while ritual is actual life and
the stage drama is not, nevertheless the actual life of
ritual does become penetrated with the qualities of all
the fine arts. Ritual, indeed, as found in the most elaborated Church ceremonials, may contain a combination
of all the arts which any stage could exhibit, and accordingly may produce the effects of drama without itself
being drama. The real secret of its dignity and majesty
will be its inward truth, its subjective realism, the fact

that the actor is what he personates, that the deed is an actual event in the life of those who participate in it, and that all the circumstances of the occasion are in fact precisely as they are set forth to be. This subjective kind of truth is so potent in enhancing beauty that in ritual a thousand accessories of the various arts may be lacking, coarse may be the materials that affront the eye, defective the proportions of the building, harsh the voices of the ministrant and the singers, awkward the postures and gestures of the celebrants — all these details falling far below the trappings of the stage — and yet

> how much more doth beauty beauteous seem
> By that sweet ornament which truth doth give!

In ritual we become aware that art and life together are more than art alone.

In the light of the foregoing analysis it will be seen that any person errs egregiously who says that those who are naturalistic in religion can never hope to elaborate a ritual splendid enough to compete with the stained-glass windows, the organs and orchestras, the variegated marbles, the embroidered and bedizened vestments, and the "long-drawn aisle and fretted vault," such as allure the senses in the scenes of Catholic ceremony; and that therefore they ought not to attempt to construct and practise a ritual which shall embody their own ideas. It is a mistake for a humanistic democrat to think: "When we want the strength and comfort of ritual, let us go to Roman cathedrals or Anglican abbeys; but when we are true to our own religious principles, let it suffice us to argue and debate and make speeches."

To do the latter is quite wise, and to abstain from a ritual of our own may perhaps be temporarily thrust upon us by circumstances. But that those who have discarded supernaturalism should enter sympathetically into a ritual

2 B

which must be interpreted supernaturalistically or have no
significance at all, is a moral and psychological impossibility. If the spectator of a Catholic ritual has no faith
in supernatural agencies, all its mere art sinks infinitely
below the level of a good play on the stage. For in a
good play what is represented is always human nature,
the besieging realities of everyday suffering and hope,
human principles and human ideals. The art of the
theatre is good when it is true to life in general. But
of what universal reality is the Catholic ritual, as it is
interpreted by the supernaturalist in religion, a sign and
token to the naturalist? Of nothing. The practice of the
Mass, to have any meaning, must be interpreted as the
outward sign of an inward and spiritual grace which is
being communicated from a supernatural source. Now
if a man has with a whole soul's protest abandoned communion with any supernatural agents whatsoever, how
can he yield himself for spiritual strength and solace to a
sign to him signifying nothing? In proportion, therefore,
as through the Roman ritual his senses are stormed by
the idea which underlies it, his whole spirit must rise up
in armed defence, as to beat off a ghostly enemy. Suppose
a man's whole life is animated by the principle embodied
in Emerson's injunction, "Trust thyself!" how can he
yield his mind to a ritual which insinuates into the very
arteries and tissues of the devotee an absolute moral self-
distrust? All that the believer in democracy and the law
of cause and effect counts a spiritual menace is transformed
by Rome into loveliness and majestic mien. If he submits
to it, it stands smiling before his eyes, it sings blinding sweet
into his ear, exhales fragrance into the air he breathes,
until, soothed into oblivion of his moral selfhood, he falls
entranced and is henceforth Rome's, to do with as she wills.
Behold what power an idea, although an enemy to knowledge and spiritual self-control, may have over us when it

is concreted into a cultus, if only we are unwary enough to submit to it !

Unless fully convinced that that which it symbolizes is the very life of life, no one except a degenerate would yield his senses to any ritual. To participate in a ritual for enjoyment's sake or for beauty's sake disintegrates the mental fibre. To amuse oneself with ritual is to play with fire. Only when that which the ritual bodies forth is believed to be the source of life, and therefore is accepted by a man as his redemption and his God, does it make him manly. Then it renders him invincible. It renders more real, powerful, vivid, and intimate than appetite the sacrifice of self for the good of all.

Such being the psychology of ritual, it follows inevitably that to a democratic and scientifically trained mind the meagrest beginnings of a ritual consonant with his principles would have more meaning and communicate more strength and peace than the most beautiful ritual conceivable, the principles of which he counted false and pernicious. If the thing it signifies is worse than nothing, no incidental accompaniments lent by the fine arts can give it vigour. The persons who do not believe in supernaturalism and yet are allured are only those who do not believe in anything, and have no idealistic convictions. Such are the lovers of art for art's sake instead of for life's sake.

CHAPTER XX

DEMOCRATIC FORMS OF PUBLIC WORSHIP

1. *Symbolism*

In another sense than that which I have dwelt upon, there is a kinship between the fine arts and ritual. The fine arts themselves are not simply embodiments of pure and universal beauty. Indeed, there are whole schools of artists and philosophers of art who maintain that the essence of art is not the beautiful in the sense of a form perfect in itself, a manifold variety of parts unified by some inherent principle within them all — a flower is beautiful in itself, a sunset, a landscape is beautiful within itself, a human face and the human form may be beautiful in this way; but there is also such a thing as the expression of a meaning which transcends the form itself. A form may point to a unity and variety beyond itself. A human face not beautiful in form may be expressive of a type of character transcendently beautiful and harmonious in itself. There is an irradiation of the soul from within, which transfigures faces by no means comely in themselves. Such a face is, as it were, an outward and visible sign of an inward and spiritual grace, and not the revelation of a charm of its own, as is the case with absolute and perfect beauty. The purely artistic sense of beauty rests in the self-revelation of the concrete object presented in colour before the eye, or in tone-structure through the ear. But an artist may be more than an artist; without degrading his art he may add to this pure beauty an extra charm, in that the outward form becomes a sign of a moral meaning.

A public far from appreciating pure beauty may be swayed and moved to admiration by every hint of higher meaning. Thus it comes about that symbolism is rife in certain schools of art; and in so far their art is allied to ritual. Signs are chosen of which they know the public will understand the inner meaning. They know that the mind of the beholder will instantly pass from the sign to the meaning, and that the meaning once astir in his mind will arouse all the emotions with which it has hitherto been associated. Artists thus appeal to the patriotic emotions, to reverence for children, to respect for motherhood, to admiration for martyrs. What is called the literary value of a picture is often the only element commendable in it. And yet, to the indignation of the pure artist, it may be so powerful that the community mistake it for beautiful. Take an object with no beauty of form, like the American Stars and Stripes; yet even men of the most disciplined judgment in the moment of patriotic emotion will find it a blessing to the eye.

Religious symbolism is in so far art as the mere use of an outward act, or colour or shape of any object arbitrarily selected to stand for some invisible reality, may be called art. And many do so call it, but possibly to the detriment of art and to the concealment of the real nature and power of ritual. Not to call symbolism art is not to deny its astonishing hold upon the imagination, and through it upon the intellect, the emotions, and the will. This effect of ritual is incalculably great. And if the thing symbolized is a thing to which we count it well that a man should turn his admiring attention, because the effect upon him is beneficent, we are grateful for the instrumentality which achieves it. But if the effect is one we deplore, we hate the means. The power of ritual, however, is undeniable. "The effect," says Mr. Lowes Dickinson in his essay entitled " Religion : A Criticism and a Forecast," "even of a ritual which we do not understand, or one with the intellectual basis of which we are out of touch, may be immense upon a sensitive spirit. How much more that of one which should really and adequately express our conviction and feeling about life and the world! For those who can accept the Christian view, the Christian ritual must be their most precious possession; but for those who cannot — and they are, as I think, an increasing number of not the least religious souls — their lack of intellectual assent to the faith weakens or even nullifies the effect of the symbol. And if, as I think will be the case, the men in whom the religious instinct is strongest move farther and farther from the Christian postulates, a ritual which shall express their new attitude will become, perhaps is already, one of their chief spiritual needs."

Unluckily for the new humanism, very few of those who accept its postulates, however much they need a ritual which shall express their new attitude, consciously want it. It would seem that with most of them the exclusive association of ritual with ideas they count pernicious will never be removed until they actually have an object-lesson in the new ritual. Hence the necessity that the pioneers of that religion which Mr. Lowes Dickinson forecasts should group themselves together and establish assemblings with song and book, with brick and stone. The world must receive ocular and oral demonstration, before it will believe that the new attitude can be made concrete to the senses.

2. *Through the Senses*

It is a little strange that persons who boast themselves free to think upon religious subjects should entertain a horror of ritual on the ground that it charms the senses. In the first place, why should the senses not be charmed?

Can we afford to leave them to be corrupted by un-scrupulous, unpatriotic, money-making syndicates who pander to the senses instead of purifying them? Or shall we become rank puritans, who not only want no beauty in outward form, but would banish even symbolic expressions of inward meanings? When we remember what symbolism is, furthermore, we shall realize that the appeal is never *to* the senses, but only *through* them. Further be it remembered, that all the wiser, more efficient, and humane methods of education embody the principle of communicating abstract ideas through signs, symbols, and associations which through the senses suggest the unseen.

Probably underlying the strong opposition of rational-istic religionists to ritual is the notion that any appeal to the senses is not quite fair and honest. An appeal should be made only to the reason and judgment of a man whom one is attempting to convert and to interest in any system of religion. "If you allure through the senses," it is asked, "have you not abandoned the fundamental principle of rationalism, and resorted to the very means which have caused the revolt of men of intellectual integrity against the old cults? Yet now you come in with a new appeal to the senses. You hope to win men by indirect methods. You mean to attach them by extraneous and adventitious associations of ideas, instead of by convincing them of the truth of your position. You mean to draw men by the cords not of reason, but of emotion, senti-ment, and possibly even of self-interest or family attach-ment or patriotic prejudice. You mean to commit a man first, and then convince him; whereas the rationalist would convince him first, and then there would be no occasion for any systematic effort to commit him."

In meeting this position one notices, in the first place, that it is inspired by a radical suspicion and distrust of a man's whole psychological make-up, except in so far as he is a logical thinker. It emanates from the presupposition that every man must beware not only of the crafts and assaults of priests and fascinating demagogues, but of his own eyes and ears, of the very laws of association of ideas by which the child-mind constructs the chaos of primal sensations into the beauty, order, and meaning of a rational cosmos within the forms of space and time. For the first three years of a child's life the power to think logically is not only not self-conscious, it is not even regulative. The confused materials of the sensations of touch and sight and sound build themselves up into windows, chairs, and human faces solely by means of frequency of repetition of appearance in the same associations. No psychologist denies that it is by seeing a certain shape and colour often together and then by seeing the colour sometimes with another shape and size, that the child learns to discriminate colour from shape and size. This process is not logical. It is not rational. There is no question of self-contradiction, although, of course, there is on the other hand no violation of the laws of identity and of difference. There is no question as to whether the shapes, colours, and sizes tally with an outside universe or violate some system of abstract thought. We further note that in the child's mind the objects which it grows to discern as distinct and connected become to it also, at the same time, symbols. Scarcely does the mother's face pass from the stage of an undiscerned sensation into a distinct perception, but, thanks to the law of association, the child takes a reappearance of that face in perception as an outward and visible sign of the veritable presence of that other reality from which emanate tender care, relief from pain, and the agreeable sensations which the child welcomes. Now, can any rationalist who accepts this psychological process as legitimate in a child find any possible ground for his int se distrust of it in the grown-up man? At what age f adolescence must this process be checked? And if it be not pernicious in youth, but, on the contrary, the very prerequisite of all rationality, how and why does it suddenly lose its beneficence and begin to destroy the very framework and constitution of the rational universe which itself has made, and which reason, after it has appeared, sanctions as altogether good?

What does the ritualist do but imitate that psychological process to which all naturally gifted teachers and all trained experts in education and all philosophic pedagogists turn as the very model and ideal for the teacher's conscious art? For instance, the rationalistic ritualist would say to himself, "In order that a man by the age of twenty-one shall see the full rationality of ethical idealism, I must begin with him when he is only five years of age to tell him stories which will interest him quite irrespectively of their ultimate significance in a scheme of religious thought and yet will at the same time illustrate the principles of that thought. But I must tell him such stories not only once a year or once in six months, but every week, and repeat them and have him repeat them. I must draw incidents from history, I must search out analogies in physical nature. Thus years before he can think for himself on abstract questions, he will have been receiving the material, and that material more or less prearranged, which will make it easy for him to judge for himself years afterwards." But the rationalistic ritualist will also say, "I want the child's mind to associate a particular building and a particular room with the religion which I mean to teach him, so that whenever he thinks of this religion a mental image of the room, its size and colour and arrangements of furniture, shall appear in his mind. All the sensations and emotions associated with that room must be agreeable; unpleasant associations would make the man in later years turn from the idea, for memories would recall sensations and emotions from which he shrinks instinctively. He must never be forced by threats of punishment to go to the room which is to be identified in his mind with rational religion. When he comes, he must not be compelled to stay longer for a lesson or any systematic work than a child's nature can well endure. The room must not be so cold as to chill the child; else this physical shrinking will extend even to the thought of what is taught in the room. The people present must be kindly, loving, considerate, and deferential to the child's individuality." And as children love to sing, the ritualist will teach him songs embodying humanistic sentiments, perfectly sure that the melodies will flow into his mind years afterwards, bearing the words and the words bearing the meaning of the message which the child could not fully comprehend. And the lights of the room must be bright — and yet not too bright. In short, the place must be like a home; and every one knows how a mother and father instinctively, if they are able, provide the comforts which shall make the home physically attractive to every inmate. Indeed, what is a home but a place of comfort and welcome for body and mind? So the ritualist would go on, putting books into the hands of the child which would lead his thought to those great factors in life which the teacher believes ultimately the child will acknowledge as deserving supreme reverence and devotion. The humanistic ritualist will not discard any agreeable if innocent association of the senses or affections, which might attach the child ultimately to the principles of reason.

Now this method, merely as method, is exactly the same as that of Roman Catholic and other ritualists, who have no faith in reason whatever, but fall back upon con-

ventional tradition.   Yet there is a world-wide difference
in the thing taught and the effect on the child's will.   There
is an absolute antagonism between the rationalistic and the
non-rationalistic ritualist, for the latter means never to
appeal to reason.   He trusts wholly to associations and
indirect attachments.   He knows how well-nigh impossible
it is for most persons at the age of thirty to throw off the
mere outward associations of a lifetime.   He knows further that, there being no principle of reason at the heart of
all the associations which he has been systematically ar-
ranging in children's experience, their power to think for
themselves will never enable them to discover any law of
rationality in the religion given to them.   But, still
further, he knows that the craving for rationality, not
having been stimulated through the growing lifetime of
the mind, will have almost died at the root.

What, however, is the position of the humanistic ritualist?   Every year of his pupil's life progressively, from the
age of five on, he will have been making more frequent and
profound appeals to the moral and scientific judgment
of the child.   He will be passing continually from the
concrete to the abstract.   But always at each step he
will be guiding and challenging the child to judge for
himself of what is right and what is wrong, of what
is verifiable truth and what is unfounded prejudice;
until finally, at the age of eighteen or twenty, the child
will have been brought to a height of judgment from
which he can survey the widest fields of speculative
thought and of moral responsibility.   But when the
pupil attains this point, all the pleasant associations, all
the lovable and tender memories of his lifetime will re-
enforce his judgment and his reason.   He will not suffer
the painful discovery that the treasure of his heart lies in
one direction and the responsibility of duty and integrity
in another.   He will rejoice in finding out that the principles

which his own judgment now accepts as right and true have from the first been the providential laws which regulated the full and varied interests of his life from the first.

Is it fair to say that humanistic ritual betrays reason by alluring the senses? Does not the word "allure" itself beg the question by implying that the senses are so appealed to as to oppose reason?

It must be remembered that many things which are not reason are nevertheless not against reason. For instance, the processes of association, the affections, the craving for agreeable sensations in the child and the man, the love of the approbation of others — these are not the love of a system of thought without contradiction, these are not the craving to reduce all phenomena to unity; but nevertheless they are not against reason. It is quite possible that a man is only one per cent. reason, and that the other ninety-nine parts of him consist of processes and cravings of a totally different kind. If so, what narrowness and inhuman bigotry it is to appeal solely to a child's power to think! Many rationalists make the preposterous blunder, in speaking of appealing to reason, of forgetting that one must always appeal also to sensations, experiences, perceptions, emotions, and volitions as the material which reason is to explain. To think that a child can spin a true religion out of his reason, unrelated to the experience of man throughout history and to the extra-rational parts of man's nature, is a more preposterous superstition than to fall back wholly upon tradition and an external revelation. For reason with no material of experience to work up and to classify is absolutely empty and void.

Not simply in reference to a child is it foolish to trust to reason alone without a mass of friendly associated ideas; it is downright madness of policy to expect to overthrow by an appeal merely to reason the entrenched prejudices which for twenty-five years have been systematically built up in the mind of an adult. What is the use of trying to convince a man that his religion is irrational when he does not care whether it be rational or not, when he has never been trained from his youth to respect the rational and his capacity both to judge and to respect it has become atrophied? Suppose, however, one does wish to bring more rational views of religion to the mind of a man trained to believe in the authority of priest and book as final. What is the only possible and the only legitimate method? It may be late in the day to begin, but even at the age of forty, if a man is to be drawn away from a false system of religion, he must be drawn — in proportion as he has little capacity and in order to develop his capacity for rationality — by bringing about in his mind new agreeable associations with those principles of which he has scarcely heard. He may meet by chance a man of the type of manners and character that he has always loved and respected; then, if he incidentally hears that the man is a humanist, instantly the whole of his attachment to that person will move out in friendly anticipation to the new ideas. He will want to know more of them. He is already, if not prejudiced in their favour, sympathetically curious to be informed. His mind is open. Nothing under heaven could have made him receptive but a preliminary indirect attachment of this sort. He is astonished, for he had supposed that only persons socially "impossible" ever entertained unorthodox views of religion. He already has discovered one error, and he says to himself, "Perhaps the ideas themselves are no less admirable than the man who entertains them."

Or suppose it is a question as to what sort of meeting-place humanists will choose for the presentation of their ideas and how the meeting shall be conducted. From the point of view of the rigorous anti-ritualist and jealous

deifier of reason, it will make no difference in what sort of
room the meeting is to be held, or whether the speaker use
good English or violate all the conventional canons of
speech, or whether in debate he show deference to others
or not.

But the ritualist will say that because of the power of the
association of ideas no one of these adventitious circumstances should be allowed to give offence, and that every
particular object or event or circumstance that can be used
as an outward sign to signify the real character of the
new idealism shall be appropriated and used. Indeed, a
humanistic rationalist himself, if he be a ritualist, will dedicate not only his reasoning, but all his other powers to the
service of reason. He will be not only ready to give his
time and risk his reputation and suffer ostracism, but he
will resort to less heroic forms of sacrifice. He will dedicate all the minor incidents of life so that they shall not
occasion unnecessary offence or prejudice.

I have dwelt thus long upon the prejudice against
ritual entertained by persons who hold fundamental
principles like my own, because nearly all the men and
women of taste who abandon the old interpretations of religion, upon ceasing to attend church, never dream of the
possibility of entering into fellowship with others of their
own newer belief. Yet the reason for this shrinking from
new religious coöperation is almost wholly due to a dread
of the crudities in methods of propaganda, and of the over-
emphasis of mere logical appeals to reason, which have prevailed among those who, coming out of the old churches,
have set up new centres of propaganda.

There is another and profounder reason for the public
celebration of a humanistic ritual. The real enemy of
the idealistic humanist, as I have pointed out in an earlier
chapter, is not, after all, the supernaturalistic religionist.
It is the same enemy which, from the first, Christianity and

Judaism themselves have been fighting: the world, which accepts selfishness as the regulative principle of conduct. I recur to this fact again, in order to bring it into connection with the psychological principle of the association of ideas. The child from the age of five, besides any association built up by his religious teachers, is constantly, by his meeting with all sorts and conditions of people and by all sorts and conditions of accidental experience and observation, forming associations which allure him towards the practices of lying, physical self-indulgence, and love of power and display. If great care be not taken, by the time he is twenty-one years of age he will have been committed, by a thousand habits and desires and by the expectations of others, to a life of shrewd, systematic service of himself at the expense of others. One need not even cite the case of the still lower order of intelligences where the self-seeking and self-gratification are neither shrewd nor far-sighted, but the character is marked by an effeminate and weak yielding to momentary impulse. In either case the moral calamity has come about by a gradual association of ideas which committed the whole mind to one or the other form of pleasing oneself without consideration of others. How, I ask, can an appeal to reason unsupplemented by an elaborated scheme of counteracting associations ever rescue such individuals and the society into which they are born from the calamity of moral downfall? Ethical ritual, then, really means moral propaganda by methods which a knowledge of psychological processes suggests to every teacher.

3. *Ethical Ceremony*

But deep and radical is the ordinary rationalist's opposition to outward and visible signs of inward and spiritual grace, even if that grace be the idealism of reason itself.

It is maintained among all who oppose ritual, but chiefly by its extremest opponents, the rationalists, that through-out the history of religious organizations ceremonial has been at enmity with the ethical tendency, and has often extinguished it. This opposition is to be met by challenging both psychologically and historically the truth of the statement that ceremonial in itself tends to check the ethical element in religion. Of course, it goes with-out saying that an immoral ceremonial will not have moral effects, but the very opposite. It also goes without saying that a non-moral ceremonial will have not moral effects, but again a very opposite. For the ethical has two opposites, the unethical and the non-ethical; and of the two, in the actual history of society and of each individual mind, the non-ethical is, as a fact, a greater enemy to the positively ethical than is actual self-conscious wickedness. The diabolically bad is a comparatively small factor in human life compared to apathy, indifference, preoccupation, interest in the things of the senses and of worldly prosperity. Yet, surely, in considering whether ceremonial religion be antagonistic to ethical religion, we must bar out ceremonials non-ethical and anti-ethical, and ask only whether an ethical religion which resorts to ritual as a means of communicating its principles and enthusiasm is in danger of a suicidal absorption in the details of the ceremonial. Is an ethical religion which resorts to outward signs apt to forget the things signified, in its attention to the efficiency of the signs? If it did absorb its attention in the signs so as to make them ex-quisitely perfect in efficiency, could such a development of symbolism obscure the very grace it was meant to symbolize? Or would the effort to make the signs supremely efficient somehow degenerate without knowing it into making them inefficient? My contention is that there are no psychological processes known to us which would justify our fearing that an ethical ceremonial would so absorb the interest of teachers and preachers and organizers of the ethical life as to induce them to forget the ethical life or to sacrifice it to the ceremonial.

Even if we admitted that all the ceremonials of the past and present did and do militate against the interests of ethical life, we should have also to concede that the grace signified by these ceremonials was not social, not humanistic, not naturalistic. A supernaturalistic ceremonial diverts men from social responsibility and thus injures the ethical life; yet not because it is ceremonial, but because it is supernaturalistic. In such a ritual the personal agents propitiated are not one's fellow human beings, but agents without human bodies, agents not recognized by the law, agents who are not subjects of rights and privileges, and who cannot be punished by public opinion and the criminal law, agents who cannot be made legislators, administrators, or judges. The opponents of ceremonial must point to a purely ethical ritual and show that the ritual has had an unethical or non-ethical effect. But that would be very difficult to prove. When such an effect is shown, the ceremonial is proved not to have been what at the outset it was assumed to be.

With the spiritistic rituals of the churches of the past one must contrast a humanistic, social, naturalistic ritual. And one must not attribute to ritual in itself any evil effect which can be traced directly to the spiritistic presuppositions out of which it has grown.

But to be just to the rituals of Judaism and Christianity, we must admit that they are essentially ethical rituals. The real problem before us is not Jewish and Christian *versus* ethical; the problem is to decide between two ethical rituals, the one spiritistic and the other socialistic.

Judaism and Christianity have hitherto been spiritistic

2 C

ethical religions. They are, as I believe, vitiated to a great extent by their spiritism. But despite these vitiating elements they are superbly ethical. The result is that their rituals are relatively very great and good; and, as compared with no ritual and no ethical religion, they are infinitely precious. What is more, when we turn to the facts of Jewish and Christian church discipline, a comparison of the more and the less ritualistic communions by no means confirms the statement that ritual militates against the ethical life. On the contrary, where there is most ritual there is often the most intense ethical enthusiasm and self-sacrifice. It is true that the spiritistic element increases in efficiency with the ritual; but the ethical element increases proportionately and holds its own against the non-ethical and anti-ethical effects of the spiritistic error. We find, for instance, in England that the High Churchmen who seem to spend a great proportion of time and thought upon details of ritual are as a direct effect of that ceremonial so heightened in enthusiasm of self-sacrifice for the poor that they stand an object of moral admiration to persons of all religions and of no religion. It must be further remembered that the Roman Catholic Church by its very ritual has created such domination and ascendency of the idea of sacrifice for the poor that it stands to this hour preëminent for its charities, its consolations to the lonely and the suffering, and its attention to the education of its children. What we do find is the aloofness both of Protestant churches and of the Roman Catholic communion from national and municipal politics, from the modern interests of science and art, and from the whole movement of women and the working people for economic emancipation. But the spiritism at the heart of Christian dogma as it has hitherto been interpreted is quite enough to account for this aloofness. The trust of Christianity has thus far been in supernatural agencies, outside the political organism. Its supreme interest for a thousand years has been in a world beyond death. The fact that despite this moral aberration it still has been so intensely ethical in its discipline upon the human soul is one of the strongest proofs that notwithstanding its dogma its supreme passion was human righteousness. Even within the sphere of individual ethics we see the adverse influence of its spiritism. This spiritism, not being verifiable in experience, has caused the churches, if not positively to discourage, at least to overlook the claims of intellectual honesty and of bold, free investigation of truth. But the ritualism is in no wise to blame for these deficiencies.

When we investigate the ceremonial and ethical aspects of Judaism, we find that the ceremonial has been a tremendous aid to the moral character of the Jews and a strengthening of the Jewish people such as has made it a two thousand years' wonder to all the other races of the world. We must remember that the Temple service as illustrated in the Psalms was that of the second Temple. The people had lost their political independence. The ruling classes had been banished for seventy years in the Babylonian Exile. There the greatest of the ethical prophets, Ezekiel, not excelled by Isaiah in moral insight and passion, was statesman enough to see that with the political independence gone, a psychological substitute must be found which would focus the people's hope and confidence upon those lines of conduct which in the end lead to national independence and prosperity. He hit upon the notion of a splendid Temple ritual as the means of focussing steadfastly and reverently the whole people's heart upon the supreme means of the ultimate blessings of life. It was ritual, it was ceremonial, it was a system of signs for inward and ethical tribal grace, that kept the Jews from 432 B.C. until 70 A.D. from losing their national idealism, and has preserved them to this day not without hope, and now at last has brought the establishment of a Jewish kingdom nearer to the domain of practical politics than it has been for two thousand years.

4. *Good Deeds and Public Worship*

Take the elements of ceremonial as contrasted with the ethical life of social justice. A ceremonial that aims at social justice cannot but prove the most powerful ally conceivable of the teaching and preaching of morality, of discipline, of the sanction of public opinion, and of the moral atmosphere of a community where social justice is practised and illustrated.

Ceremonial religion involves the keeping of holydays, because the community must agree upon times of ceremonial worship. Now in modern life one of the greatest questions dividing the ordinary rationalist from the traditionalist in religion is this one of keeping the Sabbath Day holy. Says the rationalist, "All days are holy." Says the traditional ritualist, "Sunday must be kept sacred to religion irrespective of reasons of social expediency." But now comes into the argument the humanistic ritualist. He maintains that one day in seven is needed for ethical meditation, concentration, and commitment; that a day must be set apart and kept holy, guarded against the inroads and encroachments of sport and athletics, art, and mere intellectual science. Is it conceivable that a whole nation devoting one day in seven to the problems and principles and policy of social justice should not thereby advance ethically in ten years to a moral stage which otherwise they could scarcely attain in a hundred years? An ethical Sabbath would be the most powerful moral asset conceivable for a nation if its ethics were based upon science and social democracy instead of upon unverifiable dogmas devised to secure trust in invisible agencies beyond society.

And when you have secured the ethical holyday there must be the assemblings. In these assemblies every available sign must be utilized to make real in presence and power the claims of the national ideal. There must be song and book. And the necessity of housing the multitudes means a temple building.

A disproof of the utility of an ethical ritual would require a demonstration that a nation's attention can be fixed upon the ends and means of social justice without influencing politics. Or, if not this, it will require a demonstration that men and women will be as ethical if they do not pay attention to the means and ends of social justice as if they do. But neither of these attitudes can be defended. Grown men will not spontaneously attend even so much as children to the claims of social justice, unless their minds be systematically turned thereto. Nor is there any evidence to justify the belief that people would do right if the right were never taught them.

The senses of every human being are constantly solicited by objects which in close proximity would gratify instincts and impulses. These objects, presenting themselves to the senses, carry with them an overpowering feeling of their reality.

The problem of the ethical teacher is, how to give a corresponding impression of reality to the claims of Duty, the invisible Laws of the universe, and the Ideals and Visions of a perfect order of society. How can these be made as present and immediate as the visible and audible world of the senses? There is only one way. If their reality is to be brought home to people, and their force is to become dominant and to master appetites, ambitions, and vanities, we must find outward, visible, and audible signs which, by the law of association, suggest powerfully to the imagination their presence and reality.

The universal, the ideal, the moral order, the state of things which ought to be but is not yet, the great ends of society — all these, prefigured in the constitution of man, but not actualized in his daily life and institutions, can be by means of outward signs so vividly suggested as to create a mystic sense of their real presence.

It is the function of symbolism, through the eye, the ear, and the other senses, thus to bring home the reality of the supersensible world, *i.e.* the world of ideals, of principles, of types and tendencies, of universal conceptions of humanity, of visions of the perfect city, the true State and the honest man.

If these did not possess by divine right validity and necessity and binding power, it would be an unpardonable playing with the mind of another to create such an impression by ritual. It would be scarcely less than black art to attempt by some outward and palpable sign to secure for them the sense of reality. But according to reason and in the moral judgment these supersensible things are the supreme realities.

Were we not deceived and ensnared by the false claims of objects which obtrude themselves upon the senses by appealing to purely physical instincts and impulses, we should never for a moment doubt the reality of the fundamental order of nature and the universal principles and standards of right reason. But because of the obtrusiveness of objects of the senses and because of the devices and intrigues of cunning and unscrupulous human beings, every man is in danger of forgetting the claims of duty and the remote consequences of present deeds.

To bring the future as powerfully before the mind as is the present, to obtrude the claims of persons unknown as intensely as those obtrude their own who clamour upon their knees before us — to do this is impossible except as the future, the absent, the invisible, the supersensible, the moral order are represented by signs or counters or marks which will not let us forget that they stand before our very eyes and ears as the proxies of those realities which are invisible.

The power and claim of what we aspire to be in our moments of selfless meditation are apt to be overlooked by the busy, the inexperienced, the thoughtless, the perplexed. Only ethical symbolism can find for the supersensible order a foothold in the world of sense upon which it may plead for the higher ends of life.

But there is still another form which the objection to ritual assumes in the minds of those who have turned away from supernaturalistic ceremonials. These persons are apt to retort, not without great plausibility: "What need has an ethical idealism for outward signs? Let every deed of our daily conduct speak for our religion. Let our deeds testify to our principles. For those whose religion is a cult of the supernatural, there may be occasion for symbolic acts, like the making of the sign of the Cross in the air, like the partaking of a meal that is not a real meal, and the like; but for us whose religion is ethical, not a minute of the day passes that does not give us a chance of illustrating the ideas by which we live." This is all very beautiful in motive, but, if I am not in error, it is wholly a mistake. It is not as a fact true that specific deeds of duty reveal the principles, dispositions, motives, presuppositions, and ideals which animate them. The spectator will interpret any deed of human kindness or mercy or justice done by another in the light of the principles which would animate him if he were to do the deed. Our deeds are not self-revealing as to their inmost secret. You cannot discover from a man's giving a cup of cold water to a dying neighbour whether he acted from a Mohammedan,

Buddhist, Roman Catholic, Anglican, Agnostic, or Mystic view of duty and the world. Our deeds do not point unequivocally to our principles — except to our own introspective observation. Our deeds point, on the contrary, to each spectator's own principles which might have produced them. If a man works among the poor as a philanthropist in a neighbourhood where hitherto only devout Christians have done so, every act of his will be interpreted by the neighbourhood as being done in the name and for the sake of Jesus Christ — or for whatever motive is customarily assigned to Christian philanthropists. If a Jew whose features do not betray his race does philanthropic work among the Gentile poor, all the neighbours will draw the inference that he is working as a disciple of Christ. If an Agnostic do the same, not a living mortal could infer his "heresy" from his deeds. Or suppose a modern humanitarian was assisted by a Japanese in delivering some suffering dumb animal from acute pain — how could any bystander detect that the humanitarian's deed emanated from a direct love for all sentient beings, while the Japanese was but illustrating his belief that some ancestor might be incarnate in the cat or dog and that on that account it should be relieved from pain? What possible difference in the deed of mercy could be detected which would cause the Occidental's act to point to humanism and that of the Oriental to spiritistic ancestor-worship? It becomes quite clear that if you wish to disclose your motives, ideas, doctrines, or creed, you must resort to the practice of symbolic acts arbitrarily chosen and understood to signify adherence to exactly those ideas and doctrines. The only alternative to symbolic acts is simply talking. With one's lips one must declare oneself Agnostic, Buddhist, Mohammedan; or else one must undergo some ceremonial act. And, indeed, even the declaration with one's lips, if hunted down, is found to be an arbitrary sign, outward and audible, for an inward and spiritual truth. The community agrees that a man who declares himself a Roman Catholic is a Roman Catholic. By making that sign he actually throws in the weight of his influence on the side of Catholicism. Therefore to the community at large the public profession of faith with the lips is a symbolic deed which pledges a man. To know that a man is a Roman Catholic, we must have evidence that he has participated in some rite distinctive of that communion.

I may have succeeded in convincing some readers that such a thing as a humanistic ritual is not only right, but necessary as a means of propaganda and to the building up of a national love of righteousness.

5. *A Spiritual Atmosphere*

Many adhere to the prevalent opinion that nothing but a belief in supernatural powers can create in a religious assembly what is called a spiritual atmosphere. Yet it is just the creation of an atmosphere in which one is filled with a sense of the infinite and of the supersensible and of the reality of an unseen universe, that a ritual purely human and scientific in its implications is preëminently fitted to achieve.

What is, after all, the most sublime Reality, the supreme spiritual Power, in response to which the individual human will and heart vibrate? I say, without a moment's hesitation, it is the indwelling principle of righteousness animating a social group, the idealizing will of a community of human beings. Whoever surrenders himself to the good of the community and to the cause of the good in the world as it is organizing, guiding, and inspiring the lives of a group of brave men and women, knows that he is experiencing that which is the Absolute Reality for the rational will of every finite soul. As he reads the account of devout and religious men of every creed, however supernaturalistic, he sees that what they are describing as God is the reality which he himself has found and by which he lives. In terms of psychology and sociology he may describe it simply as the spirit of humanity or the general will of the community; but however cautiously and restrainedly he thus designates it, he knows it and loves it as the Consoler, the Inspirer, the Saviour.

In a meeting where there is no thought of personal agencies outside of the spiritual organism of human society, every individual person may be flooded, thrilled, and transfigured in the sense of the glory and power, the dignity and presence of the spiritual organism in which he lives and moves and has his being, and to which he gladly surrenders himself. In such a meeting of idealistic humanists one may find one's own private wish and desire merging and growing into the mighty creative will that blends millions of men in one organic nation.

If it is a man's first experience of this moral transfiguration, he forthwith undergoes what is called religious conversion. If, despite previous experience and a full knowledge of its meaning and blessing, he has been living a life of base and abject subservience to petty interests, he will be filled with remorse and suffer the pain of cleansing fire.

In a meeting where all present are filled with one idea, and that a great and humane one, where all are moved by one purpose and each is conscious of his own responsible contribution towards its fulfilment, no scoffer, no hardened sinner can escape the sense of the reality of a Power not himself and yet himself that makes for righteousness.

> The tidal wave of deeper souls
> Into our inmost being rolls,
> And lifts us unawares
> Out of all meaner cares.

There may be those who have not even so much as heard that the higher will, the combined effort of many in the cause of humanity, is a Holy Spirit. Much less may they have heard the claim here made for it that it is *the* Holy Spirit, the same reality revealed to the world and rightly named by the earliest Christians. It was they who discovered it in that first losing and finding of themselves in their combined effort to spread the Gospel.

There may possibly be reasons why the formative spirit of a group of human beings bound in devotion to the moral ideal should not be called God or the Holy Ghost; but it is hard to see why any human being, professedly Christian or not, should deny himself the blessing of being filled, cleansed, and strengthened by its power. If we analyze the spiritual atmosphere of religious meetings, we always find humanistic factors which adequately account for it.

In the first place, not every religious meeting where those present believe in supernatural agencies can boast of a spiritual atmosphere. On the contrary, the organizers and leaders of all denominations openly confess, and with infinite grief, that days, months, and years pass where there is no such outpouring of the Holy Ghost as is to be desired. The mere belief in supernatural agents as the source of spiritual blessings by no means secures those blessings. Where there is pride and vainglory, where the preacher is believed to be a hypocrite, where the music is theatrical, where the living pillars of the church are known to be the supporters of iniquitous commercial enterprises, the congregation does not experience a season of the outpouring of the Spirit. On the other hand, where the preacher is brave, humane, spiritually minded, indefatigable and self-sacrificing in his ministry, and the people hunger and thirst after righteousness, there at any moment it requires only concentration of attention to the end of deepening the inner experience, and a moral revival begins.

But over and above such general conditions, one notes that this atmosphere dominates religious meetings in proportion as all present have met more than halfway the purpose of the preacher and of the church. When each person comes with his mind already predisposed, disciplined by private and secret meditation and prayer, when each comes with his mind fixed upon the vision of perfect manhood and a perfect fellowship, the very bearing and faces of men and women as they enter the church reveal their mind. When every member of a congregation is thus held by the Ideal, an unwonted serenity, a sweet peace, pervades the meeting. Every person present is reënforced by the consciousness that all are devoted to one end and are moving in spirit to the same goal.

In speaking of the purpose and devotion of each individual present at a meeting, I have touched upon the fundamental source of a spiritual atmosphere. In a church service where religion is interpreted wholly in a humanistic sense, every cause of spiritual redemption operates not less but more powerfully than where redemption is regarded as a miracle. For the human understanding now coöperates with the other psychic energies, social and personal, which induce redemption.

It is in religion as it is in physics. A man may deny the vibratory theory, but the light takes no umbrage, and the sun blesses the man who misunderstands it, as well as the plant and animal which are wholly innocent of any theory whatsoever. Yet, on the other hand, a knowledge of the laws of light might lead to a new mastery of it in the service of man. For the same reason, we must attack supernaturalistic theories of the spiritual life, for the hastening of the Kingdom of Righteousness, without denying the untold benefit which the world has derived from the spiritistic religions of the past.

INDEX

THE following pages contain advertisements of
books by the same author or on kindred subjects

SOCIAL WORSHIP

For Use in Families, Schools, and Churches

Compiled and edited by STANTON COIT, Chairman of the West London Ethical Society; formerly Head Worker of the New York University Settlement. The Music Edited by CHARLES KENNEDY SCOTT. Issued on Behalf of the West London Ethical Society as a Memorial of Its Twenty first Anniversary.

Two volumes, royal octavo, $12.50 net; carriage extra

EXTRACTS FROM THE COMPILER'S INTRODUCTION

The publication of "Social Worship" sprang from the conviction of the Members of the West London Ethical Society, that no more fitting memorial could be found for the first twenty-one years of their pioneer work as propagandists of humanistic religion. But by a fitting memorial they meant not simply something that would reflect what the society has been and done, but something that would advance the cause they had at heart. They believed that a book embodying in the best form accessible the ideals, principles and policies to which they have been devoted, might carry their gospel, within a short period of years, to a far larger portion of the world than any personal propaganda which they could initiate. . . . They have felt, in short, that the Religion of Science, Democracy and Personal Responsibility in the Service of Humanity must become, like Buddhism, Christianity and Mohammedanism, a religion of a book. . . . Our ambition has been, to do — so far as could be feasible, after only twenty-one short years of organized effort — for the enthusiasms, visions and motives which have drawn us into religious fellowship, what the writers and compilers of the New Testament did for their own religious experiences and those of their immediate predecessors, in collecting the sayings and traditions current among them ; or what the editors of the Old Testament did for the moral idealism of their race. . . .

". . . the most valuable book of the kind that has ever been published. Its selection of material from the great moral and religious literatures of the world is made with great care, is thoroughly catholic in spirit and represents a range which is simply astonishing. The Bible, Eastern Scripture, Plato, Milton, Sir Thomas More, Shakespeare, Bacon, Goethe, Wordsworth, Emerson, Whitman, Browning, Henry George, Huxley, Bernard Shaw, Ibsen, Zangwill — these are only a few of the authors quoted, but they show at least the many and wide sources which have been tapped. Especially helpful is the classification of these selections and the running summary at the head of each. The book also contains services for special occasions such as funeral and marriage services, and numerous introductory and dismissory sentences which are exceedingly useful for the practical purposes of public worship. All in all, I feel that this book is almost as indispensable to the modern minister as the traditional Old and New Testament."
— *Dr. John Haynes Holmes.*

THE MACMILLAN COMPANY

Publishers   64-66 Fifth Avenue   New York

Work and Wealth : A Human Valuation

By J. A. HOBSON, M.A.

Author of " Industrial Society," " John Ruskin, Social Reformer," etc.

Cloth, 8vo, $2.00 net

Mr. Hobson is an economist of established reputation whose writings have for years been eagerly read by his fellow-economists. The purpose of this, his latest work, is to present a just and formal exposure of the inhumanity and vital waste of modern industries by the close application of the best approved formulas of individual and social welfare, and to indicate the most hopeful measures of remedy for a society sufficiently intelligent, courageous and self-governing to apply them. The wholly satisfying fashion in which the author has achieved this purpose results in a suggestive and stimulating review from a novel standpoint of problems in which all students of economy are interested. Not only is the book an important contribution to the literature of its field; it is no less valuable in its bearing on general questions of the day with which other than purely professional economists are concerned.

Where and Why Public Ownership Has Failed

By YVES GUYOT

Cloth, 12mo, $1.50 net

What have state ownership and operation accomplished in the way of tax and other reforms in those cases where they have been tried? Yves Guyot, statesman, traveler, editor, economist, here answers this question in perhaps the most exhaustive treatise thus far published upon the subject. A glance at a few of the topics covered is a sufficient index of the comprehensive character of the work : — Municipal Activity of the United Kingdom, The United States, Germany, Russia, France, Austria-Hungary, Italy, Denmark, Switzerland, Belgium, Sweden; State Operation of Railroads; State and Municipal Bookkeeping and Finances; Private versus Public Initiative; The Housing of the Working Class; State and Municipal Extravagance; Political and Social Consequences of a Socialist Program.

THE MACMILLAN COMPANY

Publishers   64-66 Fifth Avenue   New York

Violence and the Labor Movement

By ROBERT HUNTER
Author of "Poverty," "Socialists at Work," etc.

Cloth, 12mo, $1.50 net

This book deals with the mighty conflict that raged throughout the latter part of the last century for possession of the soul of labor. It tells of the doctrines and deeds of Bakounin, Netchayeff, Kropotkin, Ravachol, Henry, Most and Caserio. It seeks the causes of such outbursts of rage as occurred at the Haymarket in Chicago in 1886 and are now being much discussed as Syndicalism, Haywoodism and Larkinism. It is a dramatic, historical narrative in which terrorism, anarchism, syndicalism and socialism are passionately voiced by their greatest advocates as they battle over programs, tactics and philosophies.

Progressivism and After

By WILLIAM ENGLISH WALLING
Author of "The Larger Aspects of Socialism,"
"Socialism As It Is," etc.

Cloth, 12mo, $1.50 net

This is a book which every thoughtful socialist, social reformer and those to whom social reform makes any appeal, ought to read. Mr. Walling views social and economic questions as a thinker and student, never merely as a theorist or partisan. In the political events of the last few years Mr. Walling sees much that is significant not only for the present but for the future. What the progress of affairs in the next generation is to be he outlines in this work in a fashion that is as convincing as it is unusual from the socialistic standpoint. Of particular interest are his analyses of President Wilson, Colonel Roosevelt and other prominent leaders, while his description of that which has been and that which is to come is trenchant and keen. Whether one agrees with his predictions or not, the force and clearness with which the issues are indicated distinguish the volume for all kinds of readers.

THE MACMILLAN COMPANY
Publishers   **64-66 Fifth Avenue**   **New York**

Progressive Democracy

By HERBERT CROLY
Author of " The Promise of American Life "

Cloth, 8vo, $2.00 net

The object of the author in this book is threefold. He has in the first place analyzed the modern progressive democratic movement in this country in order to separate its essential from its nonessential ingredients to discover whether there is any real issue between American progressivism and American conservatism. In the second place he has tried to reconstruct the historical background of progressivism to see what roots or lack of roots it has in the American political and economic tradition. And finally he has attempted to trace what we may reasonably expect from the progressive movement, to show what tools it must use in order to carry out its program and what claims it has on the support of patriotic Americans. The work seeks, therefore, to express for the first time a consistently educational theory of democracy.

Democracy and Race Friction: A Study in Social Ethics

By JOHN MOFFATT MECKLIN, Ph.D.
Professor of Philosophy in the University of Pittsburg

Cloth, 12mo, $1.25 net

Professor Mecklin's purpose in this volume is not to present a solution of the race problem, which he believes to be insoluble, but rather to indicate as clearly as possible what the problem really involves. With this end in view he has brought to bear upon the subject the results of the work recently done in social psychology by such men as Tarde, Baldwin, McDougall, Ross, and others. An analysis of the social principles by which the individual lives himself into the lives of the group and at the same time attains mental and moral maturity is followed by an examination of race traits with special reference to the Negro to determine how far they influence the process of becoming social and solid with one's fellows. The results thus gained are utilized to explain the imperfect way in which the Negro has assimilated the civilization of the white and why the color line appears universally where whites and blacks are brought together in large numbers. The book closes with an attempt at a restatement of the meaning of democracy.

THE MACMILLAN COMPANY
Publishers   64-66 Fifth Avenue   New York